Swahili

PHRASEBOOK & DICTIONARY

Acknowledgments

Publisher Mina Patria
Associate Product Director Angela Tinson
Product Editor Elin Berglund
Series Designer James Hardy
Language Writer Dr Martin Benjamin
Cover Image Researcher Naomi Parker

Thanks

Elizabeth Jones, Chris Love, Kate Mathews, Wayne Murphy, John Taufa, Branislava Vladisavljevic, Tony Wheeler

---

Published by Lonely Planet Publications Pty Ltd
ABN 36 005 607 983

5th Edition – August 2014
ISBN 978 1 74321 196 0
Text © Lonely Planet 2014
Cover Image Maasai tribesmen in Paje, Tanzania, Ellen Rooney/Corbis ©
Printed in China   10 9 8 7 6 5 4 3 2

Contact lonelyplanet.com/contact

Although the authors and Lonely Planet try to make the information as accurate as possible, we accept no responsibility for any loss, injury or inconvenience sustained by anyone using this book.

Paper in this book is certified against the Forest Stewardship Council™ standards. FSC™ promotes environmentally responsible, socially beneficial and economically viable management of the world's forests.

MIX
Paper from responsible sources
FSC™ C021741
www.fsc.org

acknowledgments

This edition of Lonely Planet's *Swahili phrasebook* is based on the previous edition by the Lonely Planet Language Products team and Dr Martin Benjamin, who provided the translations and cultural information, and wrote a concise guide to Swahili grammar. Martin is an anthropologist who has lived and worked in Tanzania for many years as a researcher and consultant on issues of development, health and gender. In addition to teaching Swahili and Anthropology at Wesleyan University, he is the founder and editor of the Kamusi Project Internet Living Swahili Dictionary at Yale University. Readers who wish to advance their Swahili can use the online lessons that he is developing in the Learning Guide at www.kamusiproject.org, and all travellers to East Africa are invited to visit the How to Help page of this site to learn how to contribute photos to the cause of Swahili education.

Martin wishes to thank Charles Mironko and Anne Geoghegan for their work on the previous edition of this phrasebook – many of their words have found their way into the current edition. Thanks also to Ben and Branislava for all their work preparing and editing this book. My deepest thanks for making it possible for me to (almost) meet my deadlines go to my wife Veronica, who yielded me to this project in the weeks right after our wedding.

acknowledgments

make the most of this phrasebook ...

Anyone can speak another language! It's all about confidence. Don't worry if you can't remember your school language lessons or if you've never learnt a language before. Even if you learn the very basics (on the inside covers of this book), your travel experience will be the better for it. You have nothing to lose and everything to gain when the locals hear you making an effort.

finding things in this book

For easy navigation, this book is in sections. The Basics chapters are the ones you'll thumb through time and again. The Practical section covers basic travel situations like catching transport and finding a bed. The Social section gives you conversational phrases, pick-up lines, the ability to express opinions – so you can get to know people. Food has a section all of its own: gourmets and vegetarians are covered and local dishes feature. Safe Travel equips you with health and police phrases, just in case. Sustainable Travel, finally, completes this book. Remember the colours of each section and you'll find everything easily; or use the comprehensive Index. Otherwise, check the two-way traveller's Dictionary for the word you need.

being understood

Throughout this book you'll see coloured phrases on each page. They're phonetic guides to help you pronounce the language. Start with them to get a feel for how the language sounds. The pronunciation chapter in Basics will explain more, but you can be confident that if you read the coloured phrase, you'll be understood. As you become familiar with the spoken language, move on to using the actual text in the language which will help you perfect your pronunciation.

communication tips

Body language, ways of doing things, sense of humour – all have a role to play in every culture. 'Local talk' boxes show you common ways of saying things, or everyday language to drop into conversation. 'Listen for ...' boxes supply the phrases you may hear. They start with the phonetic guide (because you'll hear it before you know what's being said) and then lead in to the language and the English translation.

CONTENTS

5

swahili

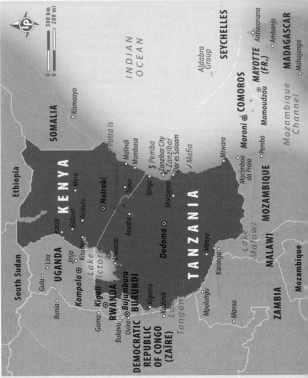

- national language
- widely spoken

For more details, see the **introduction**.

Swahili is one of the most widely spoken African languages and is internationally recognised as the key language of communication in the East African region. It belongs to the Bantu group of languages from the Niger-Congo family and can be traced back to the first millenium AD. This Bantu origin is clearly visible in the distinctive grammar and sound system of Swahili.

Although the number of speakers of Swahili throughout East Africa is estimated to be well over 50 million, it's the mother tongue of only about 4–5 million people, and is predominantly used as a second language or a lingua franca by speakers of other African languages. Swahili is the national language of Tanzania and Kenya and is widely used in Uganda, Rwanda and Burundi, as well as in the eastern part of the Democratic Republic of Congo and on the Indian Ocean islands of Zanzibar and the Comoros. There are speakers of Swahili in the southern parts of Ethiopia and Somalia, the northern regions of Mozambique and Zambia, and even on the northwestern coast of Madagascar.

The development of Swahili through time is an interesting story of contact between nations, reflecting many political and social changes in this part of the world. Originally spoken by indigenous people along the coast and on the

at a glance ...

language name: Swahili

name in language:
Kiswahili kee·swa·hee·lee

language family:
Niger-Congo

key countries:
Tanzania, Kenya

approximate number of speakers: 4–5 million as first language, over 50 million as second language or lingua franca

close relatives:
Bantu languages
(eg Pokomo, Mijikenda, Comorian)

donations to English:
safari, simba (lion)

introduction

9

islands, it was the main language of coastal trade, and therefore from the 7th century heavily influenced by Arabic, principally in the vocabulary – the word 'Swahili' itself comes from an Arabic word for 'coastal'. With the arrival of European explorers and colonisers and the rise of the slave trade in the 19th century, Swahili spread inland. Apart from Arabic, there are influences from Persian, Portuguese, and of course, English (words like *baisikeli*, *penseli* and *kompyuta* have only been adapted slightly to reflect Swahili pronunciation).

It's hardly surprising that in an area as vast as East Africa many different dialects of Swahili can be found, but you shouldn't have problems being understood if you stick to the standard coastal form, as used in this book. Standard Swahili developed from the urban dialect of Zanzibar City, dominant from pre-colonial times. The missionaries and colonial governments in Kenya and Tanzania used it first to communicate with the locals and later encouraged its use in administration, which led to its official status in the post-colonial period.

Even though Swahili grammar can seem a bit daunting, you should find the pronunciation pretty much straightforward. The writing system is based on the Roman alphabet, which will make using this phrasebook and learning Swahili much easier.

So wherever you go throughout the East African region, you'll find Swahili greatly useful and attempts to communicate with locals in the language will be greatly appreciated. This book gives you the practical phrases you need to get by, as well as the fun, spontaneous phrases that lead to a better understanding of East African people and their culture. Local knowledge, new relationships and a sense of satisfaction are on the tip of your tongue. So don't just stand there, say something!

abbreviations used in this book:

a	adjective	n	noun
adv	adverb	pl	plural
f	feminine	prep	preposition
Ken	Kenya	sg	singular
m	masculine	Tan	Tanzania
lit	literal translation	v	verb

The pronunciation of Swahili is relatively simple, since most of the sounds in this language are also found in English. Once you learn a few basic rules you won't have any problems reading or pronouncing it, but we've included a pronunciation guide throughout this book to make it even easier.

vowel sounds

Vowels are short and each one is pronounced clearly, even when not stressed. There are no diphthongs in Swahili (ie vowel sound combinations, like in English 'how' or 'day').

symbol	english equivalent	swahili example	transliteration
a	father	*dada*	*da·da*
ay	may	*wewe*	*way·way*
ee	bee	*sisi*	*see·see*
oh	role	*moja*	*moh·ja*
oo	moon	*duka*	*doo·ka*

consonant sounds

Most consonants in Swahili have equivalents in English. The only one that might be a bit unusual for an English speaker is the sound ng. It can be a bit tricky at first, but with a little practice it should come easily – try saying 'sing along' a few times and then dropping the 'si', and that's how it sounds at the beginning of a word.

The sounds th and dh occur only in words borrowed from Arabic.

Swahili speakers make only a slight distinction between r and l. Instead of the hard 'r', try pronouncing a light 'd'.

symbol	english equivalent	swahili example	transliteration
b	big	*betri*	*bay*·tree
ch	chilli	*chakula*	cha·*koo*·la
d	din	*duka*	*doo*·ka
dh	this	*dhambi*	*dham*·bee
f	fun	*sufu*	*soo*·foo
g	go	*gari/ghali*	*ga*·ree/*ga*·lee
h	hat	*tarehe*	ta·*ray*·hay
j	jam	*jiwe*	*jee*·way
k	kick	*ukuta*	oo·*koo*·ta
l	loud	*uliza*	oo·*lee*·za
m	man	*mwanamume*	m·wa·na·*moo*·may
n	no	*nunua*	noo·*noo*·a
ng	sing	*ng'ombe*	ng·*ohm*·bay
ny	canyon	*nyasi*	*nya*·see
p	pig	*chupa*	*choo*·pa
r	run (but softer, more like a light 'd')	*dirisha*	dee·*ree*·sha
s	so	*kisu*	*kee*·soo
sh	ship	*shida*	*shee*·da
t	tin	*tochi*	*toh*·chee
th	thing	*thelathini*	thay·la·*thee*·nee
v	van	*vumbi*	*voom*·bee
w	win	*wazo*	*wa*·zoh
y	yes	*yoyote*	yoh·*yoh*·tay
z	zoo	*ziwa*	*zee*·wa

regional variations

Being used over a huge geographical area, Swahili has many dialectical variations, which can be grouped as northern, central and southern dialects, with a further basic distinction between urban and rural dialects. The form of Swahili in this phrasebook is the standard form which is based on Kiunguja, the coastal dialect spoken in Zanzibar City. When you travel across East Africa, you should be understood using this book, as all the regional variations are generally mutually intelligible and also increasingly influenced by this standard form, which is used in all the media.

word stress

In Swahili, words are almost always stressed on the second-last syllable. There are only a handful of words that break this rule, and these are mostly loanwords. In our pronunciation guide, the stressed syllable is always in italics.

stressing the point

• Changing the stress in a word can sometimes make a whole lot of difference. Make sure to get the stress in the right place on *barabara* ba·*ra*·ba·ra (amazing). If you say ba·ra·*ba*·ra, you're simply saying 'road'!

• Many words in Swahili come from English, but the pronunciation changed slightly. Be sure to stress the second-last syllable in the word *tiketi* tee·*kay*·tee (ticket), rather than the first syllable (*tee*·kay·tee) as you would in English. *Tikiti* tee·*kee*·ti is used instead of *tiketi* in many areas – listen to the locals' pronunciation and follow their lead.

reading & writing

Swahili was traditionally written in a modified Arabic script (used mostly for writing epic poetry). The Roman-based alphabet, in use since the mid-19th century, was formalised in the 1930s. It consists of 24 letters (all the letters of the English alphabet except 'q' and 'x').

The correspondence between the written language and the pronunciation is consistent. As a general rule, every written letter is pronounced. When two vowels appear together, each one must be pronounced separately. For example, *kawaida* (usual) is pronounced ka·wa·*ee*·da. However, if the same vowel is repeated twice at the end of a word, it's pronounced as one syllable and the stress falls on that (last) syllable, rather than the second-last one: *sikukuu* see·koo·*koo* (holiday).

There are only a few two-letter combinations in written Swahili that don't follow the general rule of pronouncing every letter separately: *ch, dh, gh, ng, ny, sh* and *th* all represent single sounds (see **consonant sounds**, page 12). Our coloured pronunciation guides indicate the correct pronunciation so don't worry if you can't remember these rules.

The symbol ' which appears in written Swahili after the letter combination *ng*, as in *ng'ombe* ng·*ohm*·bay (cow), is called a glottal stop, which is similar to the tightening of the throat that happens when you cough. You can also hear it in the word 'bottle' when the double 't' is swallowed. It's not represented in the pronunciation guide, as it only serves to show in writing that *ng'* should be pronounced as one syllable. Without it, these two letters belong to separate syllables, as in *changu chan*·goo (finger).

alphabet					
A a a	*B b* bee	*C c* see	*D d* dee	*E e* ay	*F f* ayf
G g jee	*H h* *ay*·chee	*I i* ee	*J j* jay	*K k* kay	*L l* ayl
M m aym	*N n* ayn	*O o* oh	*P p* pee	*R r* ar	*S s* ays
T t tee	*U u* oo	*V v* vee	*W w* *dab*·al·yoo	*Y y* wa·ee	*Z z* *zayd*·ee

a–z phrasebuilder
tengeneza sentensi

contents

The index below shows the grammatical structures you can use to say what you want. Look under each function – listed in alphabetical order – for more information on how to build your own phrases. For example, to tell the taxi driver where your hotel is, look for **giving directions/orders** and you'll be directed to information on **location**, **prepositions** and **requests**. A glossary of grammatical terms is also included at the end of this chapter. The label 'survival Swahili' used after some forms in this chapter means that the form won't be fully correct, but will generally be understood. You can find detailed explanations and grammar exercises in the Learning Guide at www.kamusiproject.org.

adjectives & adverbs

Adjectives always come after the noun they describe.

good news   *habari nzuri*   ha·*ba*·ree n·*zoo*·ree
                    (lit: news good)

Many adjectives in the **dictionary** have a hyphen in front. The hyphen indicates the space for a prefix, which varies depending on certain qualities of the thing being described. The rules are complicated and there are many exceptions, but the basic groups are listed here.

noun qualities	prefix	swahili example	english example
person or animal sg	m-	*mtoto mzuri* m·*toh*·toh m·*zoo*·ree *tembo mkubwa* taym·boh m·*koo*·bwa	good child big elephant
person or animal pl	wa-	*watoto wazuri* wa·*toh*·toh wa·*zoo*·ree *tembo wakubwa* taym·boh wa·*koo*·bwa	good children big elephants
object sg&pl (survival swahili)	n- or j- or no prefix	*habari nzuri* ha·*ba*·ree n·*zoo*·ree *pikipiki kubwa* pee·kee·*pee*·kee koo·bwa	good news big motorcycle

Many Swahili nouns can become adjectives by using the word 'of' before them. The word used for 'of' changes depending on the qualities of the thing being described, as shown in the table on the next page. The word 'of' is also used to express possession. (For more details on the forms for 'of' see also **possession**.)

noun qualities	'of'	swahili example	english example
person or animal sg&pl	wa	*tembo **wa** kijivu* taym·boh wa kee·jee·voo	gray elephant
		*mbu **wa** jioni* m·boo wa jee·oh·nee	evening mosquitos
object sg (survival swahili)	ya	*baisikeli **ya** kisasa* ba·ee·see·kay·lee ya kee·sa·sa	modern bike
object pl (survival swahili)	za	*boti **za** mbao* boh·tee za m·ba·oh	wooden boats

Adverbs also go after the verb they're modifying. Often, the word *kwa* appears before the adverb – in that case, *kwa* resembles the English suffix '-ly' (eg 'nicely').

I walked a lot.
　Nilitembea sana.　　　　　　　nee·lee·taym·*bay*·a *sa*·na
　(lit: I-*past*-walk much)

She speaks in a hurry.
　Anasema kwa haraka.　　　　　a·na·*say*·ma kwa ha·*ra*·ka
　(lit: she-*present*-talk with hurry)

articles

describing things • naming things/people

Swahili doesn't have articles (a/an, the). To refer to a specific object (ie 'the' thing), use a demonstrative pronoun ('this' book) or a possessive pronoun ('his' book) (see **demonstratives** & **possession**). To refer to 'a' thing (ie an unspecified thing in a generic sense), use the adjective *-moja* for 'one' (preferably with the appropriate prefix – see **adjectives** & **adverbs**):

a flower　　　　　*ua moja*　　　　　oo·a *moh*·ja
　　　　　　　　　　　(lit: flower one)

'Some' is expressed with the phrase *baadhi ya*, which is used before the noun, or *kadhaa*, which comes after the noun.

some people	*baadhi ya watu* (lit: some people)	*ba·dhee ya wa·too*
	watu kadhaa (lit: people some)	*wa·too ka·dha*

be

doing things · making a statement · negating

In the present tense, the verb 'be' (*kuwa*) is incredibly easy. No matter what the subject, the word for 'am/is/are' is *ni*.

I am English.
Mimi ni Mwingereza.   *mee·mee nee mween·gay·ray·za*
(lit: I am English)

We are Africans.
Sisi ni Waafrika.   *see·see nee wa·a·free·ka*
(lit: we are Africans)

It's just as easy to form negative statements – the form of 'be' is *si* for all persons in singular and plural.

I am not a doctor.
Mimi si daktari.   *mee·mee see dak·ta·ree*
(lit: I am-not doctor)

We are not students.
Sisi si wanafunzi.   *see·see see wa·na·foon·zee*
(lit: we are-not students)

However, many things that you can 'be' in English are things you can 'have' in Swahili (see **have**).

In the past and future tenses the verb 'to be' has a different form for each person, as shown in the next table.

past tense

I	was	nilikuwa	nee·lee·koo·wa
you sg	were	ulikuwa	oo·lee·koo·wa
he/she (person)*	was	alikuwa	a·lee·koo·wa
it (object) (survival swahili)		ilikuwa	ee·lee·koo·wa
we	were	tulikuwa	too·lee·koo·wa
you pl		mlikuwa	m·lee·koo·wa
they (person)*		walikuwa	wa·lee·koo·wa
they (object) (survival swahili)		zilikuwa	zee·lee·koo·wa

future tense

I	will be	nitakuwa	nee·ta·koo·wa
you sg		utakuwa	oo·ta·koo·wa
he/she (person)*		atakuwa	a·ta·koo·wa
it (object) (survival swahili)		itakuwa	ee·ta·koo·wa
we		tutakuwa	too·ta·koo·wa
you pl		mtakuwa	m·ta·koo·wa
they (person)*		watakuwa	wa·ta·koo·wa
they (object) (survival swahili)		zitakuwa	zee·ta·koo·wa

* or animal(s)

demonstratives

naming things/people • pointing things out

When you want to point something out (eg 'this thing' or 'those things'), remember that in Swahili the demonstrative comes after the noun it refers to:

this child	mtoto huyu (lit: child this)	m·toh·toh hoo·yoo
those giraffes	twiga wale (lit: giraffes those)	twee·ga wa·lay

noun qualities	this/these	that/those
person or animal sg	*huyu* hoo·yoo	*yule* yoo·lay
person or animal pl	*hawu* ha·wa	*wale* wa·lay
object sg (survival swahili)	*hii* hee	*ile* ee·lay
object pl (survival swahili)	*hizi* hee·zee	*zile* zee·lay

have

doing things • making a statement • possessing

In Swahili, the verb 'have' (*kuwa na*) is very similar to the verb 'be' (*kuwa*) – essentially, it translates as 'to be with'. Many things that you 'are' in English are things that you 'have' in Swahili:

I am hungry.
　Nina njaa. 　　　　　　　　 *nee*·na n·*ja*
　(lit: I-have hunger)

She is cold.
　Ana baridi. 　　　　　　　　 *a*·na ba·*ree*·dee
　(lit: she-has cold)

In the present tense, the verb is irregular, but not difficult, as you can see in the tables that follow. In the past and future tenses, simply add the word *na* after the correct form of the verb 'be' in the table on page 20.

I	have	*nina*	*nee*·na
you sg		*una*	*oo*·na
he/she (person or animal)	has	*ana*	*a*·na
it (object) (survival swahili)		*ina*	*ee*·na
we	have	*tuna*	*too*·na
you pl		*mna*	m·*na*
they (person or animal)		*wana*	*wa*·na
they (object) (survival swahili)		*zina*	*zee*·na

I	don't have	*sina*	*see*·na
you sg		*huna*	*hoo*·na
he/she (person)*	doesn't have	*hana*	*ha*·na
it (object) (survival swahili)		*haina*	ha·*ee*·na
we	don't have	*hatuna*	ha·*too*·na
you pl		*hamna*	*ham*·na
they (person)*		*hawana*	ha·*wa*·na
they (object) (survival swahili)		*hazina*	ha·*zee*·na

* or animal(s)

location

To say that something is 'here' or 'there' requires two parts – variations on the verb 'be' and a locative suffix (ie a verb ending that indicates location). Swahili divides location into three general areas – 'here', 'there', and 'inside', with these corresponding suffixes:

here	*-po*	·poh
there	*-ko*	·koh
inside	*-mo*	·moh

I will be at the market at noon.
   *Nitakuwe**ko***   nee·ta·koo·*way*·koh
   *so**ko**ni saa sita.*   soh·*koh*·nee sa *see*·ta
   (lit: I-*future*-be-there market-at hour six)

In addition, if something is at a specific place, the word for that place will often take the suffix -*ni*:

store	*duka*	*doo*·ka
at the store	*dukani*	doo·*ka*·nee

In the present tense, the locative suffixes are used with the subject prefixes in the table below, depending on the person or thing whose location is pointed out:

subject prefixes used when making statements			
I	ni-	we	tu-
you sg	u-	you pl	m-
he/she (person)*	yu-	they (people)*	wa-
it (object) (survival swahili)	i-	they (objects) (survival swahili)	zi-

subjects prefixes used for negating			
I	si-	we	hatu-
you sg	hu-	you pl	ham-
he/she (person)*	hayu-	they (people)*	hawa-
it (object) (survival swahili)	hai-	they (objects) (survival swahili)	hazi-

* or animal(s)

Is she at school?
Yuko shuleni?   yoo·koh shoo·*lay*·nee
(lit: she-there school-at)

She is not here.
Hayupo.   ha·*yoo*·poh
(lit: she-not-here)

For past and future tenses, use the forms of the verb 'be' from page 20 and attach the suffix directly to the verb. Adding the locative suffix will always change the stress of the verb to the syllable immediately before the suffix. Swahili speakers often change the final -wa to -we before adding the locative suffix.

Was he at the hotel?
Alikuwako gestini?   a·lee·koo·*wa*·koh gay·*stee*·nee
(lit: he-*past*-be-there hotel-at)

We won't be here tomorrow.
Hatutakuwepo kesho.   ha·too·ta·koo·*way*·poh *kay*·shoh
(lit: not-we-*future*-be-here tomorrow)

negatives

Negative verbs are formed in a similar way to positive verbs (see **verbs**), but with different subject prefixes and different tense markers.

negative subject prefixes			
I	si-	we	hatu-
you sg	hu-	you pl	ham-
he/she (person)*	ha-	they (person)*	hawa-
it (object) (survival swahili)	hai-	they (object) (survival swahili)	hazi-

* or animal(s)

Negative tense markers for past and future tense are -*ku*- and -*ta*- respectively:

I didn't know.   *Si**ku**jua.*   see·koo·*joo*·a
                     (lit: not-me-*past*-know)
It won't rain.   *Hai**ta**nyesha.*   ha·ee·ta·*nyay*·sha
                     (lit: not-it-*future*-rain)

In the present tense, however, no tense marker is used, but there's a twist – if the verb ends in an -*a*, that final -*a* changes to an -*i*.

know   -*jua*   ·*joo*·a
I don't know.   *Sijui.*   see·*joo*·ee
                     (lit: not-me-know)

For negative forms of the verb **be**, see page 19.

nouns

describing things • naming things/people

Nouns in Swahili are divided into groups with similar qualities or characteristics called 'noun classes'. What noun class something belongs to determines many other things in a sentence – for example, the subject prefix or object infix of the verb, the prefix of any associated adjectives, and the demonstrative and possessive pronouns to use.

Although Swahili has 16 noun classes, you can get by with the basic sets of rules shown in all the tables of this chapter. The others cover concepts you can explore if you're inspired to study Swahili in greater depth. Most noun classes come in pairs for the singular and the plural (with a different prefix for the two forms). The prefixes for noun classes that will allow you to get by are given in pairs below:

noun classes			
prefix sg	**example**	**prefix pl**	**example**
m- (person or animal)	*mke* m·kay wife	wa- (person or animal)	*wake* wa·kay wives
m-	*mto* m·toh river	mi-	*mito* mee·toh rivers
no prefix	*embe* aym·bay mango	ma-	*maembe* ma·aym·bay mangoes
ji-	*jicho* jee·choh eye	ma-	*macho* ma·choh eyes
ki-	*kiatu* kee·a·too shoe	vi-	*viatu* vee·a·too shoes
ch-	*choo* choh toilet	vy-	*vyoo* vyoh toilets
u-	*ukuta* oo·koo·ta wall	no prefix	*kuta* koo·ta walls

Many nouns are the same in the singular and the plural – the only way to tell whether a speaker is referring to one or several things is by looking at the associated grammatical elements within the sentence:

This bird flies.
> *Ndege huyu anaruka.*   n·*day*·gay *hoo*·yoo a·na·*roo*·ka
> (lit: bird this it-*present*-fly)

These birds fly.
> *Ndege hawa wanaruka.*   n·*day*·gay *ha*·wa wa·na·*roo*·ka
> (lit: bird these they-*present*-fly)

personal pronouns

doing things • making a statement

Personal pronouns in Swahili have just one form for both sub-ject (eg 'I', 'they') and object ('me', 'them') in a sentence.

I/me	*mimi*	*mee*·mee
you sg	*wewe*	*way*·way
he/she/him/her/it	*yeye*	*yay*·yay
we/us	*sisi*	*see*·see
you pl	*ninyi/nyinyi*	*nee*·nyee/*nyee*·nyee
they/them	*wao*	*wa*·oh

Personal pronouns are often not necessary as subject of a sentence, as the form of Swahili verbs already indicates who that is. Using the personal pronoun in such a case often has the same effect as putting an exclamation point at the end of your sentence:

I want food.
> *Ninataka chakula.*   nee·na·*ta*·ka cha·*koo*·la
> (lit: I-*present*-want food)

I want food!
> *Mimi ninataka chakula.*   *mee*·mee nee·na·*ta*·ka cha·*koo*·la
> (lit: I I-*present*-want food)

You can sometimes, however, use the personal pronoun in-stead of a verb construction in answer to a direct question:

BASICS

Who wants food?
  Nani anataka chakula?   na·nee a·na·ta·ka cha·koo·la
  (lit: who *third-person-sg-present*-want food)

I do.
  Mimi.   mee·mee
  (lit: me)

possession

To say that a thing belongs to someone or something, you can either use the word 'of' with the name of the possessor, or you can use a possessive pronoun. The possessive pronouns have a prefix and a suffix, which change according to different patterns. The suffix changes according to who or what is the possessor:

english equivalent	pronoun suffix	
my	-angu	·an·goo
your sg	-ako	·a·koh
his/her/its	-ake	·a·kay
our	-etu	·ay·too
your pl	-enu	·ay·noo
their	-ao	·a·oh

This is our camera.
  Hii ni kemra yetu.   hee nee kaym·ra yay·too
  (lit: this be camera our)

Both the possessive pronoun prefix and the word 'of' change according to the noun class qualities of the thing being possessed:

noun qualities	pronoun prefix	'of'	swahili example	english example
person or animal sg&pl	w-	wa	mtoto **wangu** m·*toh*·toh *wan*·goo	my child
object sg (survival swahili)	y-	ya	pikipiki **yako** pee·kee·*pee*·kee *ya*·koh	your motorcycle
object pl (survival swahili)	z-	za	nyumba **zetu** nyoom·ba *zay*·too	our houses

If you use the word 'of' instead of the pronoun, this word and the name of the possessor always go after the thing being possessed:

today's news   *habari za leo*   ha·*ba*·ree za *lay*·oh
              (lit: news of today)

prepositions

giving directions/orders · indicating location

Prepositions always come before the word they go with:

since yesterday   *tangu jana*   *tan*·goo *ja*·na

across from, opposite	ng'ambo ya	ng·*am*·boh ya
after	baada ya	ba·*a*·da ya
at	kwenye	*kway*·nyay
before	kabla	*ka*·bla
from	kutoka	koo·*toh*·ka
in	katika	ka·*tee*·ka
on	juu ya	joo ya
since	tangu	*tan*·goo
to	hadi	*ha*·dee

questions

To ask a question in Swahili, use the word *je*. It essentially means 'hey, I'm asking a question' and can go either at the beginning or the end of a sentence:

What's your name?
Jina lako ni nani, je?   jee·na *la*·koh nee *na*·nee jay
  (lit: name your be who *question*)

The word *je* has one other function – if you attach it directly to the verb in a sentence, it serves as the question word 'how?':

How do you say …?
Unasemaje …?   oo·na·say·*ma*·jay …
  (lit: you-*present*-say-how)

You can also turn most statements into questions simply by raising intonation at the end of a sentence.
  For question words, see the **dictionary**. To answer a direct question, see **personal pronouns**.

requests

Basic requests are very easy. To tell one person to do something, simply use the verb stem (dictionary form of a verb). To tell more than one person to do something, add the suffix *-ni* to the verb stem (if the verb stem ends in an *-a*, it changes to an *-e*).

english	verb stem	request sg	request pl
run	*-kimbia* keem·*bee*·a	*kimbia* keem·*bee*·a	*kimbieni* keem·bee·*ay*·nee
return	*-rudi* roo·dee	*rudi* roo·dee	*rudini* roo·*dee*·nee
speak	*-sema* say·ma	*sema* say·ma	*semeni* say·*may*·nee

A few verbs have irregular request forms:

english	verb stem	request sg	request pl
come	*-ja* ·ja	*njoo* n·joh	*njooni* n·joh·nee
go	*-enda* ·ayn·da	*nenda* nayn·da	*nendeni* nayn·*day*·nee

there is/are

making a statement • negating • pointing things out

The word *kuna* corresponds to both 'there is' and 'there are'. The word *hakuna* is used for 'there isn't' and 'there aren't'.

There are two passengers.
Kuna abiria wawili.   koo·na a·bee·*ree*·a wa·*wee*·lee
(lit: there-are passengers two)

There isn't any toilet paper.
Hakuna karatasi ya choo.   ha·*koo*·na ka·ra·*ta*·see ya *choh*
(lit: there-are-not paper of toilet)

verbs

doing things

Most verbs in Swahili follow a very regular (although often quite complex) set of rules. The Swahili verb has slots for different elements. A basic verb consists of a subject prefix, a tense marker and a verb stem. The table below shows these and other slots (such as object infix and suffix) that can be filled within the structure of a verb:

verb slots				
subject prefix	tense marker	object infix	verb stem	suffix
a-	*-na-*	*-tu-*	*-pik(a)-*	*-ia*

He is cooking for us.
  Anatupikia.   a·na·too·peek·*ee*·a
  (lit: he-now-us-cooks-for)

As you can see in the table below, the subject prefix changes
depending on the noun class of the subject ('he'), while the
object infix depends on the noun class of the object ('us').

noun qualities	subject prefix	negative subject prefix	object infix
I/me	*ni-*	*si-*	*-ni-*
you sg	*u-*	*hu-*	*-ku-*
he/she (person or animal – often begins with *m-*)	*a-*	*ha-*	*-m-/-mw-*
it (object) (survival swahili)	*i-*	*hai-*	*-i-*
we/us	*tu-*	*hatu-*	*-tu-*
you pl	*m-*	*ham-*	*-wa-*
they (person or animal – often begins with *wa-*)	*wu-*	*hawa-*	*-wa-*
they (object) (survival swahili)	*zi-*	*hazi-*	*-zi-*

As the example below shows, both the direct object ('the
book') and the indirect object ('me') use the same set of infixes,
although if you have both a direct and an indirect object in the
sentence, only the indirect object will be marked in the object
slot within the verb.

He gave the book to me.
  Alinipa kitabu.   a·lee·*nee*·pa kee·*ta*·boo
  (lit: he-*past*-me-give book)
He gave it.
  Alikipa.   a·lee·*kee*·pa
  (lit: he-*past*-it-give)

The following are the most common tense markers that you'll come across:

tense	tense marker	swahili example	english example
present	-na-	ninasoma nee·na·soh·ma	I am reading
past (completed action)	-li-	nilisoma nee·lee·soh·ma	I read
past (recent or ongoing action)	-me-	nimesoma nee·may·soh·ma	I have read
future	-ta-	nitasoma nee·ta·soh·ma	I will read

If you take one subject prefix, one tense marker, and one verb stem, you can make a basic verb:

He said … *Alisema …* a·lee·*say*·ma …
(lit: he-*past*-say)

If your sentence has an object, put the appropriate infix between the tense marker and the verb stem.

I will marry you. *Nitakuoa.* nee·ta·koo·*oh*·a
(lit: I-will-you-marry)

For information on negative verbs, see **negatives**.

word order

making a statement

Swahili sentences are usually constructed in the order subject-verb-object, just like in English:

The elephants eat grass.
Tembo wanakula nyasi. *taym*·boh wa·na·*koo*·la *nya*·see
(lit: elephants eat grass)

For word order in questions and negative statements, see **questions** and **negatives**.

glossary

adjective	a word that describes something – 'a **long** journey'
adverb	a word that explains how an action was done – 'he walked **slowly**'
article	the words 'a/an' and 'the'
demonstrative pronoun	a word like 'this/these' or 'that/those' used to point something out
infix	syllable(s) inserted in the middle of a word, eg to show what the object in the sentence is
locative suffix	syllable(s) added to the end of a word to indicate location
noun	a thing, person or idea, eg 'table'
object	the thing or person in the sentence that has the action directed to it, eg in 'Please bring me the menu', 'the menu' is the direct object and 'me' is the indirect object
possesive pronoun	a word that conveys the meaning 'mine', 'yours', 'ours', 'theirs', etc
prefix	syllable(s) added to the beginning of a word, eg to show who the subject in the sentence is
preposition	a word like 'from' or 'after' in English
pronoun	a word that means 'you', 'she', etc

subject	the thing or person in the sentence that does the action – 'I took the train'
suffix	syllable(s) added to the end of a word to modify its meaning, eg -**ly** is added to 'happy' to make 'happily'
tense marker	*infix* in a verb which shows the time an action takes place, ie past, present, future
verb	the word that tells you what action happened – eg 'I **saw** the book'
verb stem	the dictionary form of a verb, which doesn't change – 'search' in 'searched' and 'searching'

Do you speak (English)?
Unasema (Kiingereza)? oo·na·*say*·ma (kee·een·gay·*ray*·za)

Does anyone speak (English)?
Kuna mtu yeyote koo·na m·too yay·*yoh*·tay
kusema (Kiingereza)? koo·*say*·ma (kee·een·gay·*ray*·za)

Do you understand?
Unaelewa? oo·na·ay·*lay*·wa

Yes, I understand.
Ndiyo, naelewa. n·*dee*·yoh na·ay·*lay*·wa

No, I don't understand.
Hapana, sielewi. ha·*pa*·na see·ay·*lay*·wee

I understand.
Naelewa. na·ay·*lay*·wa

I don't understand.
Sielewi. see·ay·*lay*·wee

speaking sheng

While travelling around Kenya, you might come across Sheng, a mixture of Swahili and English with a fair sprinkling of other local languages. It's spoken almost exclusively by young people. Unless you're reasonably fluent in Swahili, you probably won't even realise Sheng is being spoken, so listen out for *sassa sa*·sa (distinctive greeting between friends). The response can be either *besht* baysht, *mambo mam*·boh or *fit* feet (all variations of 'hello').

I speak (English).
    Nasema (Kiingereza).   na-*say*-ma (kee-een-gay-*ray*-za)

I don't speak (Swahili).
    Sisemi (Kiswahili).   see-*say*-mee (kee-swa-*hee*-lee)

I speak a little.
    Nasema kidogo.   na-*say*-ma kee-*doh*-goh

What does *'asante'* mean?
    Neno 'asante' lina   *nay*-noh a-*san*-tay *lee*-na
    maana gani?   ma-*a*-na *ga*-nee

How do you …?		
pronounce this	*Unatamkaje?*	oo-na-tam-*ka*-jay
write *'asante'*	*Unaandikaje*	oo-na-an-dee-*ka*-je
	'asante'?	a-*san*-tay

Could you please …?	*Tafadhali …*	ta-fa-*dha*-lee …
repeat that	*sema tena*	*say*-ma *tay*-na
speak more	*sema pole*	*say*-ma *poh*-lay
slowly	*pole*	*poh*-lay
write it down	*andika*	an-*dee*-ka

---

knock knock!

The word for 'stranger' in Swahili, *mgeni* m-*gay*-nee, is also the word for 'guest', and many East Africans enjoy welcoming strangers as guests not only to their countries but to their homes too.

You'll always be greeted with *karibu* ka-*ree*-boo (welcome). It's an all-purpose word, used to welcome visitors to the home, the business or even the country. It also means 'you're welcome' (when someone thanks you).

When entering someone's home or office, you should always announce your presence and your intent to come in by calling out *hodi* hoh-dee (Hello, may I enter?) before crossing the threshold. It can be accompanied by knocking on the door. Even if you're being escorted in by the inhabitant, it's polite to pause at the door and say *hodi*.

cardinal numbers

namba kamili

0	*sifuri*	see·*foo*·ree
1	*moja*	*moh*·ja
2	*mbili*	m·*bee*·lee
3	*tatu*	ta·too
4	*nne*	n·nay
5	*tano*	ta·noh
6	*sita*	see·ta
7	*saba*	sa·ba
8	*nane*	na·nay
9	*tisa*	tee·sa
10	*kumi*	koo·mee
11	*kumi na moja*	koo·mee na *moh*·ja
12	*kumi na mbili*	koo·mee na m·*bee*·lee
13	*kumi na tatu*	koo·mee na ta·too
14	*kumi na nne*	koo·mee na n·nay
15	*kumi na tano*	koo·mee na ta·noh
16	*kumi na sita*	koo·mee na see·ta
17	*kumi na saba*	koo·mee na sa·ba
18	*kumi na nane*	koo·mee na na·nay
19	*kumi na tisa*	koo·mee na tee·sa
20	*ishirini*	ee·shee·ree·nee
21	*ishirini na moja*	ee·shee·ree·nee na moh·ja
30	*thelathini*	thay·la·thee·nee
40	*arobaini*	a·roh·ba·ee·nee
50	*hamsini*	ham·see·nee
60	*sitini*	see·tee·nee
70	*sabini*	sa·bee·nee
80	*themanini*	thay·ma·nee·nee
90	*tisini*	tee·see·nee
100	*mia moja*	mee·a moh·ja
1,000	*elfu*	ayl·foo
100,000	*laki*	la·kee

ordinal numbers

For persons and animals, use *wa* wa. For objects, use *ya* ya before the cardinal number – '1st' and '2nd' are irregular though:

1st	*wa/ya kwanza*	wa/ya *kwan*·za
2nd	*wa/ya pili*	wa/ya *pee*·lee
3rd	*wa/ya tatu*	wa/ya *ta*·too
4th	*wa/ya nne*	wa/ya *n*·nay
5th	*wa/ya tano*	wa/ya *ta*·noh

fractions

sehemu

a quarter	*robo moja*	*roh*·boh *moh*·ja
a third	*theluthi moja*	thay·*loo*·thee *moh*·ja
a half	*nusu*	*noo*·soo
three-quarters	*robo tatu*	*roh*·boh *ta*·too
all	*jumla*	*joom*·la
none	*hakuna*	ha·*koo*·na

useful amounts

kiasi zenye manufaa

How much?	*Kiasi gani?*	kee·*a*·see *ga*·nee
How many?	*Ngapi?*	n·*ga*·pee
(Please) give me ...	*(Tafadhali) nipe ...*	(ta·fa·*dha*·lee) *nee*·pay ...
less	*chache zaidi*	*cha*·chay za·*ee*·dee
(just) a little	*kidogo (tu)*	kee·*doh*·goh (too)
a lot	*kingi*	*keen*·gee
more	*zaidi*	za·*ee*·dee
some	*kiasi*	kee·*a*·see

telling the time

kusema saa

The word for time, *saa* sa, also means 'hour', 'watch' and 'clock'. Time and hours are distinguished by different noun classes, so *saa mbili* sa m·*bee*·lee (lit: clocks two) means '2 o'clock Swahili time/8 o'clock European time' while *masaa mawili* ma·*sa* ma·*wee*·lee (lit: hours two) means 'two hours'. (For more on noun classes, see the **phrasebuilder**.)

What time is it?
  Ni saa ngapi?   nee sa n·*ga*·pee

It's (ten) o'clock.
  Ni saa (nne).   nee sa (*n*·nay)

Five past (ten).
  Ni saa (nne) na tano. nee sa (*n*·nay) na *ta*·noh

Quarter past (ten).
  Ni saa (nne) na robo. nee sa (*n*·nay) na *roh*·boh

Half past (ten).
  Ni saa (nne) na nusu. nee sa (*n*·nay) na *noo*·soo

Quarter to (ten).
  Ni saa (nne) kasarobo. nee sa (*n*·nay) ka·sa·*roh*·boh

Twenty to (ten).
  *Ni saa (nne) kasoro
  ishirini.*   nee sa (*n*·nay) ka·*soh*·roh
                           ee·she·*ree*·nee

what's the time?

The Swahili time system starts six hours later compared to the international one. It begins at sunrise which occurs at about 6am all year round. This system causes endless confusion for visitors to East Africa, especially as many people set their watches using the international system and then try to read them according to the Swahili system. Your best bet is to verify which system is being used – international time, *saa za kizungu* sa za kee·zoon·goo, or Swahili time, *saa za kiswahili* sa za kee·swa·*hee*·lee. Since people usually specify what period of the day they're talking about, you can determine which time system they're using from context.

International time	Swahili time	
midnight	6	*saa sita usiku*
1am	7	*saa saba usiku wa manane*
2	8	*saa nane usiku wa manane*
3	9	*saa tisa usiku wa manane*
4	10	*saa kumi alfajiri*
5	11	*saa kumi na moja alfajiri*
6am (sunrise)	12	*saa kumi na mbili asubuhi*
7	1	*saa moja asubuhi*
8	2	*saa mbili asubuhi*
9	3	*saa tatu asubuhi*
10	4	*saa nne asubuhi*
11	5	*saa tano asubuhi*
noon	6	*saa sita mchana*
1pm	7	*saa saba mchana*
2	8	*saa nane mchana*
3	9	*saa tisa mchana*
4	10	*saa kumi mchana*
5	11	*saa kumi na moja jioni*
6pm (sundown)	12	*saa kumi na mbili jioni*
7	1	*saa moja jioni*
8	2	*saa mbili usiku*
9	3	*saa tatu usiku*
10	4	*saa nne usiku*
11	5	*saa tano usiku*
midnight	6	*saa sita usiku*

morning	*asubuhi*	a·soo·*boo*·hee
afternoon	*mchana*	m·*cha*·na
evening	*jioni*	jee·*oh*·nee

At what time ...?	... *saa ngapi?*	... sa n·*ga*·pee
At (ten).	*Saa (nne).*	sa (*n*·nay)
At (7.57pm).	*Saa (mbili*	sa (m·*bee*·lee
	kasoro dakika	ka·*soh*·roh da·*kee*·ka
	tatu jioni).	*ta*·too jee·*oh*·ni)

the calendar

kalenda

days

Monday	*Jumatatu*	joo·ma·*ta*·too
Tuesday	*Jumanne*	joo·ma·*n*·nay
Wednesday	*Jumatano*	joo·ma·*ta*·noh
Thursday	*Alhamisi*	al·ha·*mee*·see
Friday	*Ijumaa*	ee·joo·*ma*
Saturday	*Jumamosi*	joo·ma·*moh*·see
Sunday	*Jumapili*	joo·ma·*pee*·lee

months

Swahili has two systems for counting months: one consisting of English soundalikes that foreigners like to use and the one that Swahili speakers commonly use. It's best, however, to use the second system, which simply counts months as ordinal numbers starting with January. At a pinch, though, many people will understand the English version.

time & dates

41

January	mwezi wa kwanza	mway·zee wa kwan·za
February	mwezi wa pili	mway·zee wa pee·lee
March	mwezi wa tatu	mway·zee wa ta·too
April	mwezi wa nne	mway·zee wa n·nay
May	mwezi wa tano	mway·zee wa ta·noh
June	mwezi wa sita	mway·zee wa see·ta
July	mwezi wa saba	mway·zee wa sa·ba
August	mwezi wa nane	mway·zee wa na·nay
September	mwezi wa tisa	mway·zee wa tee·sa
October	mwezi wa kumi	mway·zee wa koo·mee
November	mwezi wa kumi na moja	mway·zee wa koo·mee na moh·ja
December	mwezi wa kumi na mbili	mway·zee wa koo·mee na m·bee·lee

dates

What date is it today?

| *Leo ni tarehe gani?* | *lay*·oh nee ta·*ray*·hay *ga*·nee |

It's (18 October).

| *Ni (tarehe kumi na nane, mwezi wa kumi).* | nee (ta·*ray*·hay koo·mee na na·nay mway·zee wa koo·mee) |

seasons

The seasons in East Africa don't correspond to those of other parts of the world. They vary greatly depending on altitude and latitude. *Kiangazi* kee·an·*ga*·zee (lit: dry-season), which roughly corresponds to June, July and August, can be cold in the southern highlands of Tanzania, pleasant on the coast and hot in the northern regions of Kenya. People may refer to the following seasons but have different times of year in mind:

... season	*kipindi ...*	kee·*peen*·dee ...
cold	*cha baridi*	cha ba·*ree*·dee
harvest	*cha kuvuna*	cha koo·*voo*·na
hot	*cha joto*	cha *joh*·toh
rainy	*cha mvua*	cha m·*voo*·a

present

now	*sasa*	*sa*·sa
today	*leo*	*lay*·oh
tonight	*leo usiku*	*lay*·oh oo·*see*·koo

this...		
morning	*asubuhi hii*	a·soo·*boo*·hee hee
afternoon	*mchana huu*	m·*cha*·na hoo
week	*wiki hii*	*wee*·kee hee
month	*mwezi huu*	*mway*·zee hoo
year	*mwaka huu*	*mwa*·ka hoo

past

day before yesterday	*juzi*	*joo*·zee
(three) days ago	*siku (tatu) zilizopita*	*see*·koo (*ta*·too) zee·lee·zo·*pee*·ta
(three) months ago	*miezi (mitatu) iliyopita*	mee·*ay*·zee (mee·*ta*·too) ee·lee·yoh·*pee*·ta
since (May)	*tangu (mwezi wa tano)*	*tan*·goo (*mway*·zee wa *ta*·noh)

last ...		
night	*jana usiku*	*ja*·na oo·*see*·koo
week	*wiki jana*	*wee*·kee *ja*·na
month	*mwezi uliopita*	*mway*·zee oo·lee·oh·*pee*·ta
year	*mwaka uliopita*	*mwa*·ka oo·lee·oh·*pee*·ta

yesterday ...	*jana ...*	*ja*·na ...
morning	*asubuhi*	a·soo·*boo*·hee
afternoon	*mchana*	m·*cha*·na
evening	*jioni*	jee·*oh*·nee

future

day after tomorrow	*kesho kutwa*	*kay*·shoh *koot*·wa
in (six days)	*baada ya (siku sita)*	ba·*a*·da ya (*see*·koo *see*·ta)
until (June)	*mpaka (mwezi wa sita)*	m·*pa*·ka (*mway*·zee wa *see*·ta)
next ...	*... kesho*	... *kay*·shoh
week	*wiki*	*wee*·kee
month	*mwezi*	*mway*·zee
year	*mwaka*	*mwa*·ka
tomorrow ...	*kesho ...*	*kay*·shoh ...
morning	*asubuhi*	a·soo·*boo*·hee
afternoon	*mchana*	m·*cha*·na
evening	*jioni*	jee·*oh*·nee

during the day

afternoon	*mchana*	m·*cha*·na
dawn	*alfajiri*	al·fa·*jee*·ree
day	*siku*	*see*·koo
evening	*jioni*	jee·*oh*·nee
midday	*saa sita mchana*	sa *see*·ta m·*cha*·na
midnight	*saa sita usiku*	sa *see*·ta oo·*see*·koo
morning	*asubuhi*	a·soo·*boo*·hee
night	*usiku*	oo·*see*·koo
sunrise	*macheo*	ma·*chay*·oh
sunset	*magharibi*	mag·ha·*ree*·bee

How much is it?
Ni bei gani? — ni bay *ga*·nee

It's free.
Ni bure. — nee *boo*·ray

It's (500) shillings.
Ni shilingi (mia tano). — nee shee·*leen*·gee (*mee*·a *ta*·noh)

Can you write down the price?
Andika bei. — an·*dee*·ka bay

There's a mistake in the bill.
Kuna kosa kwenye bili. — koo·na koh·sa kwayn·yay bee·le

Do you accept …?	*Mnakubali …*	m·na·koo·*ba*·lee …
credit cards	*kadi ya benki*	*ka*·dee ya *bayn*·kee
travellers	*hundi ya*	*hoon*·dee ya
cheques	*msafiri*	m·sa·*fee*·ree
I'd like to …	*Nataka …*	na·*ta*·ka …
cash a cheque	*kulipwa fedha*	koo·*leep*·wa *fay*·dha
	kutokana	koo·toh·*ka*·na
	na hundi	na *hoon*·dee
change a	*kubadilisha*	koo·ba·dee·*lee*·sha
travellers	*hundi ya*	*hoon*·dee ya
cheque	*msafiri*	m·sa·*fee*·ree
change money	*kubadilisha*	koo·ba·dee·*lee*·sha
	hela	*hay*·la
get a cash	*kupata hela*	koo·*pa*·ta *hay*·la
advance	*ya awali*	ya *a*·wa·lee
withdraw money	*kuondoa hela*	koo·ohn·*doh*·a *hay*·la

Where's ...?	... iko wapi?	... ee·koh wa·pee
an automated teller machine	mashine ya kutolea pesa	ma·shee·nay ya koo·toh·lay·a pay·sa
a foreign exchange office	foreks	foh·rayks

What's the ...?	... ni nini?	... nee nee·nee
charge	gharama yake	ga·ra·ma ya·kay
exchange rate	kiwango cha kubadilisha hela	kee·wan·goh cha koo·ba·dee·lee·sha hay·la

I'd like ..., please.	Nataka ..., tafadhali.	na·ta·ka ... ta·fa·dha·lee
a refund	unirudishie hela	oo·nee·roo·dee·shee·ay hay·la
a receipt	risiti	ree·see·tee
my change	chenji yangu	chayn·jee yan·goo
to return this	kurudisha kitu hiki	koo·roo·dee·sha kee·too hee·kee

coast, island or town?

The Swahili name for Zanzibar Island is Unguja. It's often used locally to distinguish the island from the Zanzibar Archipelago (which also includes Pemba), as well as from Zanzibar Town (called Mji Mkongwe or Stone Town).

The word 'Zanzibar' comes from the Arabic Zinj el-Barr (lit: Land of the Blacks). It was used by Arab traders from the 8th century to refer to both the archipelago and the adjacent coast. Now, the name refers exclusively to the archipelago.

getting around

kutembea

Which ... goes	*... ipi huenda*	*...* ee·pee hoo·*ayn*·da
to (Mbeya)?	*(Mbeya)?*	(m·*bay*·a)
Is this the ...	*Hii ni ... kwenda*	hee nee *...* kwayn·da
to (Mombasa)?	*(Mombasa)?*	(mohm·*ba*·sa)
boat	*Boti*	*boh*·tee
bus	*Basi*	*ba*·see
ferry	*Kivuko*	kee·*voo*·koh
minibus	*Daladala/*	da·la·*da*·la/
	Matatu Tan/Ken	ma·*ta*·too
train	*Treni*	*tray*·nee
When's the	*Basi ...*	*ba*·see ...
... bus?	*itaondoka lini?*	ee·ta·ohn·*doh*·ka *lee*·nee
first	*ya kwanza*	ya *kwan*·za
last	*ya mwisho*	ya *mwee*·shoh
next	*ijayo*	ee·*ja*·yoh

Is the ... going today/tomorrow?
... itaenda leo/kesho? ... ee·ta·*ayn*·da *lay*·oh/*kay*·shoh

What time does it leave?
Itaondoka saa ngapi? ee·ta·ohn·*doh*·ka sa n·*ga*·pee

What time does it get to (Kisuma)?
Itafika (Kisumu) ee·ta·*fee*·ka (kee·*soo*·moo)
saa ngapi? sa n·*ga*·pee

How long will it be delayed?
Itachelewa kwa
muda gani?

ee·ta·chay·*lay*·wa kwa
moo·da *ga*·nee

Is this seat free?
Kuna nafasi hapa?

koo·na na·*fa*·see *ha*·pa

That's my seat.
Hiki ni kiti changu.

hee·kee nee *kee*·tee *chan*·goo

Please tell me when we get to (Moshi).
Niambie tukifika
(Moshi).

nee·am·*bee*·ay too·kee·*fee*·ka
(*moh*·shee)

Please stop here.
Simama hapa,
tafadhali.

see·*ma*·ma *ha*·pa
ta·fa·*dha*·lee

How long do we stop here?
Tutakaa hapa kwa
muda gani?

too·ta·*ka ha*·pa kwa
moo·da *ga*·nee

I'm sorry, I've changed my mind.
Samahani,
nimebadili nia.

sa·ma·*ha*·nee
nee·may·ba·*dee*·lee *nee*·a

hop on, hop off

The most common word people call out to get a bus to stop is *shusha shoo*·sha (drop off). It's also considered slang. Pay attention to the way East Africans deliver the line. If you casually call *shusha* the same way when you want to get off, you can sometimes bring an entire bus to laughter.

On the other hand, if you're standing by the side of the road and you want to get a local bus to stop, simply extend your arm fully and flap your hand like a whale's tail.

tickets

A ... ticket to (Iringa).	*Tiketi moja ya ... kwenda (Iringa).*	tee·*kay*·tee *moh*·ja ya ... *kwayn*·da (ee·*reen*·ga)
1st-class	*daraja la kwanza*	da·*ra*·ja la *kwan*·za
2nd-class	*daraja la pili*	da·*ra*·ja la *pee*·lee
child's	*mtoto*	m·*toh*·toh
one-way	*kwenda tu*	*kwayn*·da too
return	*kwenda na kurudi*	*kwayn*·da na koo·*roo*·dee
student	*mwanafunzi*	mwa·na·*foon*·zee

I'd like a/an ... seat.	*Nataka kiti ...*	na·*ta*·ka *kee*·tee ...
aisle	*jirani ya njia*	jee·*ra*·nee ya n·*jee*·a
nonsmoking	*kutovuta sigara*	koo·toh·*voo*·ta see·*ga*·ra
smoking	*kuvuta sigara*	koo·*voo*·ta see·*ga*·ra
window	*jirani ya dirisha*	jee·*ra*·nee ya dee·*ree*·sha

Is there (a) ...?	*Kuna ...?*	*koo*·na ...
air conditioning	*a/c*	*ay*·see
blanket	*blanketi*	blan·*kay*·tee
sick bag	*mfuko wa kutapikia*	m·*foo*·koh wa koo·ta·pee·*kee*·a
toilet	*choo*	choh

Where do I buy a ticket?
Ninunue tiketi wapi?   nee·noo·*noo*·ay tee·*kay*·tee *wa*·pee

Do I need to book?
Ni lazima nifanye buking?   nee *la*·zee·ma nee·*fa*·nyay *boo*·keeng

How much is it?
Ni bei gani?   nee bay *ga*·nee

How long does the trip take?

Safari huchukua	sa·*fa*·ree hoo·choo·*koo*·a
muda gani?	*moo*·da *ga*·nee

Is it a direct route?

Njia ni moja	n·*jee*·a nee *moh*·ja
kwa moja?	kwa *moh*·ja

Can I get a stand-by ticket?

Naweza kununua	na·*way*·za koo·noo·*noo*·a
tiketi kutumia kama	tee·*kay*·tee koo·too·*mee*·a ka·ma
nafasi ikipatikana?	na·*fa*·si ee·kee·pa·tee·*ka*·na

Can I get a sleeping berth?

Naweza kupata	na·*way*·za koo·*pa*·ta
kitanda?	kee·*tan*·da

What time should I check in?

Ripoting ni saa ngapi?	ree·*pot*·eeng nee sa n·*ga*·pee

I'd like to ... my ticket, please.	*Nataka ... tiketi yangu tafadhali.*	na·*ta*·ka ... tee·*kay*·tee *yan*·goo ta·fa·*dha*·lee
cancel	*kufuta*	koo·*foo*·ta
change	*kubadilisha*	koo·ba·dee·*lee*·sha
confirm	*kuhakikisha*	koo·ha·kee·*kee*·sha

---

listen for ...

dirisha la tiketi	dee·*ree*·sha la tee·*kay*·tee	ticket window
hii	hee	this one
hiyo	*hee*·yoh	that one
imeche leweshwa	ee·may·chay lay·*waysh*·wa	delayed
imefutwa	ee·may·*foot*·wa	cancelled
imejaa	ee·may·*ja*	full
mgomo	m·*goh*·moh	strike
ratiba	ra·*tee*·ba	timetable
stendi	*stayn*·dee	platform
uwakala wa safiri	oo·*wa*·ka·la wa sa·*fee*·ree	travel agent

luggage

mizigo

Where can I find …?	… iko wapi?	… ee·koh wa·pee
the baggage claim	Sehemu ya kuchukulia mizigo	say·hay·moo ya koo·choo·koo·lee·a mee·zee·goh
the left-luggage office	Chumba cha kuwekea mizigo	choom·ba cha koo·way·kay·a mee·zee·goh
a luggage locker	Sanduku la kuhifadhia mizigo	san·doo·koo la koo·hee·fa·dhee·a mee·zee·goh
a trolley	Kigari	kee·ga·ree

My luggage	Mizigo	mee·*zee*·goh
has been ...	yangu ...	*yan*·goo ...
damaged	imeharibiwa	ee·may·ha·ree·*bee*·wa
lost	imepotea	ee·may·poh·*tay*·a
stolen	imeibwa	ee·may·*eeb*·wa

That's mine.
Ni yangu. nee *yan*·goo

That's not mine.
Si yangu. see *yan*·goo

Can I put my bag here?
Naweza kuweka na·*way*·za koo·*way*·ka
mzigo wangu hapa? m·*zee*·goh *wan*·goo *ha*·pa

Can I have some coins?
Nataka sarafu. na·*ta*·ka sa·*ra*·foo

plane

ndege

Where does flight (number 432) arrive/depart?
Ndege (namba mia n·*day*·gay (*nam*·ba *mee*·a
nne thelathini n·nay thay·la·*thee*·nee
na mbili) itafika/ na m·*bee*·lee) ee·ta·*fee*·ka/
itaondoka wapi? ee·ta·ohn·*doh*·ka *wa*·pee

I'd like to charter a plane to ...
Nataka kukodisha na·*ta*·ka koo·koh·*dee*·sha
ndege kwenda ... n·*day*·gay *kwayn*·da ...

Where's (the) ...?	... iko wapi?	... ee·koh *wa*·pee
airport	Basi ya uwanja	ba·see ya oo·*wan*·ja
shuttle	wa ndege	wa n·*day*·gay
arrivals hall	Wanaofika	wa·na·oh·*fee*·ka
departures hall	Wanaoondoka	wa·na·oh·ohn·*doh*·ka
duty-free shop	Duty-free	doo·tee·*free*
gate (3)	Mlango (tatu)	m·*lan*·goh (*ta*·too)

PRACTICAL

mizigo inayozidi	mee-*zee*-goh ee-na-yoh-*zee*-dee	**excess baggage**
mizigo ya kubebea	mee-*zee*-goh ya koo-bay-*bay*-a	**carry-on baggage**
pasipoti	pa-see-*poh*-tee	**passport**
pasi ya kuingilia	*pa*-see ya koo-een-gee-*lee*-a	**boarding pass**
wanaohamisha	wa-na-oh-ha-*mee*-sha	**transfer passengers**
wanaopita	wa-na-oh-*pee*-ta	**transit passengers**

bus & coach

mabasi

Can you recommend a reliable/safe bus company?
Kampuni gani ina mabasi yenye uaminifu/usalama? — kam-*poo*-nee *ga*-nee ee-na ma-*ba*-see *yay*-nyay oo-a-mee-*nee*-foo/oo-sa-*la*-ma

How often do buses come?
Mabasi hufika muda gani? — ma-*ba*-see hoo-*fee*-ka *moo*-da *ga*-nee

What time is this bus leaving?
Basi hili litaondoka saa ngapi? — *ba*-see *hee*-lee lee-ta-ohn-*doh*-ka sa n-*ga*-pee

Does it stop at (Tanga)?
Linasimama (Tanga)? — lee-na-see-*ma*-ma (*tan*-ga)

What's the next stop?
Kipi ni kituo kijacho? — *kee*-pee nee kee-*too*-oh kee-*ja*-choh

I'd like to get off at (Bagamoyo).

Nataka kushusha (Bagamoyo). na·*ta*·ka koo·*shoo*·sha (ba·ga·*moh*·yoh)

Drop me off here!

Nishushe hapa! nee·*shoo*·shay *ha*·pa

city bus	*daladala/* *matatu* Tan/Ken	da·la·*da*·la/ ma·*ta*·too
express bus	*basi ya moja kwa moja*	*ba*·see ya *moh*·ja kwa *moh*·ja
intercity	*baini ya miji*	ba·*ee*·nee ya *mee*·jee
local bus	*basi linalosimama katika kila kituo*	*ba*·see lee·na·loh·see·*ma*·ma ka·*tee*·ka *kee*·la kee·*too*·oh

train

treni

What station is this?

Hiki ni stesheni gani? *hee*·kee nee stay·*shay*·nee *ga*·nee

What's the next station?

Stesheni ijayo itakuwa mji gani? stay·*shay*·nee ee·*ja*·yoh ee·ta·*koo*·wa m·jee *ga*·nee

Does it stop at (Dodoma)?

Itasimama (Dodoma)? ee·ta·see·*ma*·ma (doh·*doh*·ma)

Do I need to change?

Itabidi nibadilishe? ee·ta·*bee*·dee nee·ba·dee·*lee*·shay

Is it …?	**Ni …?**	nee …
direct	*treni hii kwa safari nzima*	*tray*·nee hee kwa sa·*fa*·ree n·*zee*·ma
express	*moja kwa moja kwa haraka*	*moh*·ja kwa *moh*·ja kwa ha·*ra*·ka

Which carriage is (for) …?	**Behewa gani ni (kwa) …?**	bay·*hay*·wa *ga*·nee nee (kwa) …
1st class	*daraja la kwanza*	da·*ra*·ja la *kwan*·za
dining	*kula*	*koo*·la
Tabora	*Tabora*	ta·*boh*·ra

| express train | treni ya moja kwa moja kwa haraka | *tray*·nee ya *moh*·ja kwa *moh*·ja kwa ha·*ra*·ka |
| ordinary train | treni ya kawaida | *tray*·nee ya ka·wa·*ee*·da |

boat

What's the sea like today?
Bahari ikoje leo?   ba·*ha*·ree ee·*koh*·jay *lay*·oh

Are there life jackets?
Kuna jaketi la kuokolea?   koo·na ja·*kay*·tee la koo·oh·koh·*lay*·a

Which island is this?
Hiki ni kisiwa gani?   *hee*·kee nee kee·*see*·wa *ga*·nee

Which beach is this?
Huu ni ufukwe gani?   hoo nee oo·*fook*·way *ga*·nee

I feel seasick.
Nahitaji kutapika.   na·hee·*ta*·jee koo·ta·*pee*·ka

boat	boti	boh·tee
cabin	kibini	kee·*bee*·nee
car deck	sitaha ya magari	see·*ta*·ha ya ma·*ga*·ree
deck	sitaha	see·*ta*·ha
ferry n	kivuko	kee·*voo*·koh
lifeboat	mashua ya kuokolea	ma·*shoo*·a ya koo·oh·koh·*lay*·a
life jacket	jaketi la kuokolea	ja·*kay*·tee la koo·oh·koh·*lay*·a
row boat	mtumbwi	m·*toom*·bwee
ship n	meli	*may*·lee
small wooden boat	mashua	ma·*shoo*·a
traditional sailing boat	dhau	dha·oo
yacht	mashua ya anasa	ma·*shoo*·a ya a·*na*·sa

taxi

The majority of taxis in East Africa have no signs. As taxis can be scarce, it's not unusual to share a taxi with strangers, and each person usually agrees on a price individually. Another option is to hire a *bodaboda/teksi ya baisikeli* Ken/Tan boh·da·*boh*·da/ *tayk*·see ya ba·ee·see·*kay*·lee – a short-haul bicycle taxi.

I'd like a taxi ...	Nataka teksi ...	na·*ta*·ka *tayk*·see ...
at (9am)	saa (tatu asubuhi)	sa (*ta*·too a·soo·*boo*·hee)
now	sasa	*sa*·sa
tomorrow	kesho	*kay*·shoh
for the whole day	kwa siku nzima	kwa *see*·koo n·*zee*·ma
for (three) hours	kwa masaa (matatu)	kwa ma·*sa* (ma·*ta*·too)
to run various errands	kufanya shughuli mbalimbali	koo·*fa*·nya shoo·*goo*·lee m·*ba*·lee·m·*ba*·lee
to the airport	kwenda kwenye uwanja wa ndege	*kwayn*·da *kway*·nyay oo·*wan*·ja wa n·*day*·gay
to the harbor	kwenda bandarini	*kwayn*·da ban·da·*ree*·nee

Where's the taxi rank?
Stendi ya teksi iko wapi?	*stayn*·dee ya *tayk*·see ee·koh *wa*·pee

Is this taxi free?
Teksi hii inapatikana?	*tayk*·see hee ee·na·pa·tee·*ka*·na

Please take me to (this address).
Tafadhali niendeshe — ta·fa·*dha*·lee nee·ayn·*day*·shay
mpaka (anwani hii). — m·*pa*·ka (an·*wa*·nee hee)

Please put the meter on.
Tumia mita ya — too·*mee*·a *mee*·ta ya
kupima nauli. — koo·*pee*·ma na·*oo*·lee

How much should I expect to pay to …?
Nitarajie kulipa — nee·ta·ra·*jee*·ay koo·*lee*·pa
shilingi ngapi — shee·*leen*·gee n·*ga*·pee
kwenda …? — *kwayn*·da …

How much is it to …?
Ni bei gani kwenda …? — nee bay *ga*·nee *kwayn*·da …

How much is it?
Ni shilingi ngapi? — nee shee·*leen*·gee n·*ga*·pee

That's too expensive!
Ni ghali mno! — nee *ga*·lee *m*·noh

Please lower the price.
Punguza bei, tafadhali. — poon·*goo*·za bay ta·fa·*dha*·lee

Would you like to share a taxi to …?
Ungependa kugawa — oon·gay·*payn*·da koo·*ga*·wa
teksi kwenda …? — *tayk*·see *kwayn*·da …

Can we share a taxi?
Tugawe teksi? — too·*ga*·way *tayk*·see

Please …	*Tafadhali …*	ta·fa·*dha*·lee …
slow down	*endesha*	ayn·*day*·sha
	polepole	poh·lay·*poh*·lay
stop here	*simama hapa*	see·*ma*·ma *ha*·pa
wait here	*subiri hapa*	soo·*bee*·ree *ha*·pa

car & motorbike

car & motorbike hire

Are you willing	Unaweza	oo·na·way·za
to hire out ...?	kunikodisha ...?	koo·nee·koh·dee·sha ...
your car	gari lako	ga·ree la·koh
your	pikipiki	pee·kee·pee·kee
motorbike	yako	ya·koh

I'd like to hire	Nataka	na·ta·ka
a/an ...	kukodi ...	koo·koh·dee ...
4WD	forbaifor	fohr·ba·ee·fohr
automatic	otomatiki	oh·toh·ma·tee·kee
car	gari	ga·ree
manual	kwa mkono	kwa m·koh·noh
motorbike	pikipiki	pee·kee·pee·kee

With ...	Kwenye ...	kway·nyay ...
air conditioning	a/c	ay·see
a driver	dereva	day·ray·va

How much	Ni bei gani	nee bay ga·nee
for ... hire?	kukodi kwa ...?	koo·koh·dee kwa ...
daily	siku	see·koo
hourly	saa	sa
weekly	wiki	wee·kee

Does that include insurance/mileage?

Bei inazingitia   bay ee·na·zeen·gee·tee·a
bima/umbali?   bee·ma/oo·m·ba·lee

Do you have a guide to the road rules in English?

Mna mwongozo wa   m·na mwohn·goh·zoh wa
sheria za barabara kwa   shay·ree·a za ba·ra·ba·ra kwa
Kiingereza?   kee·een·gay·ray·za

Do you have a road map?

Mna ramani?   m·na ra·ma·nee

on the road

What's the speed limit?
Mwendo gani
unaruhusiwa?
    *mwayn-*doh *ga-*nee
    oo-na-roo-hoo-*see-*wa

Is this the road to (Embu)?
Hii ni barabara
kwenda (Embu)?
    hee nee ba-ra-*ba-*ra
    *kwayn-*da (*aym-*boo)

Where's a petrol station?
Kituo cha mafuta
kiko wapi?
    kee-*too-*oh cha ma-*foo-*ta
    *kee-*ko *wa-*pee

Please fill it up.
Jaza tangi/tanki.
    *ja-*za *tan-*gee/*tan-*kee

I'd like ... litres.
Nataka lita ...
    na-*ta-*ka *lee-*ta ...

diesel	*dizeli*	dee-*zay-*lee
leaded	*na risasi*	na ree-*sa-*see
regular	*kawaida*	ka-wa-*ee-*da
premium unleaded	*super*	*soo-*payr
unleaded	*isiyo na risasi*	ee-*see-*yoh na ree-*sa-*see

windscreen
kiwambo upepo
kee-*wam-*boh
oo-*pay-*poh

petrol/gas
mafuta
ma-*foo-*ta

battery
betri
*bay-*tree

engine
injini
*een-*jee-nee

tyre
tairi
ta-*ee-*ree

headlight
taa ya mbele
ta ya m-*bay-*lay

Can you check the ...?	*Angalia ...?*	an·ga·lee·a ...
oil	*mafuta*	ma·foo·ta
tyre pressure	*upepo*	oo·pay·poh
water	*maji*	ma·jee

(How long) Can I park here?
Naweza kuegesha na·way·za koo·ay·gay·sha
hapa (kwa muda gani)? ha·pa (kwa moo·da ga·ni)

Do I have to pay?
Ni lazima nilipe? nee la·zee·ma nee·lee·pay

problems

I need a mechanic.
Nahitaji fundi. na·hee·ta·jee foon·dee

I've had an accident.
Nimepata ajali. nee·me·pa·ta a·ja·lee

The car/motorbike has broken down (at Chalinze).
Gari/Pikipiki ga·ree/pee·kee·pee·kee
imeharibika (Chalinze). ee·may·ha·ree·bee·ka (cha·leen·zay)

The car/motorbike won't start.
Gari/Pikipiki haiwaki. ga·ree/pee·kee·pee·kee ha·ee·wa·kee

I have a flat tyre.
Nina pancha. nee·na pan·cha

I've lost my car keys.
Nimepoteza nee·may·poh·tay·za
funguo za gari. foon·goo·oh za ga·ree

I've locked the keys inside.

Nimefunga	nee·may·*foon*·ga
funguo ndani.	foon·*goo*·oh n·*da*·ni

I've run out of petrol.

Mafuta yamekwisha.	ma·*foo*·ta ya·may·*kwee*·sha

Can you fix it (today)?

Utaweza	oo·ta·*way*·za
kuitengeneza (leo)?	koo·ee·tayn·gay·*nay*·za (*lay*·oh)

How long will it take?

Itachukua muda gani?	ee·ta·choo·*koo*·a *moo*·da *ga*·nee

bicycle

I'd like ...	*Nataka ...*	na·*ta*·ka ...
my bicycle	*kutengeneza*	koo·tayn·gay·*nay*·za
repaired	*baisikeli yangu*	ba·ee·see·*kay*·lee *yan*·goo
to buy a	*kununua*	koo·noo·*noo*·a
bicycle	*baisikeli*	ba·ee·see·*kay*·lee
to hire a	*kukodisha*	koo·koh·*dee*·sha
bicycle	*baisikeli*	ba·ee·see·*kay*·lee
I'd like	*Nataka*	na·*ta*·ka
a ... bike.	*baisikeli ...*	ba·ee·see·*kay*·lee ...
mountain	*yenye gia*	*yay*·nyay *gee*·a
	kupanda	koo·*pan*·da
	milima	mee·*lee*·ma
racing	*yenye gia*	*yay*·nyay *gee*·a
	kukimbia	koo·keem·*bee*·a
	mbio	m·*bee*·oh
second-hand	*isiyo mpya*	ee·*see*·yoh m·pya
How much is	*Ni bei gani*	nee bay *ga*·nee
it per ...?	*kwa ...?*	kwa ...
day	*siku*	*see*·kuu
hour	*saa*	sa

Do I need a helmet?
   Ni lazima nivai   nee *la*·zee·ma nee·*va*·ee
   helmeti?   hayl·*may*·tee

Is there a bicycle-path map?
   Kuna ramani ya njia   *koo*·na ra·*ma*·nee ya n·*jee*·a
   za baisikeli?   za ba·ee·see·*kay*·lee

I have a puncture.
   Nina pancha.   *nee*·na *pan*·cha

local transport

Can I pay for a ride in your truck?
   Naweza kulipa kwa lifti   na·*way*·za koo·*lee*·pa kwa *leef*·tee
   katika lori lako?   ka·*tee*·ka *loh*·ree *la*·koh

How much to …?
   Ni bei gani kwenda …?   nee bay *ga*·nee *kwayn*·da …

Are you waiting for more people?
   Unangojea watu   oo·na·n·goh·*jay*·a *wa*·too
   wengine?   wayn·*gee*·nay

How many people can ride on this?
   Watu wangapi   *wa*·too wan·*ga*·pee
   wanaweza   wa·na·*way*·za
   kusafirishwa kwa hili?   koo·sa·fee·*ree*·shwa kwa *hee*·lee

Could I ride in the front?
   Naomba kukaa mbele.   na·*ohm*·ba koo·*ka* m·*bay*·lay

I don't want to ride on top.
   Sitaki kukaa juu.   see·*ta*·kee koo·*ka* joo

Could I contribute to the petrol cost?
   Naweza kuchangia   na·*way*·za koo·chan·*gee*·a
   sehemu ya bei ya mafuta?   say·*hay*·moo ya bay ya ma·*foo*·ta

Thanks for the ride.
   Asante kwa lifti.   a·*san*·tay kwa *leef*·tee

border crossing

kuvuka mpaka

I'm …	Mimi ni …	mee·mee nee …
in transit	safarini	sa·fa·ree·nee
on business	kwa biashara	kwa bee·a·sha·ra
on holiday	kwa likizo	kwa lee·kee·zoh

I'm here for …	Nipo kwa …	nee·poh kwa …
(three) days	siku (tatu)	see·koo (ta·too)
(four) months	miezi	mee·ay·zee
	(minne)	(mee·n·nay)
(two) weeks	wiki (mbili)	wee·kee (m·bee·lee)

Do I require a/an …?	Ni lazima niwe na …?	nee la·zee·ma nee·way na …
I have a/an …	Nina …	nee·na …
entry permit	hati ya kuingia	ha·tee ya koo·een·gee·a
customs form	fomu ya forodha	foh·moo ya foh·roh·dha
health certificate	cheti cha afya	chay·tee cha af·ya
pass/permit	cheti	chay·tee
police report	ripoti ya polisi	ree·poh·tee ya poh·lee·see

listen for …

familia	fa·mee·lee·a	family
kundi	koon·dee	group
pasipoti	pa·see·poh·tee	passport
peke yake	pay·kay ya·kay	alone
visa	vee·sa	visa

I'm going to (Malindi).
Naenda (Malindi). na-*ayn*-da (ma-*leen*-dee)

I'm staying at (the Pendo Inn).
Nakaa (Pendo Inn). na-*ka* (*payn*-doh een)

The children are on this passport.
Watoto wanasafiri wa-*toh*-toh wa-na-sa-*fee*-ree
kwenye pasipoti. *kway*-nyay pa-see-*poh*-tee hee

at customs

I have nothing to declare.
Sina ya kutaja. *see*-na ya koo-*ta*-ja

I have something to declare.
Ninacho kitu cha kutaja. nee-*na*-cho *kee*-too cha koo-*ta*-ja

Do I have to declare this?
Ni lazima nitaje hiki? nee *la*-zee-ma nee-*ta*-jay *hee*-kee

That's (not) mine.
Hiki ni (si) changu. *hee*-kee nee (see) *chan*-goo

I didn't know I had to declare it.
Sikujua ilibidi see-koo-*joo*-a ee-lee-*bee*-dee
kuitaja. koo-ee-*ta*-ja

I didn't know I couldn't take this out of the country.
Sikujua kwamba see-koo-*joo*-a *kwam*-ba
hairuhusiwi ha-ee-roo-hoo-*see*-wee
kuchukua kitu koo-choo-*koo*-a *kee*-too
hiki nje ya nchi. *hee*-kee *n*-jay ya *n*-chee

signs		
Duty-Free	doo-tee-*free*	**Duty-free**
Forodha	foh-*roh*-dha	**Customs**
Karantini	ka-ran-*tee*-nee	**Quarantine**
Udhibiti wa	oo-dhee-*bee*-tee wa	**Passport Control**
Pasipoti	pa-see-*poh*-tee	
Uhamiaji	oo-ha-mee-*a*-jee	**Immigration**

Where's (the market)?
(Soko) iko wapi? (soh·koh) ee·koh wa·pee

What's the address?
Anwani ni nini? an·wa·nee nee nee·nee

How do I get there?
Nifikaje? nee·fee·ka·jay

How far is it?
Ni umbali gani? nee oom·ba·lee ga·nee

Can you show me (on the map)?
Unaweza kunionyesha oo·na·way·za koo·nee·oh·nyay·sha
(katika ramani)? (ka·tee·ka ra·ma·nee)

It's ...	Iko ...	ee·koh ...
behind ...	nyuma ya ...	nyoo·ma ya ...
close	karibu	ka·ree·boo
here	hapa	ha·pa
in front of ...	mbele ya ...	m·bay·lay ya ...
near ...	karibu na ...	ka·ree·boo na ...
next to ...	jirani ya ...	jee·ra·nee ya ...
on the corner	pembeni	paym·bay·nee
opposite ...	ng'ambo ya ...	ng·am·boh ya ...
straight ahead	moja kwa moja	moh·ja kwa moh·ja
there	hapo	ha·poh

Turn ...	Geuza ...	gay·oo·za ...
at the corner	kwenye kona	kway·nyay koh·na
at the traffic lights	kwenye taa za barabarani	kway·nyay ta za ba·ra·ba·ra·nee
left	kushoto	koo·shoh·toh
right	kulia	koo·lee·a

... dakika	... da·kee·ka	... minutes
... kilomita	... kee·loh·mee·ta	... kilometres
... mita	... mee·ta	... metres

north	kaskazini	kas·ka·zee·nee
south	kusini	koo·see·nee
east	mashariki	ma·sha·ree·kee
west	magharibi	ma·ga·ree·bee

by ...	kwa ...	kwa ...
bus	basi	ba·see
foot	miguu	mee·goo
taxi	teksi	tayk·see
train	treni	tray·nee

What ... is this?	Hapa ni ... gani?	ha·pa nee ... ga·nee
neighbourhood	mtaa	m·ta
street	njia	n·jee·a
village	kijiji	kee·jee·jee

traffic lights
taa za barabarani
ta za ba·ra·ba·ra·nee

shop
duka
doo·ka

pedestrian
crossing
kivuko cha
wanaotembea
kee·voo·koh cha
wa·na·oh·taym·bay·a

bus
basi
ba·see

intersection
njiapanda
n·jee·a·pan·da

corner
pembe
paym·bay

taxi
teksi
tayk·see

finding accommodation

Where's a ...?	... iko wapi?	... ee·koh wa·pee
camping	Uwanja wa	oo·wan·ja wa
ground	kambi	kam·bee
guesthouse	Gesti	gay·stee
hotel	Hoteli	hoh·tay·lee
restaurant	Hoteli	hoh·tay·lee
youth hostel	Hosteli ya	hoh·stay·lee ya
	vijana	vee·ja·na
Can you	Unaweza	oo·na·way·za
recommend	kunipendeke	koo·nee·payn·day·kay
somewhere ...?	zea malazi ...?	zay·a ma·la·zee ...
cheap	rahisi	ra·hee·see
good	nzuri	n·zoo·ree
luxurious	ya anasa	ya a·na·sa
nearby	hapo	ha·poh
	karibuni	ka·ree·boo·nee
romantic	kwa wapenzi	kwa wa·payn·zee

What's the address?
Anwani ni nini?   an·wa·nee nee nee·nee

For responses, see **directions**, page 65.

local talk		
dive	mahali pabaya	ma·ha·lee pa·ba·ya
rat-infested	yenye panya	yay·nyay pa·nya
top spot	safi kabisa	sa·fee ka·bee·sa

booking ahead & checking in

I'd like to book a room, please.
Nataka kufanya
buking, tafadhali.
na·ta·ka koo·fa·nya
boo·keeng ta·fa·dha·lee

I have a reservation.
Nina buking.
nee·na boo·keeng

My name's ...
Jina langu ni ...
jee·na lan·goo nee ...

For (three) nights/weeks.
Kwa siku/wiki (tatu).
kwa see·koo/wee·kee (ta·too)

From (June 30) to (July 6).
Kutoka tarehe
(thelathini mwezi
wa sita) mpaka tarehe
(sita mwezi wa saba).
koo·toh·ka ta·ray·hay
(thay·la·thee·nee mway·zee
wa see·ta) m·pa·ka ta·ray·hay
(see·ta mway·zee wa sa·ba)

Do you have a	Kuna chumba	koo·na choom·ba
... room?	kwa ...?	kwa ...
double	watu wawili,	wa·too wa·wee·lee
(one bed)	kitanda kimoja	kee·tan·da kee·moh·ja
single	mtu mmoja	m·too m·moh·ja
twin	watu wawili,	wa·too wa·wee·lee
(two beds)	vitanda viwili	vee·tan·da vee·wee·lee

Do you have a suite?
Kuna chumba
chenye sebule?
koo·na choom·ba
chay·nyay say·boo·lay

Can I see the room?
Naomba nione chumba.
na·ohm·ba nee·oh·nay choom·ba

PRACTICAL

Imejaa.	ee·may·*ja*	**It's full.**
mapokezi	ma·poh·*kay*·zee	**reception**
pasipoti	pa·see·*poh*·tee	**passport**
Siku ngapi?	*see*·koo n·*ga*·pee	**How many nights?**
ufunguo	oo·foon·*goo*·oh	**key**

How much is	*Ni bei gani*	nee bay *ga*·ne
it per ...?	*kwa ...?*	kwa ...
day	*siku*	*see*·koo
person	*mtu*	*m*·too
week	*wiki*	*wee*·kee

That's too expensive.
Ni ghali mno.   nee *ga*·lee *m*·noh

Can you lower the price?
Naomba upunguze   na·*ohm*·ba oo·poon·*goo*·zay
bei?   bay

I'll take it.
Nataka.   na·*ta*·ka

Do I need to pay upfront?
Ni lazima nilipe   nee *la*·zee·ma nee·*lee*·pay
kwanza?   kwan·za

Can I pay	*Naweza kulipa*	na·*way*·za koo·*lee*·pa
by ...?	*kwenye ...?*	*kway*·nyay ...
credit card	*kadi ya benki*	*ka*·dee ya *bayn*·kee
travellers	*hundi ya*	*hoon*·dee ya
cheque	*msafiri*	m·sa·*fee*·ree

For other methods of payment, see **shopping**, page 77, and
money, page 45.

Hakuna Nafasi	ha·*koo*·na na·*fa*·see	**no vacancy**
Nafasi Ipo	na·*fa*·see *ee*·po	**vacancy**

accommodation

69

requests & queries

When/Where is breakfast served?
Chai ya asubuhi   cha·ee ya a·soo·*boo*·hee
inapatikana lini/wapi?   ee·na·pa·tee·*ka*·na *lee*·nee/*wa*·pee

Please wake me at (seven).
Tafadhali niamshe   ta·fa·*dha*·lee nee·*am*·shay
saa (moja).   sa (*moh*·ja)

Do you arrange tours here?
Mnapanga safari hapa?   m·na·*pan*·ga sa·*fa*·ree *ha*·pa

Do you change money here?
Mnabadilisha hela hapa?   m·na·ba·dee·*lee*·sha *hay*·la *ha*·pa

Can I use the …?	*Je, naweza*	jay na·*way*·za
	kutumia …?	koo·too·*mee*·a …
kitchen	*jiko*	*jee*·ko
laundry	*udobi*	oo·*doh*·bee
telephone	*simu*	*see*·mu

Do you have a/an …?	*Kuna …?*	*koo*·na …
elevator	*lifti*	*leef*·tee
laundry service	*dobi*	*doh*·bee
message board	*kibao cha*	kee·*ba*·oh cha
	ujumbe	oo·*joom*·bay
safe	*kasha la fedha*	*ka*·sha la *fay*·dha
swimming pool	*bwawa la*	*bwa*·wa la
	kuogelea	koo·oh·gay·*lay*·a

a knock at the door …

Who is it?	*Ni nani?*	nee *na*·nee
Just a moment.	*Subiri kidogo.*	soo·*bee*·ree kee·*doh*·goh
Come in.	*Ingia.*	een·*gee*·a
Come back later, please.	*Rudi baadaye, tafadhali.*	*roo*·dee ba·a·*da*·yay ta·fa·*dha*·lee

Could I have …, please?	Naomba …, afadhali.	na·ohm·ba … ta·fa·dha·li
a mosquito net	chandarua	chan·da·roo·a
a receipt	risiti	ree·see·tee
an extra blankt	blanketi nyingine	blan·kay·tee nyeen·gee·nay
my key	ufunguo wangu	oo·foon·goo·oh wan·goo
toilet paper	karatasi ya choo	ka·ra·ta·see ya choh

Can you wash these clothes?
Mnaweza kufua nguo hizi?
m·na·way·za koo·foo·a n·goo·oh hee·zee

air conditioning
a/c
ay·see

fan
feni
fay·nee

toilet
choo
choh

key
ufunguo
oo·foon·goo·oh

bed
kitanda
kee·tan·da

bathroom
bafuni
ba·foo·nee

TV
runinga
roo·neen·ga

washerman/ -woman	*dobi*	*doh*·bee
wash clothes	*fua nguo*	*foo*·a n·*goo*·oh
with starch	*weka stachi*	*way*·ka *sta*·chee
without starch	*usiweke stachi*	oo·see·*way*·kay *sta*·chee

Is there a message for me?
Kuna ujumbe wangu?   koo·na oo·*joom*·bay wan·goo

Can I leave a message for someone?
Naweza kumwachia   na·*way*·za koom·wa·*chee*·a
mtu ujumbe?   m·too oo·*joom*·bay

I'm locked out of my room.
Nimefungwa nje ya   nee·may·*foon*·gwa n·jay ya
chumba changu.   *choom*·ba *chan*·goo

complaints

malalimiko

It's too ...	... *mno.*	... *m*·noh
bright	*Kuna mwanga*	koo·na *mwan*·ga
cold	*Ni baridi*	nee ba·*ree*·dee
dark	*Kuna giza*	koo·na *gee*·za
expensive	*Ni ghali*	nee *ga*·lee
noisy	*Kuna kelele*	koo·na kay·*lay*·lay
small	*Ni ndogo*	nee n·*doh*·goh

The ... doesn't work.	... *haifanyi kazi.*	... ha·ee·*fa*·nyee ka·zee
air conditioning	*A/c*	ay·*see*
fan	*Feni*	*fay*·nee
toilet	*Choo*	choh
light	*Taa*	ta

PRACTICAL

72

Can I get another (blanket)?
  Inawezekana   ee·na·way·zay·ka·na
  nipate (blanketi)   nee·pa·tay (blan·kay·tee)
  nyingine?   nyeen·gee·nay

Can you clean the room?
  Inawezekana   ee·na·way·zay·ka·na
  kusafisha chumba?   koo·sa·fee·sha choom·ba

This (pillow) isn't clean.
  (Mto) huu si safi.   (m·toh) hoo see sa·fee

There's no ...	*Hakuna ...*	ha·koo·na ...
electricity	*umeme*	oo·may·may
hot water	*maji ya moto*	ma·jee ya moh·toh

checking out

kuachia chumba

What time is checkout?
  Muda wa kuachia   moo·da wa koo·ach·ee·a
  chumba ni saa ngapi?   choom·ba nee sa n·ga·pee

Can I have a late checkout?
  Naweza kuchelewa   na·way·za koo·chay·lay·wa
  kuachia chumba?   koo·ach·ee·a choom·ba

Can you call a taxi for me (for 11 o'clock)?
  Naomba teksi   na·ohm·ba tayk·si
  kwa saa (tano).   kwa sa (ta·noh)

I'm leaving now.
  Naondoka sasa.   na·ohn·doh·ka sa·sa

Can I leave my bags here?
  Naweza kuacha   na·way·za koo·ach·a
  mizigo yangu hapa?   mee·zee·goh yan·goo ha·pa

There's a mistake in the bill.
  Mmekosa kwenye   m·may·koh·sa kway·nyay
  bili yangu.   bee·lee yan·goo

Can I have my …?	Naomba …yangu.	na-*ohm*-ba …*yan*-goo
deposit	maweko	ma-*way*-koh
passport	pasipoti	pa-see-*poh*-tee
valuables	vitu vya	*vee*-too vya
	thamani	tha-ma-nee

I'll be back …	Nitarudi …	nee-ta-*roo*-dee …
in (three)	baada ya	ba-*a*-da ya
days	siku (tatu)	*see*-koo (*ta*-too)
on (Tuesday)	(Jumanne)	(joo-ma-*n*-nay)

I've been very happy here, thank you.
| Nimefurahi sana | nee-may-foo-*ra*-hee *sa*-na |
| hapa, asante. | *ha*-pa a-*san*-tay |

I'll recommend it to my friends.
| Nitawapendekezea | nee-ta-wa-payn-day-kay-*zay*-a |
| rafiki zangu. | ra-*fee*-kee *zan*-goo |

camping

kupiga kambi

Do you have …?	Kuna …?	*koo*-na …
a laundry	udobi	oo-*doh*-bee
a tent site	nafasi kupiga	na-*fa*-see koo-*pee*-ga
	hema	*hay*-ma
a car site	nafasi	na-*fa*-see
	kuegesha gari	koo-ay-*gay*-sha *ga*-ree
electricity	umeme	oo-*may*-may
hot water	maji ya moto	*ma*-jee ya *moh*-toh
shower facilities	bafuni	ba-*foo*-nee
tents for hire	hema	*hay*-ma
	kukodisha	koo-koh-*dee*-sha

How much is it	Ni bei gani	nee bay *ga*-nee
per …?	kila …?	*kee*-la …
caravan	lori	*loh*-ree
person	mtu	*m*-too
tent	hema	*hay*-ma
vehicle	gari	*ga*-ree

Can I ...?	Naweza ...?	na·*way*·za ...
camp here	kuwa hapa	koo·wa ha·pa
	kwa usiku	kwa oo·*see*·koo
park next to	kuegesha gari	koo·ay·*gay*·sha *ga*·ree
my tent	jirani ya hema	jee·*ra*·nee ya *hay*·ma

Is the water drinkable?
Je, maji ni safi jay *ma*·jee nee *sa*·fee
kunywa? *koony*·wa

Who do I ask to stay here?
Niongee na nani nee·ohn·*gay*·ay na *na*·nee
nikitaka kukaa hapa? nee·kee·*ta*·ka koo·*ka* ha·pa

Could I borrow ...?
Naomba niazimie ... na·*ohm*·ba nee·a·zee·*mee*·ay ...

renting

I'm here about	Nimekuja	nee·may·*koo*·ja
the ... for rent.	kuhusu	koo·*hoo*·soo
	kukodisha ...	koo·koh·*dee*·sha ...
Do you have	Kuna ...	*koo*·na ...
a/an ... for rent?	kukodisha?	koo·koh·*dee*·sha
apartment	fleti	*flay*·tee
cabin	kibanda	kee·*ban*·da
house	nyumba	*nyoom*·ba
room	chumba	*choom*·ba
furnished	kwenye	*kway*·nyay
	fenicha zote	*fay*·nee·cha *zoh*·tay
partly furnished	kwenye	*kway*·nyay
	fenicha kadhaa	*fay*·nee·cha ka·*dha*
unfurnished	bila fenicha	*bee*·la *fay*·nee·cha

accommodation

75

staying with locals

Can I stay at your place?
Naweza kukaa	na·*way*·za koo·*ka*
nyumbani kwako?	nyoom·*ba*·nee *kwa*·koh

Is there anything I can do to help?
Nisaidie namna gani?	nee·sa·ee·*dee*·ay *nam*·na *ga*·nee

I have my own ... *Nina ...* *nee*·na ...
mattress	*godolo langu*	goh·*doh*·loh *lan*·goo
sleeping bag	*mfuko wa*	m·*foo*·koh wa
	kulalia wangu	koo·la·*lee*·a *wan*·goo

Can I ...? *Naweza ...?* na·*way*·za ...
bring anything	*kuchangia*	koo·chan·*gee*·a
for the meal	*lisho*	*lee*·shoh
do the dishes	*safisha vyombo*	sa·*fee*·sha vyohm·boh
set/clear	*kutayarisha/*	koo·ta·ya·*ree*·sha/
the table	*kuondoa meza*	koo·ohn·*doh*·a *may*·za
take out	*kufuta*	koo·*foo*·ta
the rubbish	*takataka*	ta·ka·*ta*·ka

Thanks for your hospitality.
Asante sana kwa	a·*san*·tay *sa*·na kwa
wema wako.	*way*·ma *wa*·koh

For dining-related expressions, see **food**, page 153.

---

address: unknown

Other than downtown in some cities, exact street addresses – or even street names – are not common. The best way to find a specific person or place is often to go to the centre of a neighbourhood, eg the local bus stop, and ask for a particular landmark or a person who can lead you to your destination.

What's the	*Ni anwani*	nee an·*wa*·nee
address?	*gani?*	*ga*·nee
road	*barabara*	ba·ra·*ba*·ra
street	*njia*	n·*jee*·a

looking for ...

kutafutia

Where's a ...?	... iko wapi?	... ee·koh wa·pee
department store	Duka lenye vitu vingi	doo·ka lay·nyay vee·too veen·gee
general store	Duka lenye vitu mbalimbali	doo·ka lay·nyay vee·too m·ba·lee·m·ba·lee
market	Soko	soh·koh

Where can I buy (a padlock)?
Naweza kununua (kufuli) wapi?
na·way·za koo·noo·noo·a (koo·foo·lee) wa·pee

For phrases on directions, see **directions**, page 65.
For more on shops and services, see the **dictionary**.

making a purchase

wakati wa kununua

I'm just looking.
Naangalia tu.
na·an·ga·lee·a too

I'd like to buy (an adaptor plug).
Nataka kununua (adapta ya umeme).
na·ta·ka koo·noo·noo·a (a·dap·ta ya oo·may·may)

How much is it?
Ni bei gani?
ni bay ga·nee

shopping

Swahili speakers tend to reserve *tafadhali* ta·fa·*dha*·lee (please) for fairly formal situations, and generally don't use it in ordinary encounters such as shopping. Instead of saying 'could you' or 'I'd like' or 'please show me', a simple request such as *Nipe …* nee·pay … (give me …), *Naomba …* na·*ohm*·ba … (I request …) or *Nataka…* na·*ta*·ka … (I want …), when spoken with a pleasant tone of voice, will usually convey all the necessary politeness of casual interactions.

Can you write down the price?
Andika bei.   an·*dee*·ka bay

Do you have any others?
Kuna nyingine?   *koo*·na nyeen·*gee*·nay

Can I look at it?
Naomba nione.   na·*ohm*·ba nee·*oh*·nay

I don't like it.
Sipendi.   see·*payn*·dee

I'll take it.
Nataka.   na·*ta*·ka

Could I have it wrapped?
Funga, tafadhali.   *foon*·ga ta·fa·*dha*·lee

Does it have a guarantee?
Kuna dhamana?   *koo*·na dha·*ma*·na

Can I have it sent overseas?
Naweza kuipostia   na·*way*·za koo·ee·poh·*stee*·a
kwenye nchi za nje?   *kway*·nyay n·chee za n·jay

Can you order it for me?
Unaweza kuniagizia?   oo·na·*way*·za koo·nee·a·gee·*zee*·a

Can I pick it up later?
Naweza kuichukua   na·*way*·za koo·ee·choo·*koo*·a
baadaye?   ba·a·*da*·yay

It's faulty.
Haifanyi kazi.   ha·ee·*fa*·nyee *ka*·zee

bargain	*bei nafuu*	bay na·*foo*
bottom price	*bei ya mwisho*	bay ya m·*wee*·shoh
cheap	*rahisi*	ra·*hee*·see
rip-off	*feki*	*fay*·kee
sale	*seli*	*say*·lee
specials	*maalum*	*ma*·loom

Do you accept ...?	*Mnakubali ...*	m·na·koo·*ba*·lee ...
credit cards	*kadi ya benki*	*ka*·dee ya *bayn*·kee
travellers cheques	*hundi ya msafiri*	*hoon*·dee ya m·sa·*fee*·ree
I'd like ..., please.	*Nataka ..., tafadhali.*	na·*ta*·ka ... ta·fa·*dha*·lee
my change	*chenji yangu*	*chayn*·jee *yan*·goo
a refund	*unirudishie hela*	oo·nee·roo·dee·*shee*·ay *hay*·la
to return this	*kurudisha kitu hiki*	koo·roo·*dee*·sha *kee*·too *hee*·kee
Could I have a ..., please?	*Naomba ...*	na·*ohm*·ba ...
bag	*mfuko*	m·*foo*·koh
receipt	*risiti*	ree·*see*·tee

bargaining

kubishana bei

How much is it?
Ni bei gani? ni bay *ga*·nee

That's too expensive.
Ni ghali mno. nee *ga*·lee m·noh

Please lower the price.
Punguza bei. poon·*goo*·za bay

It's not a fair price.
Siyo bei nafuu. *see*·yoh bay na·*foo*

Do you have something cheaper?
Kuna rahisi zaidi?   koo·na ra·*hee*·see za·*ee*·dee

I'll give you (500 shillings).
Nitakupa   nee·ta·*koo*·pa
(shilingi mia tano).   (shee·*leen*·gee *mee*·a ta·noh)

clothes

My size is …	*Saizi yangu ni …*	sa·ee·zee yan·goo nee …
(40)	*(arobaini)*	(a·roh·ba·*ee*·nee)
small	*ndogo*	n·*doh*·goh
medium	*wastani*	wa·sta·nee
large	*kubwa*	*koob*·wa

Can I try it on?
Je, naweza kujaribu   jay na·*way*·za koo·ja·*ree*·boo
kuvaa?   koo·*va*

It doesn't fit.
Haifai.   ha·ee·*fa*·ee

Can you recommend a seamstress/tailor?
Unaweza kupendekeza   oo·na·*way*·za koo·payn·day·*kay*·za
mshonaji?   m·shoh·*na*·jee

Could you alter/mend this?
Unaweza kubadilisha/   oo·na·*way*·za koo·ba·dee·*lee*·sha/
kushona hii?   koo·*sho*·na hee

Could you make me a (dress)?
Unaweza kunishonea   oo·na·*way*·za koo·nee·shoh·*nay*·a
(gauni)?   (ga·*oo*·nee)

For clothing items, see the **dictionary**.

Throughout East Africa you'll come across women wearing *kanga* kan·ga – brightly coloured lengths of cotton cloth with Swahili sayings printed along the edge. Many of the sayings are social commentaries or messages often indirectly worded, or containing puns and double meanings. Others are simply a local form of advertising, such as those bearing the logo of political parties.

Here are some common Swahili proverbs that might appear on a *kanga*. It's easy to pair them with their English equivalents but the choice of words is typical for the East African culture:

Not all that glitters is gold.

Si kila mwenye	see *kee*·la *mway*·nyay
makucha huwa simba.	ma·*koo*·cha *hoo*·wa *seem*·ba
(lit: not all those that have claws are lions)	

Strike the iron while it's hot.

Ngozi ivute	n·*goh*·zee ee·*voo*·tay
ili maji.	ee·lee ma·jee
(lit: stretch the hide while it's wet)	

repairs

matengenezo

Can I have my	*Mnaweza*	m·na·*way*·za
... repaired	*kutengeneza ...*	koo·tayn·gay·*nay*·za ...
here?	*yangu hapa?*	*yan*·goo ha·pa
When will my	*... yangu*	... *yan*·goo
... be ready?	*itakuwa*	ee·ta·*koo*·wa
	tayari lini?	ta·*ya*·ree *lee*·nee
backpack	*shanta*	*shan*·ta
camera	*kemra*	*kaym*·ra
(sun)glasses	*miwani (ya jua)*	mee·*wa*·nee (ya *joo*·a)
shoes	*viatu*	vee·*a*·too

shopping

81

hairdressing

I'd like (a) ...	Nataka ...	na·ta·ka ...
colour	kuweka rangi	koo·way·ka ran·gee
haircut	kukata nywele	koo·ka·ta nyway·lay
my hair	kusuka	koo·soo·ka
braided	nywele	nyway·lay
my hair	kuosha	koo·oh·sha
washed	nywele	nyway·lay
shave	kunyoa ndevu	koo·nyoh·a n·day·voo
trim	kupunguza	koo·poon·goo·za
	nywele kidogo	nyway·lay kee·doh·goh

Don't cut it too short.
Usipunguze mno.   oo·see·poon·goo·zay m·noh

Please use a new blade.
Tumia wembe mpya.   too·mee·a waym·bay m·pya

Please use hot water.
Tumia maji ya moto.   too·mee·a ma·jee ya moh·toh

Shave it all off!
Nyoa zote!   nyoh·a zoh·tay

I should never have let you near me!
Nilikosa hata   nee·lee·koh·sa ha·ta
uliponikaribia!   oo·lee·poh·nee·ka·ree·bee·a

barber	kinyozi	kee·nyoh·zee
hairdresser for braiding	msusi	m·soo·see
hairdresser for cutting	mtengenezaji wa nywele	m·tayn·gay·nay·za·jee wa nyway·lay

For colours, see the **dictionary**.

books & reading

Do you have a book by (Ngugi wa Thiong'o)?

Kuna kitabu	koo·na kee·*ta*·boo
kuandikwa na	koo·an·*deek*·wa na
(Ngugi wa Thiong'o)?	(n·*goo*·gee wa thee·*ohng*·oh)

Is there an English-language bookshop?

Kuna duka la vitabu	koo·na *doo*·ka la vee·*ta*·boo
vya Kiingereza?	vya kee·een·gay·*ray*·za

Can you recommend a book for me?

Unaweza	oo·na·*way*·za
kunipendekezea	koo·nee·payn·day·kay·*zay*·a
kitabu?	kee·*ta*·boo

Do you have Lonely Planet guidebooks?

Mna vitabu vya	m·na vee·*ta*·boo vya
Lonely Planet?	*lohn*·lee *pla*·nayt

I'd like a ...	*Nataka ...*	na·*ta*·ka ...
dictionary	*kamusi*	ka·*moo*·see
newspaper	*gazeti (kwa*	ga·*zay*·tee (kwa
(in English)	*Kiingereza)*	kee·een·gay·*ray*·za)
notepad	*daftari*	daf·*ta*·ree

electronic goods

Where can I buy duty-free electronic goods?

Duty-free kununua	doo·tee·*free* koo·noo·noo·*noo*·a
bidhaa za umeme iko	bee·*dha* za oo·*may*·may *ee*·koh
wapi?	*wa*·pee

Will this work on any DVD player?

Itafanya kazi katika	ee·ta·*fa*·nya *ka*·zee ka·*tee*·ka
DVD zote?	dee·vee·*dee zoh*·tay

Is this a (PAL/NTSC) system?
Ni mfumo wa (PAL/NTSC)?
nee m·*foo*·moh wa (pal/ayn·tee·*ays*·see)

Is this the latest model?
Ni aina mpya kabisa?
nee a·*ee*·na m·pya ka·*bee*·sa

Is this (240) volts?
Ni volti (mia mbili arobaini)?
nee *vol*·tee (*mee*·a m·*bee*·lee a·roh·ba·*ee*·nee)

music

I'd like a ...	Nataka ...	na·*ta*·ka ...
blank tape	kanda tupo	*kan*·da *too*·poh
CD	CD	see·dee
drum	ngoma	n·*goh*·ma
xylophone	marimba	ma·*reem*·ba

I'm looking for something by (Remi Ongala).
Natafuta muziki ya (Remi Ongala).
na·ta·*foo*·ta moo·*zee*·kee ya (*ray*·mee ohn·*ga*·la)

What's their best recording?
Kanda gani yao inazidi?
kan·da *ga*·nee ya·oh ee·na·*zee*·dee

Can I listen to this?
Naomba tusikilize.
na·*ohm*·ba too·see·kee·*lee*·zay

listen for ...

Unataka msaada? oo·na·*ta*·ka m·*sa*·da	**Do you want help?**
Nyingine? nyeen·*gee*·nay	**Anything else?**
Hamna/Hakuna. *ham*·na/ha·*koo*·na	**No, we don't have any.**

photography

I need ... film for this camera.	*Nahitaji filamu ... kwa kemra hii.*	na·hee·*ta*·jee fee·*la*·moo ... kwa *kaym*·ra hee
APS	*APS*	a·pee·*ays*
B&W	*nyeusi na nyeupe*	nya·*oo*·see na nyay·*oo*·pay
colour	*ya rangi*	ya *ran*·gee
slide	*ya slaidi*	ya *sla*·ee·dee
(400) speed	*ya spidi (mia nne)*	ya *spee*·dee (*mee*·a n·nay)

Can you ...?	*Mnaweza ...?*	m·na·*way*·za ...
develop this film	*kusafisha mkanda huu*	koo·sa·*fee*·sha m·*kan*·da hoo
develop digital photos	*kusafisha picha za tarakimu*	koo·sa·*fee*·sha *pee*·cha za ta·ra·*kee*·moo
load my film	*kuweka mkanda katika kemra*	koo·*way*·ka m·*kan*·da ka·*tee*·ka *kaym*·ra
recharge the battery for my digital camera	*kuchajisha betri kwa kemra yangu ya tarakimu*	koo·cha·*jee*·sha *bay*·tree kwa *kaym*·ra yan·goo ya ta·ra·*kee*·moo
transfer photos from my camera to CD	*kuhamisha picha kutoka kemra kwenye CD*	koo·ha·*mee*·sha *pee*·cha koo·*toh*·ka *kaym*·ra *kway*·nyay see·*dee*

Please don't use a red tint.
Usitumie rangi   oo·see·too·*mee*·ay ran·gee
nyekundu nyekundu.   nyay·*koon*·doo nyay·*koon*·doo

When will it be ready?
Itakuwa tayari lini?   ee·ta·*koo*·wa ta·*ya*·ree *lee*·nee

How much is it?
Ni bei gani?   ni bay *ga*·nee

I need a passport photo taken.
Nahitaji picha ya   na·hee·*ta*·jee *pee*·cha ya
pasipoti.   pa·see·*poh*·tee

I'm not happy with these photos.
Sifurahi na picha hizi.   see·foo·*ra*·hee na *pee*·cha *hee*·zee

souvenirs

basket	*kikapu*	kee·*ka*·poo
batik	*batiki*	ba·*tee*·kee
bowl	*bakuli*	ba·*koo*·lee
candlestick holder	*mshumaa*	m·shoo·*ma*
ceramic pot	*chungu*	*choo*·ngoo
copper tray	*sinia ya shaba*	see·*nee*·a ya *sha*·ba
(folding safari) chair	*kiti*	*kee*·tee
jewellery	*vipuli*	vee·*poo*·lee
leather shield	*ngao ya ngazi*	n·*ga*·oh ya n·*ga*·zee
mask	*kinyago*	kee·*nya*·goh
plaited mat	*mkeka*	m·*kay*·ka
spear	*mkuki*	m·*koo*·kee
textiles	*vitambaa*	vee·tam·*ba*
three-legged stool	*kigoda*	kee·*goh*·da
woodcarving	*uchongaji*	oo·chohn·*ga*·jee

post office

posta

I want to send a/an ...	*Nataka kupeleka ...*	na·*ta*·ka koo·pay·*lay*·ka ...
fax	*faksi*	*fak*·see
letter	*barua*	ba·*roo*·a
parcel	*kifurushi*	kee·foo·*roo*·shee
postcard	*postkadi*	pohst·*ka*·dee
trunk (tea chest)	*sanduku*	san·*doo*·koo
I want to buy a/an ...	*Nataka kununua ...*	na·*ta*·ka koo·noo·*noo*·a ...
aerogram	*aerogramu*	a·ay·roh·*gra*·moo
envelope	*bahasha*	ba·*ha*·sha
stamp	*stempu*	*staym*·poo
customs declaration	*azimio la forodha*	a·zee·*mee*·oh la foh·*roh*·dha
domestic	*ndani ya nchi*	n·*da*·nee ya n·chee
fragile	*dhaifu*	dha·*ee*·foo
international	*nje ya nchi*	n·jay ya n·chee
mail	*barua*	ba·*roo*·a
mailbox	*sanduku la posta*	san·*doo*·koo la *poh*·sta
PO Box	*Sanduku la Posta*	san·*doo*·koo la *poh*·sta
postcode	*simbo ya posta*	*seem*·boh ya *poh*·sta

snail mail

air	*kwa ndege*	kwa n·*day*·gay
express	*ekspres*	ayk·*sprays*
registered	*barua ya rejesta*	ba·*roo*·a ya ray·*jay*·sta
sea	*kwa meli*	kwa *may*·lee
surface (land)	*kwa lori*	kwa *loh*·ree

Please send it by air/surface mail to (Australia).

Peleka kwa ndege/
meli kwenda
(Australia).

pay·*lay*·ka kwa n·*day*·gay/
may·lee kwayn·da
(a·oo·*stra*·lee·a)

It contains (souvenirs).

Kuna (kumbukumbu)
ndani.

koo·na (koom·boo·*koom*·boo)
n·*da*·nee

Where's the poste restante section?

Posta restante
iko wapi?

poh·sta ray·*stan*·tay
ee·koh *wa*·pee

Is there any mail for me?

Kuna barua zozote
zangu?

koo·na ba·*roo*·a zoh·*zoh*·tay
zan·goo

phone

simu

What's your phone number?

Nipe simu yako?

nee·pay *see*·moo *ya*·koh

Where's the nearest public phone?

Kuna simu ya kadi
wapi jirani?

koo·na *see*·moo ya *ka*·dee
wa·pee jee·*ra*·nee

Where's the nearest telecom centre?

Telekom iko wapi?

tay·lay·*kohm* *ee*·ko *wa*·pee

Can I look at a phone book?

Nionyeshe kitabu
cha namba za simu?

nee·oh·*nyay*·shay kee·*ta*·boo
cha *nam*·ba za *see*·moo

The number is ...

Namba ni ...

nam·ba ni ...

What's the area/country code for (New Zealand)?

Namba ya miito/
kimataifa kwa
(New Zealand) ni nini?

nam·ba ya mee·*ee*·toh/
kee·ma·ta·*ee*·fa kwa
(noo *zee*·land) nee *nee*·nee

I want to ...	Nataka ...	na·ta·ka ...
buy a phonecard	kununua kadi ya simu	koo·noo·noo·a ka·dee ya see·moo
call (Singapore)	kupiga simu kwa (Singapore)	koo·pee·ga see·moo kwa (seen·ga·pohr)
make a (local) call	kupiga simu (jirani)	koo·pee·ga see·moo (jee·ra·nee)
reverse the charges	kugeuza gharama	koo·gay·oo·za ga·ra·ma
speak for (three) minutes	kuongea kwa dakika (tatu)	koo·ohn·gay·a kwa da·kee·ka (ta·too)

How much for ...?	... ni bei gani?	... nee bay ga·nee
a (three)-minute call	Kupiga simu kwa dakika (tatu)	koo·pee·ga see·moo kwa da·kee·ka (ta·too)
each extra minute	Kila dakika nyingine	kee·la da·kee·ka nyeen·gee·nay

communications

89

It's engaged.
Inatumika. ee·na·too·*mee*·ka

I've been cut off.
Imekatika. ee·may·ka·*tee*·ka

The connection's bad.
Kiungo ni kibaya. kee·*oon*·goh nee kee·*ba*·ya

Hello.
Halo. ha·*loh*

It's …
Ni … nee …

Is … there?
… yuko? … *yoo*·koh

Can I speak to …?
Nataka kuongea na … na·*ta*·ka koo·ohn·*gay*·a na …

Who am I speaking to?
Naongea na nani? na·ohn·*gay*·a na *na*·nee

Please tell him/her I called.
Mwambie nilipiga m·wam·*bee*·ay nee·lee·*pee*·ga
simu. *see*·moo

Can I leave a message?
Naomba niache na·*ohm*·ba nee·*a*·chay
ujumbe? oo·*joom*·bay

My number is …
Simu yangu ni … *see*·moo *yan*·goo nee …

I don't have a contact number.
Sina simu. *see*·na *see*·moo

I'll call back later.
Nitajaribu tena nee·ta·ja·*ree*·boo *tay*·na
baadaye. ba·a·*da*·yay

---

just hang up

Swahili speakers often don't make a ceremony of saying 'goodbye' at the end of a phone call. Instead, phone conversations often end with *haya/sawa* ha·ya/*sa*·wa (OK), after which both parties hang up.

mobile/cell phone

I'd like a ...	Nataka ...	na·ta·ka ...
charger for	chaja kwa	cha·ja kwa
my phone	simu yangu	see·moo yan·goo
mobile/cell	kukodisha	koo·koh·dee·sha
phone for hire	simu ya	see·moo ya
	mkononi	m·koh·noh·nee
prepaid mobile/	kadi ya simu	ka·dee ya see·moo
cell phone	ya mkononi	ya m·koh·noh·nee
SIM card	kadi ya sim	ka·dee ya seem

What are the rates?
Ni bel gani?   nee bay *ga*·nee

(500 shillings) per (30) seconds.
(Shilingi mia tano)   (shee·*leen*·gee *mee*·a *ta*·noh)
kwa sekundi   kwa say·*koon*·dee
(thelathini).   (thay·la·*thee*·nee)

the internet

Where's the local Internet cafe?
Intanet Kafe iko wapi?   een·*ta*·nayt ka·*fay* ee·koh *wa*·pee

I'd like to ...	Nataka ...	na·ta·ka ...
check my	kusoma barua	koo·soh·ma ba·roo·a
email	pepe yangu	pay·pay yan·goo
get Internet	kutumia	koo·too·mee·a
access	intaneti	een·ta·nay·tee
use a printer	kutumia	koo·too·mee·a
	printa	preen·ta
use a scanner	kutumia	koo·too·mee·a
	skana	ska·na

Do you have …?	Kuna …?	koo·na …
Macs	Mac	mak
PCs	PC	pee·see
a Zip drive	draivu ya zip	dra·ee·voo ya zeep

How much per …?	Ni bei gani kwa …?	nee bay ga·nee kwa …
hour	saa	sa
(five) minutes	dakika (tano)	da·kee·ka (ta·noh)
page	ukurasa	oo·koo·ra·sa

How do I log on?
Nianziaje?
nee·an·zee·a·jay

Please change it to the English-language setting.
Tafadhali badilisha
kutumia Kiingereza.
ta·fa·dha·lee ba·dee·lee·sha
koo·too·mee·a kee·een·gay·ray·za

The connection is too slow.
Kiungo ni
polepole mno.
kee·oon·goh nee
poh·lay·poh·lay m·noh

It's crashed.
Imekwama.
ee·may·kwa·ma

I've finished.
Nimemaliza.
nee·may·ma·lee·za

In major urban areas you'll be able to use your overseas ATM card, make purchases at upscale locations with your credit card, and change cash or travellers cheques in foreign exchange offices.

Where's ...?	... iko wapi?	... ee·koh wa·pee
an automated teller machine	Mashine ya kutolea pesa	ma·shee·nay ya koo·toh·lay·a pay·sa
a foreign exchange office	Foreks	foh·rayks

What time does the bank open?

Benki inafungua
saa ngapi?

bayn·kee ee·na·foon·goo·a
sa n·ga·pee

Can I use my credit card to withdraw money?

Naweza kutumia kadi ya
benki kuondoa hela?

na·way·za koo·too·mee·a ka·dee ya
bayn·kee koo·ohn·doh·a hay·la

---

listen for ...

kitambulisho	kee·tam·boo·lee·shoh	**identification**
pasipoti	pa·see·poh·tee	**passport**

Hatuwezi.
ha·too·way·zee

We can't do that.

Kiungo kimekwisha.
kee·oon·goh
kee·may·kwee·sha

The connection's down.

Kuna shida.
koo·na shee·da

There's a problem.

Pesa zako zimekwisha.
pay·sa za·koh
zee·may·kwee·sha

You have no funds left.

Saini hapa.
sa·ee·nee ha·pa

Sign here.

I'd like to …	Nataka …	na·ta·ka …
cash a cheque	kulipwa fedha	koo·leep·wa fay·dha
	kutokana na	koo·toh·ka·na na
	hundi	hoon·dee
change a travellers cheque	kubadilisha hundi ya msafiri	koo·ba·dee·lee·sha hoon·dee ya m·sa·fee·ree
change money	kubadilisha hela	koo·ba·dee·lee·sha hay·la
get a cash advance	kupata hela ya awali	koo·pa·ta hay·la ya a·wa·lee
withdraw money	kuondoa hela	koo·ohn·doh·a hay·la

What's the …?	… ni nini?	… nee nee·nee
charge for that	Gharama yake	ga·ra·ma ya·kay
exchange rate	Kiwango cha kubadilisha hela	kee·wan·goh cha koo·ba·dee·lee·sha hay·la
large bill exchange rate	Kiwango cha kubadilisha noti kubwa	kee·wan·goh cha koo·ba·dee·lee·sha noh·tee koob·wa
small bill exchange rate	Kiwango cha kubadilisha noti ndogo	kee·wan·goh cha koo·ba·dee·lee·sha noh·tee n·doh·goh

The automated teller machine took my card.

Mashine ya kutolea pesa ilichukua kadi yangu.	ma·shee·nay ya koo·toh·lay·a pay·sa ee·lee·choo·koo·a ka·dee yan·goo

I've forgotten my PIN.

Nimesahau pin namba siri.	nee·may·sa·ha·oo peen nam·ba see·ree

Has my money arrived yet?

Je, hela yangu imeshafika?	jay hay·la yan·goo ee·may·sha·fee·ka

How long will it take to arrive?

Je, itachukua muda gani kufika?	jay ee·ta·choo·koo·a moo·da ga·nee koo·fee·ka

sightseeing

matembezi ya kuangalia mandhari

I'd like a ...	Nataka ...	na·ta·ka ...
guide	kiongozi	kee·ohn·goh·zee
guidebook in	kitabu cha	kee·ta·boo cha
English	kuongoza kwa	koo·ohn·goh·za kwa
	Kiingereza	kee·een·gay·ray·za
(local) map	ramani	ra·ma·nee
	(ya eneo hili)	(ya ay·nay·oh hee·lee)

Do you have	Mna maarifa	m·na ma·ree·fa
information	kuhusu	koo·hoo·soo
on ... sights?	sehemu za ...?	say·hay·moo za ...
cultural	utamaduni	oo·ta·ma·doo·nee
historical	historia	hee·stoh·ree·a
religious	dini	dee·nee
wildlife	wanyama pori	wa·nya·ma poh·ree

I'd like to see ...
Nataka kuona ...   na·ta·ka koo·oh·na ...

What's that?
Hiyo ni nini?   hee·yoh nee nee·nee

Who made it?
Ilitengenezwa na nani?   ee·lee·tayn·gay·nayz·wa na na·nee

How old is it?
Ina umri gani?   ee·na oom·ree ga·nee

Can I take a photograph (of you)?
Ni sawa nikipiga   nee sa·wa nee·kee·pee·ga
picha (ya wewe)?   pee·cha (ya way·way)

I'll send you the photograph.

Nitakutumia picha hii.   nee-ta-koo-too-mee-a pee-cha hee

Can you write down your address so I can send you the picture?

Andika anwani ili   an-dee-ka an-wa-nee ee-lee
nikutumie picha.   nee-koo-too-mee-ay pee-cha

I didn't realise I'd have to pay you.

Sikuelewa inabidi   see-koo-ay-lay-wa ee-na-bee-dee
nikulipe.   nee-koo-lee-pay

getting in

kuingia

What time does it open/close?

Inafungua/Inafunga   ee-na-foon-goo-a/ee-na-foon-ga
saa ngapi?   sa n-ga-pee

What's the admission charge?

Ni bei gani kuingia?   nee bay ga-nee koo-een-gee-a

Can I enter this building?

Inaruhusiwa kuingia   ee-na-roo-hoo-see-wa koo-een-gee-a
jengo hili?   jayn-goh hee-lee

Are women allowed in this mosque?

Wanawake huruhusiwa	wa·na·*wa*·kay hoo·roo·hoo·*see*·wa	
kuingia msikiti huu?	koo·een·*gee*·a m·see·*kee*·tee hoo	

Is there a	*Kuna upungufu*	koo·na oo·poon·*goo*·foo
discount for …?	*wa bei kwa …?*	wa bay kwa …
children	*watoto*	wa·*toh*·toh
families	*familia*	fa·mee·*lee*·a
groups	*vikundi*	vee·*koon*·dee
older people	*wazee*	wa·*zay*
students	*wanafunzi*	wa·na·*foon*·zee

tours/safaris

Safari is the Swahili word for 'trip'. It has come into English to mean 'wildlife spotting' or 'adventure travel', and is of course used so along the African safari circuit. However, it also retains its original meaning in Swahili – so don't be surprised if people use it to refer to any sort of travel, no matter how mundane.

Can you	*Unajua …*	oo·na·*joo*·a …
recommend a …?	*nzuri?*	n·*zoo*·ree
boat trip	*safari ya boti*	sa·*fa*·ree ya *boh*·tee
camel safari	*safari ya*	sa·*fa*·ree ya
	ngamia	n·ga·*mee*·a
day trip	*safari ya*	sa·*fa*·ree ya
	siku moja	*see*·koo *moh*·ja
safari/tour	*safari*	sa·*fa*·ree
walking safari	*safari ya*	sa·*fa*·ree ya
	kutembea	koo·taym·*bay*·a

When's the next (safari)?

(Safari) ijayo itakuwa	(sa·*fa*·ree) ee·*ja*·yoh ee·ta·*koo*·wa
lini?	*lee*·nee

What time should we be back?

Turudi saa ngapi?	too·*roo*·dee sa n·*ga*·pee

Is/Are ... included?	Inazingatia ...?	ee·na·zeen·ga·tee·a ...
accommodation	malazi	ma·la·zee
(before/after)	(kabla/	(ka·bla/
	baadaye)	ba·a·da·yay)
airport transfers	usafiri	oo·sa·fee·ree
	kwenda na	kwayn·da na
	kutoka uwanja	koo·toh·ka oo·wan·ja
	wa ndege	wa n·day·gay
equipment	kukodisha	koo·koh·dee·sha
rental	vifaa	vee·fa
fuel	mafuta	ma·foo·ta
food	chakula	cha·koo·la
park entrance fees	ada za hifadhi	a·da za hee·fa·dhee
tent rental	kukodisha	koo·koh·dee·sha
	hema	hay·ma
transport	usafiri	oo·sa·fee·ree

The guide has paid.
Kiongozi amelipa.   kee·ohn·goh·zee a·may·lee·pa

How large a tip should I pay?
Nilipe bakshishi   nee·lee·pay bak·shee·shee
kiasi gani?   kee·a·see ga·nee

How long is the tour?
Safari itachukua   sa·fa·ree ee·ta·choo·koo·a
muda gani?   moo·da ga·nee

How many people will be in the group?
Kundi itakuwa na   koon·dee ee·ta·koo·wa na
watu wangapi?   wa·too wan·ga·pee

What animals are we likely to see?
Tutegemee kuona   too·tay·gay·may koo·oh·na
wanyama gani?   wa·nya·ma ga·nee

We're very keen to see (elephants).
Tunataka sana   too·na·ta·ka sa·na
kuona (tembo).   koo·oh·na (taym·bo)

I've lost my group.
Nimepotea   nee·may·poh·tay·a
kundi yangu.   koon·dee yan·goo

For information on responsible travel and safaris in East Africa, see **sustainable travel**, page 195.

I'm attending a ...   *Nahudhuria ...*   na·hoo·dhoo·*ree*·a ...
- **conference**   *mikutano*   mee·koo·*ta*·noh
- **course**   *mafunzo*   ma·*foon*·zoh
- **meeting**   *mkutano*   m·koo·*ta*·noh
- **trade fair**   *maonyesho ya biashara*   ma·oh·*nyay*·shoh ya bee·a·*sha*·ra

I'm with ...   *Nipo na ...*   *nee*·poh na ...
- **(Tanzania Breweries)**   *(Tanzania Breweries)*   (tan·za·*nee*·a broo·ay·rees)
- **my colleague**   *mwenzi*   *mwayn*·zee
- **my colleagues**   *wenzi wangu*   *wayn*·zee *wan*·goo
- **(two) others**   *(wawili)*   (wa·*wee*·lee)
     wengine   wayn·*gee*·nay

I'm alone.
Nipo peke yangu.   *nee*·poh *pay*·kay *yan*·goo

I have an appointment with ...
Nina mkutano na ...   *nee*·na m·koo·*ta*·noh na ...

I'm staying at ..., room ...
Ninakaa ..., chumba ...   nee·na·*ka* ... *choom*·ba ...

I'm here for (two) days/weeks.
Nipo kwa siku/ wiki (mbili).   *nee*·poh kwa *see*·koo/ *wee*·kee (m·*bee*·lee)

What's your ...?   *... yako ni nini?*   ... *ya*·koh nee *nee*·nee
- **(email) address**   *Anwani (ya barua pepe)*   an·*wa*·nee (ya ba·*roo*·a *pay*·pay)
- **fax number**   *Namba ya faksi*   *nam*·ba ya *fak*·see
- **mobile number**   *Simu ya mkononi*   *see*·moo ya m·koh·*noh*·ni
- **work number**   *Simu ya kazi*   *see*·moo ya *ka*·zee

Here's my ...	Hii ni ... yangu.	hee nee ... yan·goo
business card	kadi ya biashara	ka·dee ya bee·a·sha·ra
(email) address	anwani (ya barua pepe)	an·wa·nee (ya ba·roo·a pay·pay)
fax number	namba ya faksi	nam·ba ya fak·see
mobile number	simu ya mkononi	see·moo ya m·koh·noh·ni
work number	simu ya kazi	see·moo ya ka·zee

Where's the ...?	... iko wapi?	... ee·koh wa·pee
business centre (eg in hotel)	Kituo ya biashara	kee·too·oh ya bee·a·sha·ra
conference	Mikutano	mee·koo·ta·noh
meeting	Mkutano	m·koo·ta·noh

I need ...	Nahitaji ...	na·hee·ta·jee ...
a computer	kompyuta	kohm·pyoo·ta
the Internet	intaneti	een·ta·nay·tee
an interpreter	mkalimani	m·ka·lee·ma·nee
more business cards	kadi zaidi za biashara	ka·dee za·ee·dee za bee·a·sha·ra
some space to set up	mahali pa kuandaa	ma·ha·lee pa koo·an·da
to send a fax	kupeleka faksi	koo·pay·lay·ka fak·see

That went very well.
Ilikwenda vizuri.　　ee·lee·kwayn·da vee·zoo·ree

Thank you for your time.
Asante kwa muda wako.　a·san·tay kwa moo·da wa·koh

Thank you all for your time.
Asanteni kwa muda wenu.　a·san·tay·nee kwa moo·da way·noo

Shall we go for a drink/meal?
Twende kwa vinywaji/　　twayn·day kwa vee·nywa·jee/
chakula?　　cha·koo·la

It's on me.
Ofa yangu.　　oh·fa yan·goo

senior & disabled travellers
watalii wazee na wasioweza

In East Africa you're very unlikely to encounter special facilities such as modified toilets or bathroom rails, accessible parking spaces, or special taxis.

I have a disability.
Nina ulemavu. *nee-na oo-lay-ma-voo*

I need assistance.
Nahitaji msaada. *na-hee-ta-jee m-sa-da*

What services do you have for people with a disability?
Kuna huduma *koo-na hoo-doo-ma*
gani kwa watu *ga-nee kwa wa-too*
wenye ulemavu? *way-nyay oo-lay-ma-voo*

Is there wheelchair access?
Kuna njia ya kuingia *koo-na n-jee-a ya koo-een-gee-a*
kwa kiti cha *kwa kee-tee cha*
magurudumu? *ma-goo-roo-doo-moo*

How wide is the entrance?
Mlango ni upana gani? *m-lan-goh nee oo-pa-na ga-nee*

How many steps are there?
Kuna ngazi ngapi? *koo-na n-ga-zee n-ga-pee*

Is there a lift?
Kuna lifti? *koo-na leef-tee*

I'm deaf.
Mimi ni kiziwi. *mee-mee nee kee-zee-wee*

I have a hearing aid.
Nina chombo cha *nee-na chohm-boh cha*
kusaidia kusikia. *koo-sa-ee-dee-a koo-see-kee-a*

Where can I buy a hearing aid battery?
Naweza kununua wapi *na-way-za koo-noo-noo-a wa-pee*
kibetri cha chombo cha *kee-bay-tree cha chohm-boh cha*
kusaidia kusikia? *koo-sa-ee-dee-a koo-see-kee-a*

I can't see well.
Siwezi kuona vizuri.   see·*way*·zee koo·*oh*·na vee·*zoo*·ree

I'm blind.
Mimi ni kipofu.   *mee*·mee nee kee·*poh*·foo

Are guide dogs permitted?

Mbwa wa kuongoza	m·bwa wa koo·ohn·*goh*·za
kipofu huruhusiwa	kee·*poh*·foo hoo·roo·hoo·*see*·wa
hapa?	*ha*·pa

Could you help me cross the street safely?

Naomba unisaidie	na·*ohm*·ba oo·nee·sa·ee·*dee*·ay
kuvuka barabara	koo·*voo*·ka ba·ra·*ba*·ra
kwa usalama.	kwa oo·sa·*la*·ma

Is there somewhere I can sit down?
Kuna kiti?   koo·na *kee*·tee

guide dog	mbwa wa kuongoza	m·bwa wa koo·ohn·*goh*·za
older person	mzee	m·*zay*
person with a disability	mtu mwenye ulemavu	m·too *mway*·nyay oo·lay·*ma*·voo
ramp	mbao wa kushukia	m·*ba*·oh wa ku·shoo·*kee*·a
walking frame	magongo ya kutembelea	ma·*gohn*·goh ya koo·taym·bay·*lay*·a
walking stick	fimbo	*feem*·boh
wheelchair	kiti cha magurudumu	*kee*·tee cha ma·goo·roo·*doo*·moo

travelling with children

kusafiri na watoto

Is there a …?	Kuna …?	koo·na …
baby change room	chumba cha kuvalia mtoto	choom·ba cha koo·va·lee·a m·toh·toh
child-minding service	anayeweza kumlea mtoto	a·na·yay·way·za koom·lay·a m·toh·toh
child-sized portion	kiasi kwa mtoto	kee·a·see kwa m·toh·toh
children's menu	menyu kwa watoto	may·nyoo kwa wa·toh·toh
crèche	wanapolea watoto wadogo	wa·na·poh·lay·a wa·toh·toh wa·doh·goh
discount for children	punguzo la bei kwa watoto	poon·goo·zoh la bay kwa wa·toh·toh
family ticket	tiketi kwa familia	tee·kay·tee kwa fa·mee·lee·a

Do you sell …?	Mnauza …?	m·na·oo·za …
baby wipes	vitambaa kupangusa watoto	vee·tam·ba koo·pan·goo·sa wa·toh·toh
disposable nappies/diapers	nepi	nay·pee
painkillers for infants	dawa la kutuliza maumivu kwa watoto	da·wa la koo·too·lee·za ma·oo·mee·voo kwa wa·toh·toh

I need a/an ...	Nahitaji ...	na·hee·ta·jee ...
baby seat	kiti cha kitoto	kee·tee cha kee·toh·toh
(English-speaking) babysitter	yaya (anayesema Kiingereza)	ya·ya (a·na·yay·say·ma kee·een·gay·ray·za)
booster seat	kiti kumpandisha mtoto juu	kee·tee koom·pan·dee·sha m·toh·toh joo
cot/crib	kitanda cha mtoto mchanga	kee·tan·da cha m·toh·toh m·chan·ga
highchair	kiti juu cha mtoto	kee·tee juu cha m·toh·toh
plastic bag	mfuko wa plastiki	m·foo·koh wa pla·stee·kee
potty	choo cha mtoto	choh cha m·toh·toh
pram/stroller	kigari cha mtoto	kee·ga·ree cha m·toh·toh

Do you hire prams/strollers?
Mnakodisha vigari vya watoto?
m·na·koh·dee·sha vee·ga·ree vya wa·toh·toh

Where can I change a nappy?
Nibadilishe nepi wapi?
nee·ba·dee·lee·shay nay·pee wa·pee

Where's a water tap?
Kuna bomba la maji wapi?
koo·na bohm·ba la ma·jee wa·pee

Are there any good places to take children around here?
Kuna mahali pazuri kwa watoto hapa eneo hili?
koo·na ma·ha·lee pa·zoo·ree kwa wa·toh·toh ha·pa ay·nay·oh hee·lee

Are children under (12) allowed?
Watoto chini ya miaka (kumi na miwili) huruhusiwa?
wa·toh·toh chee·nee ya mee·a·ka (koo·mee na mee·wee·lee) hoo·roo·hoo·see·wa

Is this suitable for (three)-year old children?
Inafaa kwa watoto wa miaka (mitatu)?
ee·na·fa kwa wa·toh·toh wa mee·a·ka (mee·ta·too)

Do you know a doctor who is good with children?
Unajua daktari ambaye   oo·na·*joo*·a dak·*ta*·ree am·*ba*·yay
watoto wanapenda?   wa·*toh*·toh wa·na·*payn*·da

If your child is sick, see **health**, page 183.

talking with children

kuongea na watoto

What's your name?
Jina lako nani?   *jee*·na *la*·koh *na*·nee

How old are you?
Una miaka mingapi?   oo·na mee·*a*·ka meen·*ga*·pee

When's your birthday?
Siku yako ya kuzaliwa   *see*·koo *ya*·koh ya koo·za·*lee*·wa
ni lini?   nee *lee*·nee

Do you go to school?
Unahudhuria shule?   oo·na·hoo·dhoo·*ree*·a *shoo*·lay?

What grade are you in?
Unasoma darasa gani?   oo·na·*soh*·ma da·*ra*·sa *ga*·nee

Do you learn English?
Unajifunza Kiingereza?   oo·na·jee·*foon*·za kee·een·gay·*ray*·za

Do you like sport?
Unapenda michezo?   oo·na·*payn*·da mee·*chay*·zoh

---

kids' talk

Children will often greet adult strangers by calling out
shikamoo shee·ka·*moh* (lit: respectful greetings), and will be
delighted if you reply with a warm marahaba ma·ra·*ha*·ba
(lit: thank you for your respectful greetings). In many areas
they'll run towards you with both hands raised above their
heads. You can kneel or squat for them to place their hands
on your forehead while they greet you. After this initial
respectful greeting you'll usually continue by exchanging
one or many of the standard greetings (see page 107).

c h i l d r e n

talking about children

Is this your first child?
Huyu ni mtoto wako wa kwanza?
hoo·yoo nee m·toh·toh wa·koh wa kwan·za

How many children do you have?
Una watoto wangapi?
oo·na wa·toh·toh wan·ga·pee

What a beautiful child!
Kumbe, huyu ni mtoto anayependeza!
koom·bay hoo·yoo nee m·toh·toh a·na·yay·payn·day·za

Is it a boy or a girl?
Je, huyu ni mvulana au msichana?
jay hoo·yoo nee m·voo·la·na a·oo m·see·cha·na

How old is he/she?
Ana umri gani?
a·na oom·ree ga·nee

What's his/her name?
Anaitwa nani?
a·na·eet·wa na·nee

He/She looks like you.
Anakufanana.
a·na·koo·fa·na·na

Does he/she go to school?
Anahudhuria shule?
a·na·hoo·dhoo·ree·a shoo·lay

Is he/she well behaved?
Ana tabia nzuri?
a·na ta·bee·a n·zoo·ree

baby talk

Attitude towards pregnancy and motherhood in East Africa can be surprising for a Western visitor. For example, breast-feeding in public is always acceptable and a permission would never be asked for in Swahili.

On the other hand, two questions you shouldn't ask expectant mothers are: 'When's the baby due?' and 'What are you going to call the baby?' With events like childbirth, many Swahili speakers prefer not to count their chickens before they hatch.

SOCIAL > meeting people

kukutana na watu

basics

misingi

Yes.	*Ndiyo.*	n·*dee*·yoh
No.	*Hapana.*	ha·*pa*·na
Please.	*Tafadhali.*	ta·fa·*dha*·lee
Thank you (very much).	*Asante (sana).*	a·*san*·tay (*sa*·na)
Thank you all (very much).	*Asanteni (sana).*	a·san·*tay*·nee (*sa*·na)
You're welcome.	*Karibu.*	ka·*ree*·boo
You're all welcome.	*Karibuni.*	ka·ree·*boo*·nee
Excuse me.	*Samahani.*	sa·ma·*ha*·nee
Forgive me.	*Nisamele.*	nee·sa·*may*·lay
Sorry.	*Pole.*	*poh*·lay

greetings & goodbyes

kusalimiana na kuaga

You can never spend too long exchanging greetings in East Africa. They vary depending on whether you're speaking to one person or several, or to an older or younger person. People often spend a few minutes with hands clasped, catching up on all the latest news.

You may notice many gestures that accompany greetings – respectful curtsies, grasped upper forearms, hand kisses or cool handshakes. Expect to shake hands often in East Africa. If your right hand is full or dirty, offer your wrist instead.

meeting people

107

hi there

The most common greeting is *habari* ha·*ba*·ree (lit: news). The variations on this greeting are many. Common ones include *salama* sa·*la*·ma (lit: safe) instead of *habari*, which may be dropped from the greeting altogether: *(Habari) Za leo?* (ha·*ba*·ree) za *lay*·oh (lit: news of today). You can use *salama* to greet anybody you pass or to reply to any greeting.

Hello./How are you?
Habari?   ha·*ba*·ree

What's the news?
Habari gani?   ha·*ba*·ree *ga*·nee

How are you all?
Habari zenu?   ha·*ba*·ree *zay*·noo

How's everyone at home?
Habari za nyumbani?   ha·*ba*·ree za nyoom·*ba*·nee

How's work?
Habari za kazi?   ha·*ba*·ree za *ka*·zee

Good ...	Habari za ...?	ha·*ba*·ree za ...
day	leo	*lay*·oh
morning	asubuhi	a·soo·boo·hee
afternoon	mchana	m·*cha*·na
evening	jioni	jee·oh·nee

You can reply to almost any *habari* greeting using *nzuri* n·*zoo*·ree, *salama* sa·*la*·ma or *safi* sa·fee (fine). If things are just OK, add *tu* too (only) after any of these replies. Even if things are really bad, most people will reply to greetings with *nzuri tu* (lit: only fine), rather than *mbaya* m·*ba*·ya (bad). If things are really good, you can add *sana* sa·na (very), or *kabisa* ka·*bee*·sa (totally) instead of *tu*.

What's your name?
Jina lako nani?   jee·na *la*·koh *na*·nee

My name is ...
Jina langu ni ...   jee·na *lan*·goo nee ...

I'd like to introduce you to ...
Huyu ni ...   *hoo*·yoo nee ...

This is my ...	Huyu ni ...	hoo·yoo nee ...
child	mtoto wangu	m·toh·toh wan·goo
colleague	mwenzi	mwayn·zee
	wangu	wan·goo
friend	rafiki yangu	ra·fee·kee yan·goo
husband	mume wangu	moo·may wan·goo
partner	mpenzi	m·payn·zee
(intimate)	wangu	wan·goo
wife	mke wangu	m·kay wan·goo

For more kinship terms, see also **family**, page 115 and the **dictionary**.

I'm pleased to meet you.	Nafurahi kukufahamu.	na·foo·ra·hee koo·koo·fa·ha·moo
See you later.	Baadaye.	ba·a·da·yay
Goodbye.	Tutaonana.	too·ta·oh·na·na
Bye.	Kwa heri.	kwa hay·ree
Good night.	Usiku mwema.	oo·see·koo mway·ma
Bon voyage!	Safari njema!	sa·fa·ree n·jay·ma

addressing people

vyeo vya watu

There are two forms of addressing women, different in the level of formality. The word *bibi* bee·bee is more informal than *bi* bee, and can be used by anyone to refer to their grandmother, and by a husband to refer to his wife. The general term *bwana* bwa·na is used for addressing men both in formal and informal situations.

Mr/Sir	Bwana	bwa·na
Mrs/Madam	Bi	bee
Ms/Miss	Bibi	bee·bee

When addressing an older person or an authority figure, the usual exchange of greetings is:

Respectful greetings.
Shikamoo. shee·ka·*moh*

Thank you for your respectful greetings.
(an older person to a younger person)
Marahaba. ma·ra·*ha*·ba

Thank you for your respectful greetings.
(a younger person to an older person)
Asante. a·*san*·tay

It's common to address people by their likely position within a family. You can call an elder man 'grandfather', a middle-aged man 'father', and a youthful man 'brother'. In addition, parents are often addressed as the mother or father of one of their children (not necessarily the first born), rather than using the parent's own name, eg *mama Amina ma*·ma a·*mee*·na (Amina's mother), *baba Flora ba*·ba *floh*·ra (Flora's father).

auntie (any elder woman)	*shangazi*	shan·*ga*·zee
brother	*kaka*	*ka*·ka
father	*baba*	*ba*·ba
grandmother	*bibi*	*bee*·bee
grandfather	*babu*	*ba*·boo
mother	*mama*	*ma*·ma
respected elder	*mzee*	m·*zay*
sister	*dada*	*da*·da
sibling/friend	*ndugu*	n·*doo*·goo
uncle (any elder man)	*mjomba*	m·*johm*·ba

For information on addressing children, see **talking with children**, page 105.

making conversation

kuzungumza

What a beautiful day!
Ni siku nzuri sana!
nee *see*·koo n·*zoo*·ree *sa*·na

Nice/Awful weather, isn't it?
Hali ya hewa ni nzuri/mbaya, sivyo?
ha·lee ya *hay*·wa nee n·*zoo*·ree/m·*ba*·ya secv·yoh

Do you live here?
Unakaa hapa?
oo·na·*ka* ha·pa

Where are you going?
Unaenda wapi?
oo·na·*ayn*·da *wa*·pee

What are you doing?
Unafanya nini?
oo·na·*fa*·nya *nee*·nee

Do you like it here?
Unapapenda hapa?
oo·na·pa·*payn*·da *ha*·pa

I love it here.
Napapenda hapa.
na·pa·*payn*·da *ha*·pa

What's this called?
Hii inaitwa nini?
hee ee·na·*eet*·wa *nee*·nee

That's beautiful, isn't it?
Inapendeza sana, sivyo?
ee·na·payn·*day*·za *sa*·na *seev*·yo

meeting people

111

Where are you coming from?	Umetoka wapi?	oo·may·toh·ka wa·pee
I'm coming from ...	Nimetoka ...	nee·may·toh·ka ...
home	nyumbani	nyoom·ba·nee
the market	sokoni	soh·koh·nee
town	mjini	m·jee·nee
Are you here on holiday?	Uko hapa kwa likizo?	oo·koh ha·pa kwa lee·kee·zoh
I'm here ...	Nipo kwa ...	nee·poh kwa ...
for a holiday	likizo	lee·kee·zoh
on business	biashara	bee·a·sha·ra
to study	masomo	ma·soh·moh

How long are you here for?
Upo kwa muda gani?   oo·poh kwa moo·da ga·nee

I'm here for (four) weeks/days.
Nipo kwa wiki/   nee·poh kwa wee·kee/
siku (nne).   see·koo (n·nay)

---

local talk

Cool.	Poa.	poh·a
Great!	Safi!	sa·fee
Hey!	We!	way
How are things?	Mambo?	mam·boh
It's OK.	Ni sawa.	nee sa·wa
Just a minute.	Subiri kidogo.	soo·bee·ree kee·doh·goh
Just joking.	Natania tu.	na·ta·nee·a too
Maybe.	Labda.	lab·da
No problem.	Hamna shida.	ham·na shee·da
No way!	Haiwezekani!	ha·ee·way·zee·ka·nee
Sure.	Sawa.	sa·wa
What's the news?	Lete habari.	lay·tay ha·ba·ree
What's up?	Vipi?	vee·pee

The following tips on East African etiquette should help you wherever you travel in the region.

● Men and women maintain a formal distance in many social situations. Public displays of affection between sexes don't happen, but friends of the same sex often hold hands when walking around town. Feel honoured if someone of your gender makes such a display of friendship.

● It's fine to wear shorts in tourist areas. However, long pants or skirts, as well as tops with sleeves, are essential when visiting government offices or people's homes, and are preferable at most other times, especially along the Muslim-dominated coast and in rural areas.

● If you accept a gift or treat from someone, they'll often anticipate some reciprocal gesture of friendship, often a meal or gift of equivalent value. Spoken thanks are not so common in East Africa, so don't be surprised if the appreciation isn't expressed verbally.

nationalities

uraia

Where are you from?
   Unatoka wapi?   oo·na·*toh*·ka *wa*·pee

I'm from …	*Natoka …*	na·*toh*·ka …
America	*Marekani*	ma·ray·*ka*·nee
Australia	*Australia*	a·oo·*stra*·lee·a
Canada	*Kanada*	*ka*·na·da
England	*Uingereza*	oo·een·gay·*ray*·za

meeting people

age

How old are you?
Una miaka mingapi?   oo·na mee·*a*·ka meen·*ga*·pee

How old is your child?
Mtoto wako ana   m·*toh*·toh wa·koh *a*·na
miaka mingapi?   mee·*a*·ka meen·*ga*·pee

I'm ... years old.
Nina miaka ...   nee·na mee·*a*·ka ...

He/She is ... years old.
Ana miaka ...   *a*·na mee·*a*·ka ...

Too old!
Mzee mno!   m·*zay* m·noh

For your age, see **numbers & amounts**, page 37.

occupations & studies

What's your occupation?
Unafanya kazi gani?   oo·na·*fa*·nya *ka*·zee *ga*·nee

I'm a ...	*Mimi ni ...*	mee·mee nee ...
business person	*mfanyabiashara*	m·fa·nya·bee·a·*sha*·ra
chef	*mpishi*	m·*pee*·shee
driver	*dereva*	day·*ray*·va
farmer	*mkulima*	m·koo·*lee*·ma
fisher	*mvuvi*	m·*voo*·vee
journalist	*ripota*	ree·*poh*·ta
soldier	*askari*	as·*ka*·ree
teacher	*mwalimu*	mwa·*lee*·moo

SOCIAL

114

I work in ...	Nafanya kazi kwenye ...	na·fa·nya ka·zee kway·nyay ...
administration	usimamizi	oo·see·ma·mee·zee
health	afya	af·ya
sales & marketing	uuzaji	oo·oo·za·jee

I'm ...		
retired	Nimestaafu.	nee·may·sta·foo
self-employed	Najiajiri.	na·jee·a·jee·ree
unemployed	Sina kazi sasa.	see·na ka·zee sa·sa

What are you studying?	Unasoma masomo gani?	oo·na·soh·ma ma·soh·mo ga·nee

I'm studying ...	Nasoma ...	na·soh·ma ...
African music/ dance	densi/muziki ya kiafrika	duyn·see/moo·zee·kee ya kee·af·ree·ka
humanities	sayansi za jamii	sa·yan·see za ja·mee
Swahili	Kiswahili	kee·swa·hee·lee
science	sayansi	sa·yan·see

family

Do you have a ...?	Una ...?	oo·na ...
I have/don't have a ...	Nina/Sina ...	nee·na/see·na ...
boyfriend	mpenzi	m·payn·zee
brother	kaka	ka·ka
daughter	binti	been·tee
girlfriend	mpenzi	m·payn·zee
grandchild	mjukuu	m·joo·koo
husband	mume	moo·may
partner/fiancé(e)	mchumba	m·choom·ba
sister	dada	da·da
son	mwana	mwa·na
wife	mke	m·kay

For more kinship terms, see the **dictionary**.

family tree

Swahili kinship connections through your father's brothers and your mother's sisters are regarded very highly. Rather than being 'uncles' and 'aunts', they're considered your parents too. If they're older than your birth parents they're *mkubwa* m·*koob*·wa ('big'), if they're younger they're *mdogo* m·*doh*·goh ('little'). However, mother's brothers and father's sisters don't get distinguished by age. Many families in East Africa consist of one husband and two or more wives. Children of co-wives generally consider themselves brothers and sisters.

aunt	*shangazi*	shan·*ga*·zee
(father's sister)		
aunt	*mama mkubwa*	*ma*·ma m·*koob*·wa
(mother's older sister)		
aunt	*mama mdogo*	*ma*·ma m·*doh*·goh
(mother's younger sister)		
uncle	*mjomba*	m·*johm*·ba
(mother's brother)		
uncle	*baba mkubwa*	*ba*·ba m·*koob*·wa
(father's older brother)		
uncle	*baba mdogo*	*ba*·ba m·*doh*·goh
(father's younger brother)		
big mother	*mama mkubwa*	*ma*·ma m·*koob*·wa
(father's wife senior to your mother – the one he married before)		
little mother	*mama mdogo*	*ma*·ma m·*doh*·goh
(father's wife junior to your mother – the one he married after)		

Do you have children?
Una watoto?   oo·na wa·*toh*·toh

How many children do you have?
Una watoto wangapi?   oo·na wa·*toh*·toh wan·*ga*·pee

Are you married?
Umeoa?/Umeolewa? m/f   oo·may·*oh*·a/oo·may·oh·*lay*·wa

I live with someone.
Naishi na mchumba.   na·*ee*·shee na m·*choom*·ba

SOCIAL

116

I'm ...

divorced	*Tumeachana.*	too·may·a·*cha*·na
married	*Nimeoa/*	nee·may·*oh*·a/
	Nimeolewa. m/f	nee·may·oh·*lay*·wa
not married	*Sijaoa/*	see·ja·oh·a/
yet	*Sijaolewa bado.* m/f	see·ja·oh·*lay*·wa *ba*·doh
separated	*Tumetengana.*	too·may·tayn·*ga*·na
single	*Mimi sina*	*mee*·mee *see*·na
	mpenzi.	m·*payn*·zee

farewells

In contrast to the amount of tIme East Africans spend greeting each other, they put relatively little energy into saying goodbye. Often farewells simply involve confirming when you'll next meet, then walking away with a simple *haya ha*·ya (OK). Saying goodbyes before a long trip is more involved: hands clasped, the traveller is wished well and told to greet everybody at their destination.

Tomorrow is my last day here.
Kesho ni siku yangu   *kay*·shoh nee *see*·koo yan·goo
ya mwisho hapa.   ya *mwee*·shoh *ha*·pa

It's been great meeting you.
Nimefurahi   nee·may·foo·*ra*·hee
kukufahamu.   koo·koo·fa·*ha*·moo

well-wishing		
Bless you!	*Heri zote!*	*hay*·ree *zoh*·tay
Bon voyage!	*Safari njema!*	sa·*fa*·ree n·*jay*·ma
Congratulations!	*Hongera!*	hohn·*gay*·ra
Good luck!	*Bahati njema!*	ba·*ha*·tee n·*jay*·ma
Happy birthday!	*Heri za siku kuu*	*hay*·ree za *see*·koo koo
	ya kuzaliwa!	ya koo·za·*lee*·wa
Merry Christmas!	*Heri za*	*hay*·ree za
	Krismasi!	krees·*ma*·see

If you come to (Scotland) you can stay with me.
Ukija (Skotland), karibu   oo·*kee*·ja (*skoht*·land) ka·*ree*·boo
sana kukaa kwetu.   *sa*·na koo·*ka kway*·too

Keep in touch!
Niwasiliane!   nee·wa·see·lee·*a*·nay

Here's my ...	*Hii ni ... yangu.*	hee nee ... *yan*·goo
address	*anwani*	an·*wa*·nee
email address	*anwani ya*	an·*wa*·nee ya
	barua pepe	ba·*roo*·a *pay*·pay
phone number	*simu*	*see*·moo

What's your ...?	*... yako ni nini?*	... *ya*·koh nee *nee*·nee
address	*Anwani*	an·*wa*·nee
email address	*Anwani ya*	an·*wa*·nee ya
	barua pepe	ba·*roo*·a *pay*·pay
phone number	*Simu*	*see*·moo

common interests

What do you do in your spare time?

Unafanya nini kwa starehe?		oo·na·*fa*·nya *nee*·nee kwa sta·*ray*·hay

Do you like ...?	*Unapenda ...?*	oo·na·*payn*·da ...
I like ...	*Ninapenda ...*	nee·na·*payn*·da ...
I don't like ...	*Sipendi ...*	see·*payn*·dee ...
bao (board game)	*bao*	*ba*·oh
cooking	*kupika*	koo·*pee*·ka
dancing	*kucheza densi*	koo·*chay*·za *dayn*·see
films	*filamu*	fee·*la*·moo
gardening	*kulima bustani*	koo·*lee*·ma boo·*sta*·nee
hiking	*kutembea*	koo·taym·*bay*·a
	porini	poh·*ree*·nee
music	*muziki*	moo·*zee*·kee
painting	*sanaa*	sa·*na*
photography	*kupiga picha*	koo·*pee*·ga *pee*·cha
reading	*kusoma*	koo·*soh*·ma
shopping	*ununuzi*	oo·noo·*noo*·zee
socialising	*kuchanganyika*	koo·chan·ga·*nyee*·ka
	na wengine	na wayn·*gee*·nay
sport	*michezo*	mee·*chay*·zoh
surfing	*kutumia*	koo·too·*mee*·a
the Internet	*intaneti*	een·ta·*nay*·tee
travelling	*kusafiri*	koo·sa·*fee*·ree
watching TV	*kutazama*	koo·ta·*za*·ma
	televisheni	tay·lay·vee·*shay*·nee

For sporting activities, see **sport**, page 141.

music

Do you ...?	Wewe ...?	way·way ...
dance	hucheza densi	hoo-chay-za dayn-see
go to concerts	huenda kuona muziki	hoo-ayn-da koo-oh-na moo-zee-kee
listen to music	husikiliza muziki	hoo-see-kee-lee-za moo-zee-kee
play an instrument	hucheza ala ya muziki	hoo-chay-za a-la ya moo-zee-kee
sing	huimba	hoo-eem-ba

Which ... do you like?	Unapenda ... gani?	oo-na-payn-da ... ga-nee
bands	vikundi	vee-koon-dee
music	muziki	moo-zee-kee
singers	waimbaji	wa-eem-ba-jee

Which African music videos do you like?
Unapenda video gani za muziki ya kiafrika?
oo-na-payn-da vee-day-oh ga-nee za moo-zee-kee ya kee-af-ree-ka

Where can I see music videos by local bands?
Niende wapi kuona video za muziki za vikundi vya hapa?
nee-ayn-day wa-pee koo-oh-na vee-day-oh za moo-zee-kee za vee-koon-dee vya ha-pa

drums	ngoma	n-goh-ma
horns	siwa	see-wa
shakers	kayamba	ka-yam-ba
tambourine	dufu	doo-foo
xylophone	marimba	ma-reem-ba

blues	muziki ya Marekani ya kusikitisha	moo·zee·kee ya ma·ray·ka·nee ya koo·see·kee·tee·sha
brass music	muziki ya ngoma	moo·zee·kee ya n·goh·ma
classical music	muziki ya Ulaya ya zamani	moo·zee·kee ya oo·la·ya ya za·ma·nee
electronic music	muziki ya Ulaya ya kilabuni	moo·zee·kee ya oo·la·ya ya kee·la·boo·nee
jazz	jazi	ja·zee
Kenyan dance music	benga	bayn·ga
pop	muziki ya kisasa	moo·zee·kee ya kee·sa·sa
rock	roki	roh·kee
popular music of Zanzibar	taarab	ta·rab
traditional music	muziki ya mila na desturi	moo·zee·kee ya mee·la na day·stoo·ree
world music	muziki ya sehemu mbalimbali za dunia	moo·zee·kee ya say·hay·moo m·ba·lee·m·ba·lee za doo·nee·a
Zairean jazz	sukosi	soo·koh·see

Off to a concert? See **tickets**, page 49 and **going out**, page 127.

cinema & theatre

sinema na tamthilia

I feel like going to a ...	Nataka kwenda ...	na·ta·ka kwayn·da ...
Did you like the ...?	Ulipenda ...?	oo·lee·payn·da ...
ballet	densi	dayn·see
film	filamu	fee·la·moo
play	tamthilia	tam·thee·lee·a

interests

121

What's showing at the cinema/theatre tonight?
Kuna filamu/tamthilia   koo·na fee·*la*·moo/tam·thee·*lee*·a
gani leo?   *ga*·nee *lay*·oh

Is it in English?
Ni kwa Kiingereza?   nee kwa kee·een·gay·*ray*·za

Does it have (English) subtitles?
kuna maandishi (ya   koo·na man·*dee*·shee (ya
Kiingereza) chini?   kee·een·gay·*ray*·za) *chee*·nee

Have you seen ...?
Umeona ...?   oo·may·*oh*·na ...

Who's in it?
Kuna waigizaji gani?   koo·na wa·ee·gee·*za*·jee *ga*·nee

It stars ...
Mwigizaji mkuu ni ...   mwee·gee·*za*·jee m·*koo* nee ...

I like ...	*Napenda ...*	na·*payn*·da ...
I don't like ...	*Sipendi ...*	see·*payn*·dee ...
action movies	*filamu zenye*	fee·*la*·moo *zay*·nyay
	misisimko	mee·see·*seem*·koh
African cinema	*filamu za*	fee·*la*·moo za
	kiafrika	kee·af·*ree*·ka
animated films	*katuni hai*	ka·*too*·nee *ha*·ee
comedies	*filamu za*	fee·*la*·moo za
	kuchekesha	koo·chay·*kay*·sha
documentaries	*filamu za hali*	fee·*la*·moo za *ha*·lee
	halisi	ha·*lee*·see
drama	*hadithi kama*	ha·*dee*·thee *ka*·ma
	riwaya	ree·*wa*·ya
Hindi cinema	*filamu za*	fee·*la*·moo za
	kihindi	kee·*heen*·dee
horror movies	*filamu za*	fee·*la*·moo za
	kutisha	koo·*tee*·sha
sci-fi	*hadithi za*	ha·*d ee*·thee za
	kubuni za	koo·*boo*·nee za
	kisayansi	kee·sa·*yan*·see
short films	*filamu fupi*	fee·*la*·moo *foo*·pee
war movies	*filamu*	fee·*la*·moo
	kuhusu vita	koo·*hoo*·soo *vee*·ta

feelings

hisia

Do you feel ...?	*Unasikia ...?*	oo·na·see·*kee*·a ...
I feel ...	*Nasikia ...*	na·see·*kee*·a ...
I don't feel ...	*Sisikii ...*	see·see·*kee* ...
cold	*baridi*	ba·*ree*·dee
happy	*furaha*	foo·*ra*·ha
hot	*joto*	*joh*·toh
hungry	*njaa*	n·*ja*
sad	*masikitiko*	ma·see·kee·*tee*·koh
thirsty	*kiu*	*kee*·oo

If feeling unwell, see **health**, page 183.

mixed feelings		
a little	*kidogo*	kee·*doh*·goh
I'm a little sad.	*Nasikitika*	na·see·kee·*tee*·ka
	kidogo.	kee·*doh*·goh
extremely/very	*sana*	*sa*·na
I'm very happy.	*Nafurahi*	na·foo·*ra*·hee
	sana.	*sa*·na
somewhat	*tu*	too
I feel just OK.	*Nasikia*	na·see·*kee*·a
	nzuri tu.	n·*zoo*·ree too

opinions

Do you like it?
Unaipenda?   oo·na·ee·*payn*·da

What do you think of it?
Unaionaje?   oo·na·ee·oh·*na*·jay

I thought it was …	Nilifikiri	nee·lee·fee·*kee*·ree
	ilikuwa …	ee·lee·*koo*·wa …
It's …	Ni …	nee …
awful	mbaya sana	m·*ba*·ya *sa*·na
boring	ya kuchosha	ya koo·*choh*·sha
great	nzuri kabisa	n·*zoo*·ree ka·*bee*·sa
interesting	ya kuvutia	ya koo·voo·*tee*·a
OK	sawa tu	*sa*·wa too
strange	siyo kawaida	*see*·yoh ka·wa·*ee*·da

politics & social issues

Conversing and debating with friends is an important part of daily life in East Africa. People express strong opinions about sport, politics and the latest local gossip.

Which party do you vote for?
Unapiga kura kwa   oo·na·*pee*·ga *koo*·ra kwa
chama gani?   *cha*·ma *ga*·nee

I support the … party.	Mimi	*mee*·mee
	napendelea	na·payn·day·*lay*·a
	chama cha …	*cha*·ma cha …
communist	kikomunisti	kee·koh·moo·*nee*·stee
democratic	demokrasia	day·moh·kra·*see*·a
green	kijani	kee·*ja*·nee
socialist	soshalisti	soh·sha·*lee*·stee

Did you hear about …?
  Ulisikia kuhusu …?   oo·lee·see·*kee*·a koo·*hoo*·soo …

I agree/don't agree with …
  Nakubali/Sikubali na …   na·koo·*ba*·lee/see·koo·*ba*·lee na …

How do people feel about …?
  Watu wana maoni   *wa*·too *wa*·na ma·*oh*·nee
  gani kuhusu …?   *ga*·nee koo·*hoo*·soo …

abortion	*kutoa mimba*	koo·*toh*·a *meem*·ba
AIDS	*ukimwi*	oo·*keem*·wee
animal rights	*haki za wanyama*	*ha*·kee za wa·*nya*·ma
crime	*uhalifu*	oo·ha·*lee*·foo
drugs	*madawa ya*	ma·*da*·wa ya
	kulevya	koo·*lay*·vya
the economy	*uchumi*	oo·*choo*·mee
education	*elimu*	ay·*lee*·moo
euthanasia	*eutanasia*	ay·oo·ta·na·*see*·a
Christian	*mamishionari*	ma·mee·shee·oh·*na*·ree
missionaries	*wakristo*	wa·*kree*·stoh
globalisation	*utandawazi*	oo·tan·da·*wa*·zee
human rights	*haki za*	*ha*·kee za
	binadamu	bee·na·*da*·moo
indigenous issues	*mada za wenyeji*	ma·*da* za way·*nyay*·jee
religious	*imani kali ya*	ee·*ma*·nee *ka*·lee ya
fundamentalism	*kidini*	kee·*dee*·nee
racism	*ubaguzi wa*	oo·ba·*goo*·zee wa
	rangi	*ran*·gee
sexism	*ubaguzi wa*	oo·ba·*goo*·zee wa
	kijinsia	kee·jeen·*see*·a
terrorism	*ugaidi*	oo·ga·*ee*·dee
unemployment	*ukosefu wa*	oo·koh·*say*·foo wa
	kazi	*ka*·zee
the war in …	*vita katika …*	*vee*·ta ka·*tee*·ka …

the environment

Is there a ... problem here?
Kuna shida ya ... hapa?   koo·na *shee*·da ya ... *ha*·pa

What should be done about ...?
Ni afadhali kufanya   nee·a·fa·*dha*·lee koo·*fa*·nya
nini kuhusu ...?   *nee*·nee koo·*hoo*·soo ...

drought	*ukame*	oo·*ka*·may
endangered species	*spishi zilizo hatarini*	*spee*·shee zee·*lee*·zoh ha·ta·*ree*·nee
genetically modified food	*chakula chenye jini iliyoumbwa*	cha·*koo*·la *chay*·nyay *jee*·nee ee·lee·yoh·*oom*·bwa
hunting	*uwindaji*	oo·ween·*da*·jee
nuclear testing	*majaribio ya nyuklia*	ma·ja·ree·*bee*·oh ya *nyook*·lee·a
ozone layer	*tabaka la hewa ya ozoni*	ta·*ba*·ka la *hay*·wa ya oh·*zoh*·nee
pesticides	*viuavisumbufu*	vee·oo·a·vee·soom·*boo*·foo
petroleum resource exploitation	*utumiaji ovyo wa maliasili ya mafuta*	oo·too·mee·*a*·jee *oh*·vyoh wa ma·lee·a·*see*·lee ya ma·*foo*·ta
poaching	*uwindaji kinyume na sheria*	oo·ween·*da*·jee kee·*nyoo*·may na shay·*ree*·a
pollution	*uchafuzi*	oo·cha·*foo*·zee
recycling programme	*mradi wa urejelezaji*	m·*ra*·dee wa oo·ray·jay·lay·*za*·jee
toxic waste	*taka za sumu*	*ta*·ka za *soo*·moo
water supply	*upatikanaji wa maji*	oo·pa·tee·ka·*na*·jee wa *ma*·jee

Is it a protected ...?   ... *inahifadhiwa?*   ee·na·hee·fa·*dhee*·wa ...

park	*Mbuga*	m·*boo*·ga
species	*Spishi*	*spee*·shee

where to go

kuenda wapi

What's there to do in the evenings?
Kuna nini kufanya koo·na *nee*·nee koo·*fa*·nya
saa za jioni? sa za jee·*oh*·nee

What's on …?	*Nini*	*nee*·nee
	inatokea …?	ee·na·toh·*kay*·a …
this weekend	*wikendi hii*	wee·*kayn*·dee hee
tonight	*usiku huu*	oo·*see*·koo hoo

I feel like going	*Nataka kwenda*	na·*ta*·ka *kwayn*·da
to a …	*kwenye …*	*kway*·nyay …
bar	*baa*	ba
beer club	*kilabu*	kee·*la*·boo
café	*mgahawa*	m·ga·*ha*·wa
casino	*kasino*	ka·*see*·noh
coffee house	*mgahawa*	m·ga·*ha*·wa
dance and	*ngoma*	n·*goh*·ma
drumming		
performance		
concert	*kusikiliza*	koo·see·kee·*lee*·za
	muziki	moo·*zee*·kee
film	*filamu*	fee·*la*·moo
karaoke bar	*karaoke*	ka·ra·*oh*·kay
nightclub	*klabu ya usiku*	*kla*·boo ya oo·*see*·koo
party	*sherehe*	shay·*ray*·hay
pub	*baa*	ba
restaurant	*hoteli kula*	hoh·*tay*·lee koo·la

Are gay people bothered here?
Wasenge huteswa hapa? wa·*sayn*·gay hoo·*tays*·wa *ha*·pa

Is there a local ... guide?	Kuna mwongozo wa mji kuhusu ...?	koo·na mwohn·goh·zoh wa m·jee koo·hoo·soo ...
entertainment	burudani	boo·roo·da·nee
film	filamu	fee·la·moo
gay	wasenge	wa·sayn·gay
music	muziki	moo·zee·kee
Where can I find ...?	... iko wapi?	... ee·koh wa·pee
clubs	Kilabu/Vilabu	kee·la·boo/vee·la·boo
gay venues	Mahali pa wasenge	ma·ha·lee pa wa·sayn·gay
places to eat	Hoteli kula	hoh·tay·lee koo·la
pubs	Baa	ba

For more on bars and drinks, see **eating out**, page 153.

invitations

mialiko

What are you doing ...?	Unafanya nini ...?	oo·na·fa·nya nee·nee ...
this weekend	wikendi hii	wee·kayn·dee hee
tonight	usiku huu	oo·see·koo hoo
Would you like to go (for a) ...?	Unataka kwenda (kwa) ...?	oo·na·ta·ka kwayn·da (kwa) ...
dancing	kucheza densi	koo·chay·za dayn·see
drink	kunywa	koo·nywa
	vinywaji	vee·nywa·jee
meal	chakula	cha·koo·la
walk	kutembea	koo·taym·bay·a

My round.
Ofa yangu.   oh·fa yan·goo

Do you know a good restaurant?
Unajua hoteli   oo·na·joo·a hoh·tay·lee
nzuri kula?   n·zoo·ree koo·la

We're having a party.
  Tutakuwa na sherehe.   too·ta·*koo*·wa na shay·*ray*·hay

You should come.
  Uje.   oo·jay

responding to invitations

Sure!
  Sawa!   *sa*·wa

Yes, I'd love to.
  Sawa, nitafurahi.   *sa*·wa nee·ta·foo·*ra*·hee

It's very kind of you to invite me.
  Wewe ni mwema   *way*·way nee *mway*·ma
  kunialika.   koo·nee·a·*lee*·ka

Where shall we go?
  Twende wapi?   *twayn*·day wa·pee

No, I'm afraid I can't.
  Asante, lakini siwezi.   a·*san*·tay la·*kee*·nee see·*way*·zee

What about tomorrow?
  Kesho, je?   *kay*·shoh jay

arranging to meet

What time will we meet?
  Tukutane saa ngapi?   too·koo·*ta*·nay sa n·*ga*·pee

Where will we meet?
  Tukutane wapi?   too·koo·*ta*·nay wa·pee

Let's meet at …	*Tukutane …*	too·koo·*ta*·nay …
(eight) o'clock	*saa (mbili)*	sa (m·*bee*·lee)
the entrance	*mlango wa*	m·*lan*·goh wa
	kuingia	koo·een·*gee*·a

I'll pick you up.
Nitakuja kukuchukua. nee·ta·*koo*·ja koo·koo·choo·*koo*·a

Are you ready?
Tayari? ta·*ya*·ree

I'm ready.
Mimi ni tayari. *mee*·mee nee ta·*ya*·ree

I'll be coming later.
Nitakuja baadaye. nee·ta·*koo*·ja ba·a·*da*·yay

See you later/tomorrow.
Tutaonana baadaye/ too·ta·oh·*na*·na ba·a·*da*·yay/
kesho. *kay*·sho

I'm looking forward to it.
Natarejea sana. na·ta·ray·*jay*·a *sa*·na

Sorry I'm late.
Samahani kwa sa·ma·*ha*·ni kwa
kuchelewa. koo·chay·*lay*·wa

Never mind.
Usijali. oo·see·*ja*·lee

For the Swahili time system, go to **time & dates**, page 39.

drugs

madawa ya kulevya

I don't take drugs.
Situmii madawa see·too·*mee* ma·*da*·wa
ya kulevya. ya koo·*lay*·vya

I take (*miraa*) occasionally.
Natumia (miraa) na·too·*mee*·a (mee·*ra*)
mara kwa mara. *ma*·ra kwa *ma*·ra

Do you want to have a smoke?
Unataka kuvuta? oo·na·*ta*·ka koo·*voo*·ta

Do you have a light?
Una kibiriti? *oo*·na kee·bee·*ree*·tee

romance
mapenzi

asking someone out

kuomba miadi

Where would you like to go (tonight)?
Unataka kwenda　　oo·na·*ta*·ka *kwayn*·da
wapi (jioni hii)?　　*wa*·pee (jee·*oh*·nee hee)

Would you like to do something (tomorrow)?
Unataka kupanga　　oo·na·*ta*·ka koo·*pan*·ga
pamoja (kwa kesho)?　pa·*moh*·ja (kwa *kay*·shoh)

Yes, I'd love to.
Asante, ndiyo.　　a·*san*·tay n·*dee*·yoh

Sorry, I can't.
Asante, siwezi.　　a·*san*·tay see·*way*·zee

local talk

He/She is a babe.
Huyu ni mrembo.　　hoo·yoo nee m·*raym*·boh

He/She is hot.
Huyu amependeza　　hoo·yoo a·may·payn·*day*·za
sana sana.　　　　*sa*·na *sa*·na

He's a bastard.
Yeye ni mshenzi.　　yay·yay nee m·*shayn*·zee

She's a bitch.
Yeye ni jahili.　　yay·yay nee ja·*hee*·lee

He/She gets around.
Yeye ni jamvi la　　yay·yay nee *jam*·vee la
wageni.　　　　　wa·*gay*·nee

romance

131

pick-up lines

Would you like a drink?
Unywe kinywaji?   oony·way keeny·*wa*·jee

You look like someone I know.
Unafanana mtu   oo·na·fa·*na*·na *m*·too
ninayejua.   nee·na·yay·*joo*·a

You're a fantastic dancer.
Wewe ni mchezadensi   *way*·way nee m·chay·za·*dayn*·se
mzuri sana.   m·*zoo*·ree *sa*·na

Can I dance with you?
Tucheze densi?   too·*chay*·zay *dayn*·see

Can I sit here?
Naomba nikae hapa?   na·*ohm*·ba nee·*ka*·ay *ha*·pa

Can I accompany you to your home?
Nikusindikize kwako?   nee·koo·seen·dee·*kee*·zay *kwa*·koh

Can I take you to my place?
Twende kwangu?   *twayn*·day *kwan*·goo

rejections

No, thank you.
Hapana, asante.   ha·*pa*·na a·*san*·tay

I'd rather not.
Nisingependa, asante.   nee·seen·gay·*payn*·da a·*san*·tay

I'm here with my girlfriend/boyfriend.
Nipo na mpenzi wangu.   *nee*·poh na m·*payn*·zee *wan*·goo

Excuse me, I have to go now.
Samahani, lazima   sa·ma·*ha*·nee *la*·zee·ma
niondoke sasa.   nee·ohn·*doh*·kay *sa*·sa

Leave me alone (now)!
Niache (sasa)!   nee·*a*·chay (*sa*·sa)

Piss off!
Toka!   *toh*·ka

getting closer

I like you very much.
Nakupenda sana.   na·koo·*payn*·da *sa*·na

You're great.
Wewe ni mzuri sana.   *way*·way nee m·*zoo*·ree *sa*·na

Can I kiss you?
Nikubusu?   nee·koo·*boo*·soo

Do you want to come inside for a while?
Unataka kuingia   oo·na·*ta*·ka koo·een·*gee*·a
ndani kidogo?   n·*da*·nee kee·*doh*·goh

Do you want a massage?
Unataka kuchuliwa?   oo·na·*ta*·ka koo·choo·*lee*·wa

Can I stay over?
Nikae usiku huu?   nee·*ka*·ay oo·*see*·koo hoo

sex

Kiss me.
Nibusu.   nee·*boo*·soo

I want you.
Nakutaka.   na·koo·*ta*·ka

Let's go to bed.
Twende kitandani.   *twayn*·day kee·tan·*dan*·ee

Touch me here.
Niguse hapa.   nee·*goo*·say *ha*·pa

Do you like this?
Unapenda hii?   oo·na·*payn*·da hee

romance

133

I like that.
Napenda hiyo.　　　　　na·*payn*·da *hee*·yoh

I don't like that.
Sipendi hiyo.　　　　　see·*payn*·dee *hee*·yoh

I think we should stop now.
Tusimame sasa.　　　　too·see·*ma*·may *sa*·sa

Do you have a condom?
Una kondom?　　　　　oo·na *kohn*·dom

I have a condom.
Nina kondom.　　　　　*nee*·na *kohn*·dom

Let's use a condom.
Tutumie kondom.　　　　too·too·*mee*·ay *kohn*·dom

I won't do it without protection.
Sitafanya bila kinga.　　see·ta·*fa*·nya *bee*·la *keen*·ga

It's my first time.
Ni mara yangu ya kwanza.　nee *ma*·ra *yan*·goo ya *kwan*·za

It helps to have a sense of humour.
Husaidia kuweza　　　　hoo·sa·ee·*dee*·a koo·*way*·za
kucheka.　　　　　　　koo·*chay*·ka

Oh my God!
Mwenyezi Mungu!　　　mway·*nyay*·zee *moon*·goo

That's great.
Safi sana.　　　　　　*sa*·fee *sa*·na

Easy, lion!
Tulia, simba!　　　　　too·*lee*·a *seem*·ba

That was ...	Ilikuwa ...	ee·lee·*koo*·wa ...
amazing	*barabara*	ba·*ra*·ba·ra
animalistic	*kama wanyama*	*ka*·ma wa·*nya*·ma
like a dream	*kama ndoto*	*ka*·ma n·*doh*·toh

love

upenzi

Will you go out with me?
Utakuwa mpenzi wangu?   oo·ta·*koo*·wa m·*payn*·zee *wan*·goo

Will you meet my parents?
Utakutana na wazazi   oo·ta·koo·*ta*·na na wa·*za*·zee
wangu?   *wan*·goo

I think we're good together.
Nafikiri tunafaa   na·fee·*kee*·ree too·na·*fa*
pamoja.   pa·*moh*·ja

I love you.
Nakupenda.   na·koo·*payn*·da

Will you marry me? (man asking woman)
Niolewe.   nee·oh·*lay*·way

Will you marry me? (woman asking man)
Nioe.   nee·*oh*·ay

is it a he or a she?

Swahili doesn't distinguish between 'he' and 'she' – the language treats all people the same, regardless of gender. The only exceptions are verbs like 'to marry' (a woman is married, while a man marries), and certain sexual terms.

romance

135

problems

Are you seeing someone else?
Umekuwa unatembea   oo·may·*koo*·wa oo·na·taym·*bay*·a
na mwengine?   na mwayn·*gee*·nay

He/She is just a friend.
Yeye ni rafiki tu.   yay·yay nee ra·*fee*·kee too

You're just using me for sex.
Unanitumia kwa   oo·na·nee·too·*mee*·a kwa
mapenzi tu.   ma·*payn*·zee too

I never want to see you again.
Sitaki kukuona   see·*ta*·kee koo·koo·*oh*·na
tena daima.   *tay*·na da·*ee*·ma

I don't think it's working out.
Sidhani inafaa.   see·*dha*·nee ee·na·*fa*

We'll work it out.
Itafanikiwa.   ee·ta·fa·nee·*kee*·wa

leaving

I have to leave (tomorrow).
Inabidi niondoke   ee·na·*bee*·dee nee·ohn·*doh*·kay
(kesho).   (*kay*·sho)

I'll keep in touch.
Nitakuwasiliana.   nee·ta·koo·wa·see·lee·*a*·na

I'll miss you.
Nitakukosa.   nee·ta·koo·*koh*·sa

I'll visit you.
Nitakutembelea.   nee·ta·koo·taym·bay·*lay*·a

beliefs & cultural differences
imani na tofauti za utamaduni

religion

What's your religion?
Wewe ni dini gani?   way·way nee *dee*·nee *ga*·nee

I'm not religious.
Sina dini.   *see*·na *dee*·nee

I'm ...	Mimi ni ...	mee·mee nee ...
agnostic	agnostiki	ag·noh·*stee*·kee
Buddhist	Mbudisti	m·boo·*dee*·stee
Catholic	Mkatoliki	m·ka·toh·*lee*·kee
Christian	Mkristo	m·*kree*·stoh
Hindu	Mhindu	m·*heen*·doo
Jewish	Myahudi	m·ya·*hoo*·dee
Lutheran	Mluteri	m·loo·*tay*·ree
Muslim	Mwislamu	mwee·*sla*·moo
Protestant	Mprotestanti	m·proh·tay·*stan*·tee
Sikh	Msiik	m·*seek*

I believe/don't believe in ...	Naamini/ Siamini mambo ya ...	na·a·*mee*·nee/ see·a·*mee*·nee mam·boh ya ...
fate	majaliwa	ma·ja·*lee*·wa
God	Mungu	*moon*·goo

Where can I ...?	Naweza ... wapi?	na·*way*·za ... *wa*·pee
attend mass	kuhudhuria misa	koo·hoo·dhoo·*ree*·a *mee*·sa
attend a service	kuhudhuria ibada	koo·hoo·dhoo·*ree*·a ee·*ba*·da
pray	kusali	koo·*sa*·lee
worship	kutoa huduma	koo·*toh*·a hoo·*doo*·ma

Could I visit the mosque?
   Naweza kutembelea   na·*way*·za koo·taym·bay·*lay*·a
   msikiti?   m·see·*kee*·tee

Have you been on a Haj?
   Umekwenda   oo·may·*kwayn*·da
   kwenye Haji?   *kway*·nyay ha·jee

Are you planning to do a Haj?
   Unategemea kwenda   oo·na·tay·gay·*may*·a *kwayn*·da
   kwenye Haji?   *kway*·nyay ha·jee

cultural differences

tofauti za utamaduni

Is this a local or national custom?
   Je, ni mila ya watu   jay nee *mee*·la ya *wa*·too
   wa hapa, au ni mila   wa *ha*·pa *a*·oo nee *mee*·la
   ya taifa nzima?   ya ta·*ee*·fa n·*zee*·ma

I don't want to offend you.
   Sitaki kukusafihi.   see·*ta*·kee koo·koo·sa·*fee*·hee

I'm not used to this.
   Sijazoea kufanya hivyo.   see·ja·zoh·*ay*·a koo·*fa*·nya *heev*·yoh

I'd rather not join in.
   Napendelea   na·payn·day·*lay*·a
   kutoshiriki.   koo·toh·shee·*ree*·kee

I'll try it.
   Nitajaribu.   nee·ta·ja·*ree*·boo

This is different.
   Ni tofauti.   nee toh·fa·*oo*·tee

This is interesting.
   Ni ya kuvutia.   nee ya koo·voo·*tee*·a

It's against my beliefs.
   Inavuka imani zangu.   ee·na·*voo*·ka ee·*ma*·nee *zan*·goo

I didn't mean to do/say anything wrong.
   Sikukusudia kufanya/   see·koo·koo·soo·*dee*·a koo·*fa*·nya/
   kusema vibaya.   koo·*say*·ma vee·*ba*·ya

When's the gallery/museum open?
Nyumba ya sanaa/   *nyoom·*ba ya sa·*na/*
makumbusho   ma·koom·*boo·*shoh
hufungua saa ngapi?   hoo·foon·*goo·*a sa n·*ga·*pee

What kind of art are you interested in?
Unapenda sanaa   oo·na·*payn·*da sa·*na*
ya aina gani?   ya a·*ee·*na *ga·*nee

What's in the collection?
Kuna sanaa gani hapa?   koo·na sa·*na ga·*nee *ha·*pa

What do you think of ...?
Unafikiriaje   oo·na·fee·kee·ree·*a·*jay
kuhusu ...?   koo·*hoo·*soo ...

It's an exhibition of ...
Ni onyesho la ...   nee oh·*nyay·*shoh la ...

I'm interested in ...
Napenda ...   na·*payn·*da ...

I like the works of ...
Napenda kazi ya ...   na·*payn·*da *ka·*zee ya ...

It reminds me of ...
Inanikumbusha   ee·na·nee·koom·*boo·*sha
kuhusu ...   koo·*hoo·*soo ...

... art	*sanaa ya ...*	sa·*na* ya ...
African	*kiafrika*	kee·a·*free·*ka
contemporary	*kisasa*	kee·*sa·*sa
figurative	*tamathali*	ta·ma·*tha·*lee
graphic	*grafu*	*gra·*foo
performance	*uigizaju*	oo·ee·gee·*za·*jee

architecture	*ujenzi*	oo-*jayn*-zee
artwork	*usanii*	oo-sa-*nee*
curator	*afisa mkuu*	a-*fee*-sa m-*koo*
	wa sanaa	wa sa-*na*
design	*usanifu*	oo-sa-*nee*-foo
drawing	*mchoro*	m-*choh*-roh
etching	*uchoraji picha*	oo-choh-*ra*-jee *pee*-cha
	kwa asidi	kwa a-*see*-dee
exhibit	*onyesho*	oh-*nyay*-shoh
exhibition hall	*chumba cha*	*choom*-ba cha
	maonyesho	ma-oh-*nyay*-shoh
installation	*ufungaji*	oo-foon-*ga*-jee
Makonde	*uchongaji wa*	oo-chohn-*ga*-jee wa
carvings	*Makonde*	ma-*kohn*-day
opening	*ufunguzi*	oo-foon-*goo*-zee
painter	*msanii wa rangi*	m-sa-*nee* wa *ran*-gee
painting	*picha ya*	*pee*-cha ya
(canvas)	*uchoraji*	oo-choh-*ra*-jee
painting	*uchoraji*	oo-choh-*ra*-jee
(the art)	*kwa rangi*	kwa *ran*-gee
period	*kipindi*	kee-*peen*-dee
permanent	*makusanyo*	ma-koo-*sa*-nyoh
collection	*ya kudumu*	ya koo-*doo*-moo
print	*picha*	*pee*-cha
sculptor	*mchongaji*	m-chohn-*ga*-jee
sculpture	*uchongaji*	oo-chohn-*ga*-jee
statue	*sanamu*	sa-*na*-moo
studio	*chumba cha*	*choom*-ba cha
	msanii	m-sa-*nee*
style	*mtindo*	m-*teen*-doh
technique	*mbinu*	m-*bee*-noo
Tingatinga	*tingatinga*	teen-ga-*teen*-ga
paintings		
wood carving	*uchongaji*	oo-chohn-*ga*-jee
	wa mbao	wa m-*ba*-oh

sporting interests

kupenda michezo

What sport	... mchezo	... m·chay·zoh
do you ...?	gani?	ga·nee
play	Unacheza	oo·na·chay·za
follow	Unafuata	oo·na·foo·a·ta
I play/do ...	Nacheza ...	na·chay·za ...
I follow ...	Nafuata ...	na·foo·a·ta ...
athletics	michezo ya riadha	mee·chay·zo ya ree·a·dha
basketball	mpira wa kikapu	m·pee·ra wa kee·ka·poo
boxing	ndondi	n·dohn·dee
football (soccer)	soka	so·ka
karate	kareti	ka·ray·tee
netball	netibali	nay·tee·ba·lee
running	kukimbia	koo·keem·bee·a
swimming	kuogelea	koo·oh·gay·lay·a
tennis	tenesi	tay·nay·see
volleyball	mpira wa wavu	m·pee·ra wa wa·voo

Do you like (cricket)?
Unapenda (kriketi)?
oo·na·payn·da (kree·kay·tee)

Yes, very much.
Ndiyo, sana.
n·dee·yoh sa·na

Not really.
Siyo sana.
see·yo sa·na

I like watching it.
Napenda kutazama.
na·payn·da koo·ta·za·ma

Who's your favourite ...?	Unapendelea ... gani?	oo·na·payn·day·lay·a ... ga·nee
long-distance runner	mkimbiaji	m·keem·bee·a·jee
sportsperson	mwanamichezo	mwa·na·mee·chay·zoh
team	timu	tee·moo

For more sports, see the **dictionary**.

going to a game

kuangalia mchezo

Would you like to go to a game?
Unataka kwenda
kwenye mchezo?
oo·na·ta·ka kwayn·da
kwa·nyay m·chay·zoh

Who are you supporting?
Unapendelea nani?
oo·na·payn·day·lay·a na·nee

Who's playing/winning?
Nani wanacheza/
wanashinda?
na·nee wa·na·chay·za/
wa·na·sheen·da

That was a bad/great game!
Mchezo ulikuwa
mbaya/safi sana!
m·chay·zoh oo·lee·koo·wa
m·ba·ya/sa·fee sa·na

scoring

What's the score?
Nini matokeo?
nee·nee ma·toh·kay·oh

It's (a) ...	Ni ...	nee ...
draw/even	sare	sa·ray
love (zero)	bila	bee·la
match point	pointi ya mechi	poh·een·tee ya may·chee
nil (zero)	sifuri	see·foo·ree

playing sport

Do you want to play?
Unataka kucheza? — oo·na·*ta*·ka koo·*chay*·za

Can I join in?
Naweza kucheza? — na·*way*·za koo·*chay*·za

That would be great.
Safi. — sa·fee

I can't.
Siwezi. — see·*way*·zee

I have an injury.
Nimejeruhiwa. — nee·may·jay·roo·*hee*·wa

Your/My point.
Pointi yako/yangu. — poh·*een*·tee ya·koh/*yan*·goo

Kick/Pass it to me!
Nitoe pasi! — nee·*toh*·ay pa·see

You're a good player.
Wewe ni mchezaji mzuri. — *way*·way nee m·chay·za·jee m·zoo·ree

Thanks for the game.
Asante kwa mchezo. — a·*san*·tay kwa m·*chay*·zoh

Where's a good place to …?	Wapi ni pazuri …?	wa·pee nee pa·zoo·ree …
fish	kuvua samaki	koo·voo·a sa·ma·kee
go horse riding	kutembea kwa farasi	koo·taym·bay·a kwa fa·ra·see
run	kukimbia	koo·keem·bee·a

Where's a ...?	Kuna ... wapi?	koo·na ... wa·pee
golf course	uwanja wa gofu	oo·wan·ja wa goh·foo
gym	kilabu ya	kee·la·boo ya
	mazoezi	ma·zoh·ay·zee
swimming	bwawa la	bwa·wa la
pool	kuogelea	koo·oh·gay·lay·a
tennis court	kiwanja	kee·wan·ja
	cha tenesi	cha tay·nay·see

What's the	Ni bei gani	nee bay ga·nee
charge per ...?	kwa ...?	kwa ...
day	siku	see·koo
game	mchezo	m·chay·zoh
hour	saa	sa
visit	kutembelea	koo·taym·bay·lay·a

Do I have to be a member to attend?

Ni lazima kuwa	nee la·zee·ma koo·wa
mwanachama	mwa·na·cha·ma
ili kuingia?	ee·lee koo·een·gee·a

Is there a women-only session?

Kuna kipindi kwa	koo·na kee·peen·dee kwa
wanawake tu?	wa·na·wa·kay too

Where are the changing rooms?

Chumba cha kubadilisha	choom·ba cha koo·ba·dee·lee·sha
nguo kiko wapi?	n·goo·oh kee·koh wa·pee

Can I hire a (court)?

Naweza kukodisha	na·way·za koo·koh·dee·sha
(kiwanja)?	kee·wan·ja

---

sports talk

What a ...!	... gani!	... ga·nee
goal	goli	goh·lee
hit	ushindi	oo·sheen·dee
kick	teke	tay·kay
pass	pasi	pa·see
performance	onyesho	oh·nyay·shoh

football/soccer

Who plays for (Yanga)?
Nani ni wachezaji   *na*·nee nee wa·chay·*za*·jee
wa (Yanga)?   wa (*yan*·ga)

He's a great (player).
Yeye ni (mchezaji)   *yay*·yay nee (m·chay·*za*·jee)
mzuri sana.   m·*zoo*·ree *sa*·na

Which team is at the top of the league?
Timu gani ni juu ya ligi?   *tee*·moo *ga*·nee nee joo ya *lee*·gee

What a great/terrible team!
Timu hiyo ni safi/   *tee*·moo *hee*·yoh nee *sa*·fee/
mbaya sana!   m·*ba*·ya sa·na

ball	*mpira*	m·*pee*·ra
fan	*mshabiki*	m·sha·*bee*·kee
goal	*mlango*	m·*lan*·goh
player	*mchezaji wa mpira*	m·chay·*za*·jee wa m·*pee*·ra
red card	*kadi nyekundu*	*ka*·dee nyay·*koon*·doo
referee	*rifa/refa*	*ree*·fa/*ray*·fa

water sports

Where's a good diving site?
Wapi ni pazuri   *wa*·pee nee pa·*zoo*·ree
kuzamia?   koo·za·*mee*·a

Can I book a lesson?
Naweza kupanga   na·*way*·za koo·*pan*·ga
mafunzo?   ma·*foon*·zoh

Is the equipment regularly maintained?
Vifaa huthibitishwa   vee·*fa* hoo·thee·bee·*tee*·shwa
vizuri?   vee·*zoo*·ree

Can I hire	Nataka	na·*ta*·ka
(a) ...?	kukodisha ...	koo·koh·*dee*·sha ...
boat	boti	*boh*·tee
canoe	mtumbwi	m·*toom*·bwee
diving gear	vifaa vya kuzamia	vee·*fa* vya koo·za·*mee*·a
kayak	kayaki	ka·*ya*·kee
life jacket	jaketi la	ja·*kay*·tee la
	kuokolea	ku·oh·koh·*lay*·a
water-skis	skii za maji	skee za *ma*·jee
wetsuit	vazi la kuzamia	va·zee la koo·za·*mee*·a

Are there	Kuna ...?	*koo*·na ...
any ...?		
currents	mikondo	mee·*kohn*·doh
reefs	miamba	mee·*am*·ba
rips	mikondo	mee·*kohn*·doh
sharks	papa	*pa*·pa
water	hatari katika	ha·*ta*·ree ka·*tee*·ka
hazards	maji	*ma*·jee
whales	nyangumi	nyan·*goo*·mee

cave	pango	*pan*·goh
coral	mwamba wa	*mwam*·ba wa
formations	tumbawe	toom·*ba*·way
diving boat	boti ya safari	*boh*·tee ya sa·*fa*·ree
	za kuzamia	za koo·za·*mee*·a
guide	kiongozi	kee·ohn·*goh*·zee
motorboat	motaboti	moh·ta·*boh*·tee
night dive	kuzamia wakati	koo·za·*mee*·a wa·*ka*·tee
	wa usiku	wa oo·*see*·koo
sailing boat	chombo	*chohm*·boh
	chenye tanga	*chay*·nyay *tan*·ga
surfboard	ubao wa	oo·*ba*·oh wa
	kutelezea	koo·tay·lay·*zay*·a
wall dive	kuzamia kwenye	koo·za·*mee*·a *kway*·nyay
	ukuta	oo·*koo*·ta
(wind)surfing	kuteleza	koo·tay·*lay*·za
	(na tanga)	(na *tan*·ga)
wreck	msambaratiko	m·sam·ba·ra·*tee*·koh

hiking

kutembea porini

Where can I ...?	*Naweza ... wapi?*	na·*way*·za ... *wa*·pee
buy supplies	*kununua*	koo·noo·*noo*·a
	mahitaji	ma·hee·*ta*·jee
find someone	*kumkuta mtu*	koom·*koo*·ta m·too
who knows	*anayejua*	a·na·yay·*joo*·a
this area	*eneo hili*	ay·*nay*·oh *hee*·lee
get a map	*kununua*	koo·noo·*noo*·a
	ramani	ra·*ma*·nee
hire hiking	*kukodisha*	koo·koh·*dee*·sha
gear	*vifaa vya*	vee·*fa*·vya
	kutembea	koo·taym·*bay*·a
	porini	poh·*ree*·nee
Do we need	*Inabidi*	ee·na·*bee*·dee
to take ...?	*tuchukue ...?*	too·choo·*koo*·ay ...
food	*chakula*	cha·*koo*·la
a sheet	*shuka na*	*shoo*·ka na
and cover	*tandiko*	tan·*dee*·koh
water	*maji*	*ma*·jee

We'd like to go wildlife spotting.
Tunataka kwenda — too·na·*ta*·ka *kwayn*·da
kutafuta wanyama pori. — koo·ta·*foo*·ta wa·*nya*·ma *poh*·ree

Can you recommend a trekking company?
Unaweza kupendekeza — oo·na·*way*·za koo·payn·day·*kay*·za
kampuni ya safari — kam·*poo*·nee ya sa·*fa*·ree
kwa miguu? — kwa mee·*goo*

Do we need a guide?
Inabidi tuwe na — ee·na·*bee*·dee *too*·way na
kiongozi? — kee·ohn·*goh*·zee

Are there guided treks?
*Kuna safari kwa miguu
kwenye viongozi?*
koo·na sa·*fa*·ree kwa mee·*goo*
kway·nyay vee·ohn·*goh*·zee

Are park fees included?
*Ada za hifadhi
zinazingatiwa?*
a·da za hee·*fa*·dhee
zee·na·zeen·ga·*tee*·wa

Will we be staying in huts?
Tutakaa kibandani?
too·ta·*ka* kee·ban·*dan*·ee

Will we be camping?
Tutapiga hema?
too·ta·*pee*·ga *hay*·ma

I'd like to hire a porter.
*Nataka kuajiri
mchukuzi.*
na·*ta*·ka koo·a·*jee*·ree
m·choo·*koo*·zee

Can I see your permit?
*Naomba kuona
kibali chako.*
na·*ohm*·ba koo·*ohn*·a
kee·*ba*·lee *cha*·koh

Which route would you recommend?
*Unapendekeza
njia gani?*
oo·na·payn·day·*kay*·za
n·*jee*·a *ga*·nee

How high is the climb?
Ni mita ngapi juu?
nee *mee*·ta n·*ga*·pee joo

How long is the trail?
Njia ni urefu gani?
n·*jee*·a nee oo·*ray*·foo *ga*·nee

Is it safe?
Ni salama?
nee sa·*la*·ma

Which is the	*Njia gani*	n·*jee*·a *ga*·nee
… route?	*… zaidi?*	… za·*ee*·dee
easiest	*ni rahisi*	nee ra·*hee*·see
shortest	*ni fupi*	nee *foo*·pee

Is the track …?	*Njia …?*	n·*jee*·a …
icy	*yenye barafu*	*yay*·nyay ba·*ra*·foo
(well-)marked	*iliotiwa*	ee·lee·oh·*tee*·wa
	alama (nzuri)	a·*la*·ma (n·*zoo*·ree)
very steep	*huongezeka*	hoo·ohn·gay·*zay*·ka
	ghafla	*ga*·fla

Does this path go to …?
Njia hii inaenda …?   n·*jee*·a hee ee·na·*ayn*·da …

Is the water OK to drink?
Maji yananywika?   ma·jee ya·nany·*wee*·ka

I think I'm suffering from altitude sickness.
Nadhani nimeugua   na·*dha*·nee nee·may·oo·*goo*·a
kwa sababu ya kimo.   kwa sa·*ba*·boo ya *kee*·moh

I need to descend immediately.
Ni lazima   nee *la*·zee·ma
nitelemke sasa hivi.   nee·tay·*laym*·kay *sa*·sa hee·vee

Thanks for running a great trek.
Asante kwa kuongoza   a·*san*·tay kwa koo·ohn·*goh*·za
safari nzuri sana.   sa·*fa*·ree n·*zoo*·ree *sa*·na

Thanks for carrying our bags.
Asante kwa kubeba   a·*san*·tay kwa koo·*bay*·ba
mizigo yetu.   mee·*zee*·goh *yay*·too

Where can I find the …?	… iko wapi?	… ee·koh *wa*·pee
camping ground	Uwanja wa kupiga kambi	oo·*wan*·ja wa koo·*pee*·ga *kam*·bee
nearest village	Kijiji jirani	kee·*jee*·jee jee·*ra*·nee
showers	Bafuni	ba·*foo*·nee
toilet	Choo	cho

active volcano	volkeno hai	vol·*kay*·noh *ha*·ee
forest	msitu	m·*see*·too
glacier	uwanja wa barafu	oo·*wan*·ja wa ba·*ra*·foo
grassland	ukanda wa mbuga	oo·*kan*·da wa m·*boo*·ga
mountain peak	kilele cha mlima	kee·*lay*·lay cha m·*lee*·ma
national park	hifadhi ya taifa	hee·*fa*·dhee ya ta·*ee*·fa
summit	kilele	kee·*lay*·lay
wildlife reserve	hifadhi ya wanyama	hee·*fa*·dhee ya wa·*nya*·ma

beach

Where's the ...	*Ufukwe ...*	oo-*fook*-way ...
beach?	*uko wapi?*	oo-koh wa-pee
nearest	*karibu zaidi*	ka-*ree*-boo za-*ee*-dee
nudist	*kwa watu uchi*	kwa *wa*-too oo-chee
public	*kwa hadhara*	kwa *ha*-dha-ra
How much	*Ni bei gani*	nee bay *ga*-nee
for a/an ...?	*kwa ...?*	kwa ...
chair	*kiti*	*kee*-tee
hut	*kibanda*	kee-*ban*-da
umbrella	*mwamvuli*	mwam-*voo*-lee
Where can	*... iko wapi?*	... ee-koh *wa*-pee
I find the ...?		
showers	*Bafuni*	ba-*foo*-nee
toilets	*Choo*	cho

Do we have to pay?
Ni lazima kulipa?　　　nee *la*-zee-ma koo-*lee*-pa

Is it safe to dive/swim here?
Ni salama kuzamia/　　nee sa-*la*-ma koo-za-*mee*-a/
kuogelea hapa?　　　　koo-oh-gay-*lay*-a ha-pa

What time is high/low tide?
Maji kujaa/kupwa　　　*ma*-jee koo-*ja*/*koop*-wa
ni saa ngapi?　　　　　nee sa n-*ga*-pee

signs		
Usipige	oo-see-*pee*-gay	**No Diving**
Mbizi	m-*bee*-zee	
Usiogelee	oo-see-oh-gay-*lay*	**No Swimming**

weather

What's the weather like?
Hali ya hewa ikoje?   ha·lee ya hay·wa ee·koh·jay

It's ...

cold	*Ni baridi.*	nee ba·*ree*·dee
hot	*Ni joto.*	nee *joh*·toh
raining	*Inanyesha mvua.*	ee·na·*nyay*·sha m·*voo*·a
snowing	*Theluji*	thay·*loo*·jee
	inaanguka.	ee·na·an·*goo*·ka
sunny	*Kuna jua.*	koo·na *joo*·a
windy	*Kuna upepo.*	koo·na oo·*pay*·poh

... season	*kipindi cha ...*	kee·*peen*·dee cha ...
cold	*baridi*	ba·*ree*·dee
dry	*kiangazi*	kee·an·*ga*·zee
harvest	*kuvuna*	koo·*voo*·na
hot	*joto*	*joh*·toh
rainy	*rnvua*	m·*voo*·a

Where can	*Ninunue*	nee·noo·*noo*·ay
I buy ...?	*... wapi?*	... *wa*·pee
a rain jacket	*koti la mvua*	*koh*·tee la m·*voo*·a
an umbrella	*mwamvuli*	mwam·*voo*·lee

flora & fauna

What ... is that?	*Ni ... gani?*	nee ... *ga*·nee
animal	*mnyama*	m·*nya*·ma
plant	*mmea*	m·*may*·a

Is it ...?	*Ni ...?*	nee ...
dangerous	*yenye hatari*	*yay*·nyay ha·*ta*·ree
endangered	*spishi zilizo*	*spee*·shee zee·*lee*·zoh
	hatarini	ha·ta·*ree*·nee
poisonous	*yenye sumu*	*yay*·nyay *soo*·moo
protected	*hifadhiwa*	hee·fa·*dhee*·wa

What's it used for?
Ina matumizi gani?   ee·na ma·too·*mee*·zee *ga*·nee

Can you eat the fruit?
Tunda linalika?   toon·da lee·na·*lee*·ka

We're very keen to see (elephants).
Tunataka sana   too·na·*ta*·ka *sa*·na
kuona (tembo).   koo·*oh*·na (*taym*·boh)

Yesterday we saw (impala).
Jana tuliona (swala).   *ja*·na too·lee·*oh*·na (*swa*·la)

local plants & animals

baobab	*mbuyu*	m·*boo*·yoo
coconut palm	*mnazi*	m·*na*·zee
mangrove	*mkoko*	m·*koh*·koh
miombo woodland	*msitu wa*	m·*see*·too wa
	miombo	mee·*ohm*·boh
rainforest	*msitu wa*	m·*see*·too wa
	mvua	m·*voo*·a
savanna	*mbuga*	m·*boo*·ga
camel	*ngamia*	nga·*mee*·a
crocodile	*mamba*	*mam*·ba
gazelle	*swala/swara*	*swa*·la/*swa*·ra
giraffe	*twiga*	*twee*·ga
hippopotamus	*kiboko*	kee·*boh*·koh
monkey	*tumbili*	toom·*bee*·lee
python	*chatu*	*cha*·too
sable antelope	*pala hala*	*pa*·la *ha*·la
spitting cobra	*swila*	*swee*·la
zebra	*punda*	*poon*·da
	milia	mee·*lee*·a

For the Big Five animals, see the box on page 197.

basics

misingi

breakfast	*chai ya asubuhi*	cha·ee ya a·soo·*boo*·hee
lunch	*chakula cha mchana*	cha·*koo*·la cha m·*cha*·na
dinner	*chakula cha jioni*	cha·*koo*·la cha jee·*oh*·nee
snack	*kumbwe*	*koom*·bway
eat v	*kula*	*koo*·la
drink v	*kunywa*	*koony*·wa

Is there food?
Kuna chakula?   *koo*·na cha·*koo*·la

Can you cook for us?
Unaweza kutupikia   oo·na·*way*·za koo·too·pee·*kee*·a
chakula?   cha·*koo*·la

I'd like ...
Nataka ...   na·*ta*·ka ...

I'm starving!
Nina njaa kali!   *nee*·na n·*ja ka*·lee

finding a place to eat

kutafuta mahali kula

Can you recommend a ...?	*Unaweza kupendekeza ...?*	oo·na·*way*·za koo·payn·day·*kay*·za ...
bar	*baa*	ba
café/coffee house	*mgahawa*	m·ga·*ha*·wa
restaurant	*hoteli kula*	hoh·*tay*·lee *koo*·la

Where would you go for …?	*Unapenda kwenda wapi kwa …?*	oo·na·*payn*·da *kwayn*·da wa·pee kwa …
a celebration	*sherehe*	shay·*ray*·hay
a cheap meal	*chakula rahisi*	cha·*koo*·la ra·*hee*·see
Chinese food	*chakula cha kichina*	cha·*koo*·la cha kee·*chee*·na
European food	*chakula cha kiulaya*	cha·*koo*·la cha kee·oo·*la*·ya
Indian food	*chakula cha kihindi*	cha·*koo*·la cha kee·*heen*·dee
local specialities	*chakula cha kienyeji*	cha·*koo*·la cha kee·ay·*nyay*·jee

I'd like to reserve a table for …	*Nataka kuhifadhi meza kwa …*	na·*ta*·ka koo·hee·*fa*·dhee *may*·za kwa …
(two) people	*watu (wawili)*	*wa*·too (wa·*wee*·lee)
(eight) o'clock	*saa (mbili)*	sa (m·*bee*·lee)
I'd like …, please.	*Naomba …*	na·*ohm*·ba …
a children's menu	*menyu kwa watoto*	*may*·nyoo kwa wa·*toh*·toh
the drink list	*orodha ya vinywaji*	oh·*roh*·dha ya veeny·*wa*·jee
a half portion	*nusu*	*noo*·soo
a menu (in English)	*menyu (kwa Kiingereza)*	*may*·nyoo (kwa kee·een·gay·*ray*·za)
a table for (five)	*meza kwa (watano)*	*may*·za kwa (wa·*ta*·noh)
the nonsmoking section	*eneo ambalo hakuna sigara*	ay·*nay*·oh am·*ba*·loh ha·*koo*·na see·*ga*·ra
the smoking section	*eneo kwa kuvuta sigara*	ay·*nay*·oh kwa koo·*voo*·ta see·*ga*·ra

Tumefunga. too·may·*foon*·ga	**We're closed.**
Tumejaa. too·may·*ja*	**We're full.**
Dakika moja. da·*kee*·ka *moh*·ja	**One moment.**
Unataka kukaa wapi? oo·na·*ta*·ka koo·*ka wa*·pee	**Where would you like to sit?**
Nikusaidiaje? nee·koo·sa·ee·dee·*a*·jay	**What can I get for you?**
Karibu. ka·*ree*·boo	**Here you go.**
Karibu chakula. ka·*ree*·boo cha·*koo*·la	**Enjoy your meal.**

Are you still serving food?
Kuna chakula bado?   *koo*·na cha·*koo*·la *ba*·doh

How long is the wait?
Inabidi kusubiri   ee·na·*bee*·dee koo·soo·*bee*·ree
kwa muda gani?   kwa *moo*·da *ga*·nee

restaurant

hoteli

What would you recommend?
Chakula gani ni   cha·*koo*·la *ga*·nee nee
kizuri?   kee·*zoo*·ree

What's in that dish?
Chakula hicho   cha·*koo*·la *hee*·choh
kinapikwaje?   kee·na·peek·*wa*·jay

I'll have that.
Nataka hicho.   na·*ta*·ka *hee*·choh

eating out

155

Does it take long to prepare?

Inachukua muda	ee·na·choo·*koo*·a moo·da
mrefu kuandaa?	m·*ray*·foo koo·an·*da*

Are the meals freshly cooked?

Milo hupikwa sasa	*mee*·loh hoo·*peek*·wa *sa*·sa
hivi au zamani kidogo?	*hee*·vee a·oo za·*ma*·ni kee·*doh*·goh

Is it self-serve?

Ni lazima kujihuduma?	nee *la*·zee·ma koo·jee·hoo·*doo*·ma

Is there a cover charge?

Kuna bei ya kuingia?	*koo*·na bay ya koo·een·*gee*·a

Is service included in the bill?

Bili inazingatia	*bee*·lee ee·na·zeen·*ga*·tee·a
huduma?	hoo·*doo*·ma

Are these complimentary?

Hizi ni bure?	*hee*·zee nee *boo*·ray

look for ...

Kiamsha Hamu	kee·*am*·sha *ha*·moo	Appetisers
Supu	*soo*·poo	Soups
Chakula Kikuu	cha·*koo*·la kee·*koo*	Main Courses
Saladi	sa·*la*·dee	Salads
Vinginevyo	veen·gee·*nay*·vyo	Side Dishes
Kitindamlo	kee·teen·da·*m*·loh	Desserts
Vinywaji	veeny·*wa*·jee	Drinks
Soda	*soh*·da	Soft Drinks
Pombe Kali	*pohm*·bay *ka*·lee	Spirits
Bia	*bee*·a	Beers
Mvinyo	m·*vee*·nyoh	Sparkling Wines
Mwenye Povu	*mway*·nyay poh·voo	
Mvinyo	m·*vee*·nyoh	White Wines
Mweupe	mway·*oo*·pay	
Mvinyo	m·*vee*·nyoh	Red Wines
Mwekundu	mway·*koon*·doo	

For more words you might see on a menu, see the **menu decoder**, page 173.

I'd like ...	Nataka ...	na·ta·ka ...
a local speciality	chakula maalum cha kienyeji	cha·koo·la ma·loom cha kee·ay·nyay·jee
a meal fit for a king	chakula kama kingefaa kwa mfalme	cha·koo·la ka·ma keen·gay·fa kwa m·fal·may
a sandwich	sandwichi	sand·wee·chee
that dish	chakula hicho	cha·koo·la hee·choh
the chicken	kuku	koo·koo

I'd like it with/ without ...	Nataka na/ bila ...	na·ta·ka na/ bee·la ...
cheese	chizi	chee·zee
chilli (sauce)	(mchuzi wa) pilipili hoho	(m·choo·zee wa) pee·lee·pee·lee hoh·hoh
garlic	kitunguu saumu	kee·toon·goo sa·oo·moo
peanuts	karanga	ka·ran·ga
oil	mafuta	ma·foo·ta
pepper	pilipili	pee·lee·pee·lee
salad	saladi	sa·la·dee
salt	chumvi	choom·vee
vinegar	siki	see·kee
tomato sauce/ ketchup	mchuzi wa nyanya	m·choo·zee wa nya·nya

For additional items, see the **menu decoder**. For other specific meal requests, see **vegetarian & special meals**, page 171.

---

listen for ...

Unapenda...? oo·na·payn·da ...	Do you like ...?
Napendekeza ... na·payn·day·kay·za ...	I suggest the ...
Unapenda kipikwaje? oo·na·payn·da kee·peek·wa·jay	How would you like that cooked?

at the table

Please bring …	Lete …	lay·tay …
a cloth	kitambaa	kee·tam·ba
	kufunika meza	koo·foo·nee·ka may·za
a (wine-)	glasi	gla·see
glass	(ya mvinyo)	(ya m·vee·nyoh)
a serviette	kitambaa cha	kee·tam·ba cha
	mikono	mee·koh·noh
the bill	bili	bee·lee

I didn't order that.
Sikuagiza hicho.   see·koo·a·gee·za hee·choh

There's a mistake in the bill.
Kuna kosa kwenye bili.   koo·na koh·sa kwayn·yay bee·lee

I'll pay!
Nitalipa!   nee·ta·lee·pa

I invited you, you're my guest.
Nilikukaribisha,   nee·lee·koo·ka·ree·bee·sha
wewe ni mgeni wangu.   way·way nee m·gay·nee wan·goo

ashtray
chombo cha majivu
chohm·boh cha ma·jee·voo

spoon
kijiko
kee·jee·koh

fork
uma
oo·ma

plate
sahani
sa·ha·nee

knife
kisu
kee·soo

wineglass
glasi ya mvinyo
gla·see ya m·vee·nyoh

glass
glasi
gla·see

table
meza
may·za

FOOD

158

talking food

I love this dish.
Napenda sana
chakula hiki.
na·*payn*·da sa·na
cha·*koo*·la *hee*·kee

I love the local cuisine.
Napenda sana
chakula cha kienyeji.
na·*payn*·da sa·na
cha·*koo*·la cha kee·ay·*nyay*·jee

That was delicious!
Chakula kitamu sana!
cha·*koo*·la kee·*ta*·moo sa·na

street food

chapati	cha·*pa*·tee	a round bread cooked like a pancake
chipsi	chee·psee	deep-fried potatoes
chipsi mayai	chee·psee ma·*ya*·ee	omelette made with chips
chungwa	choon·gwa	orange (usually eaten by squeezing the juice into your mouth)
kande	kan·day	a stew with beans & whole kernels of maize
mahindi	ma·heen·dee	grilled corn on the cob
mkate wa mayai	m·*ka*·tay wa ma·*ya*·ee	a mixture of eggs, ground meat, onion & spices, fried until brown
mishkaki	meesh·*ka*·kee	meat on a skewer, grilled until crisp
samosa/ sambusa	sa·*moh*·sa/ sam·*boo*·sa	a mixture of meat, onions, vegetables & spices fried in a triangular pastry
supu	soo·poo	soup with a piece of meat
wali maharagwe	wa·lee ma·ha·*ra*·gway	cooked rice & beans

My compliments to the chef.
   Mwambie mpishi   mwam·*bee*·ay m·*pee*·shee
   chakula ni kizuri.   cha·*koo*·la nee kee·*zoo*·ree

I'm full.
   Nimeshiba.   nee·may·*shee*·ba

This isn't very good.
   Chakula hiki si   cha·*koo*·la *hee*·kee see
   kizuri sana.   kee·*zoo*·ree *sa*·na

This is too spicy.
   Chakula hiki ni   cha·*koo*·la *hee*·kee nee
   mno chenye viungo.   *m*·noh *chay*·nyay vee·*oon*·goh

methods of preparation

mibinu ya kuandaa

I'd like it ...	*Nataka* ...	na·*ta*·ka ...
I don't want it ...	*Sitaki* ...	si·*ta*·kee ...
boiled	*ya kuchemshwa*	ya koo·*chaym*·shwa
broiled	*ya kuchomwa*	ya koo·*chohm*·wa
fried	*ya kukaangwa*	ya koo·*kan*·gwa
grilled	*ya kuchomwa*	ya koo·*chohm*·wa
mashed	*ya kuponda*	ya koo·*pohn*·da
medium	*ya kuiva*	ya koo·*ee*·va
	wastani	*wa*·sta·nee
rare	*ya kuiva*	ya koo·*ee*·va
	kidogo	kee·*doh*·goh
reheated	*kiwekwe*	kee·*wayk*·way
	moto tena	*moh*·toh *tay*·na
steamed	*ya kupikwa*	ya koo·*pee*·kwa
	kwa mvuke	kwa m·*voo*·kay
well-done	*ya kuiva sana*	ya koo·*ee*·va *sa*·na
with the	*kwenye*	*kway*·nyay
dressing/sauce	*mchuzi*	m·*choo*·zee
on the side	*pembeni*	paym·*bay*·nee
without ...	*bila* ...	*bee*·la ...

in the bar

Excuse me!
Samahani!
sa·ma·*ha*·nee

I'm next.
Zamu yangu ijayo.
za·moo *yan*·goo ee·*ja*·yoh

I'll have …
Nipe …
nee·pay …

Same again, please.
Hiki tena.
hee·kee *tay*·na

No ice, thanks.
Bila barafu, asante.
bee·la ba·*ra*·foo a·*san*·tay

I'll buy you a drink.
*Nitakununulia
kinywaji.*
nee·ta·koo·noo·noo·*lee*·a
keeny·*wa*·jee

What would you like?
Unataka nini?
oo·na·*ta*·ka *nee*·nee

I don't drink alcohol.
Sinywi pombe.
seeny·wee *pohm*·bay

It's my round.
Mzunguko wangu.
m·zoon·*goo*·koh *wan*·goo

How much is that?
Ni bei gani?
nee bay *ga*·nee

Do you serve meals here?
Kuna chakula hapa?
koo·na cha·*koo*·la *ha*·pa

listen for …

Unakunywa nini?
oo·na·*koony*·wa *nee*·nee
What are you having?

Nafikiri umekunywa ya kutosha.
na·fee·*kee*·ree oo·may·*koony*·wa
ya koo·*toh*·sha
I think you've had enough.

Maagizo ya mwisho.
ma·a·*gee*·zoh ya *mwee*·shoh
Last orders.

nonalcoholic drinks

All water sold in sealed bottles in East Africa is clean, but usually flat – the only water you'll find with bubbles is soda water.
If you can't find water in a bottle, make sure any water you
drink has been boiled.

Has this water been boiled?

Maji haya	*ma·jee ha·ya*	
yalichemshwa?	*ya·lee·chaym·shwa*	

... water	*maji ...*	*ma·jee ...*
boiled	*yaliyochemshwa*	*ya·lee·yoh·chaym·shwa*
bottled	*kwenye chupa*	*kway·nyay choo·pa*
cold	*ya baridi*	*ya ba·ree·dee*
hot	*ya moto*	*ya moh·toh*
mineral	*ya madini*	*ya ma·dee·nee*

orange juice	*maji ya*	*ma·jee ya*
	machungwa	*ma·choon·gwa*
soda water	*klub soda*	*kloob soh·da*
(cold) soft drink	*soda (ya baridi)*	*soh·da (ya ba·ree·dee)*

(cup of) ...	*(kikombe cha) ...*	*(kee·kohm·bay cha) ...*
ginger tea	*chai ya*	*cha·ee ya*
	tangawizi	*tan·ga·wee·zee*
spiced tea	*chai masala*	*cha·ee ma·sa·la*
tea	*chai*	*cha·ee*

(cup of)	*(kikombe cha)*	*(kee·kohm·bay cha)*
coffee ...	*kahawa ...*	*ka·ha·wa ...*
with milk	*na maziwa*	*na ma·zee·wa*
with lemon	*na limau*	*na lee·ma·oo*
with spices	*na viungo*	*na vee·oon·goh*
without (sugar)	*bila (sukari)*	*bee·la (soo·ka·ree)*

East Africans drink tea and coffee at all hours, even on a hot afternoon. It's different in Central Africa, where cool drinks are the go on hot days. You might be offered a soda or a beer instead of a hot drink – but it's quite common that soft drinks or beer will be served at room temperature.

... coffee	kahawa ...	ka·ha·wa ...
black	ya rangi	ya ran·gee
decaffeinated	bila kafini	bee·la ka·fee·nee
iced	baridi yenye	ba·ree·dee yay·nyay
	barafu	ba·ra·foo
strong	yenye	yay·nyay
	nguvu	n·goo·voo
weak	isiye na	ee·see·yay na
	nguvu	n·goo·voo
white	ya maziwa	ya ma·zee·wa

alcoholic drinks

pombe

Most East Africans drink their beer warm. When you order, you should specify whether you want your beer *baridi* ba·ree·dee (cold) or *ya moto* ya moh·toh (warm).

a ... of beer	... ya bia	... ya bee·a
glass	glasi	gla·see
half liter	nusu lita	noo·soo lee·ta
jug	lita	lee·ta
large bottle	chupa kubwa	choo·pa koob·wa
pint	painti	pa·een·tee
small bottle	chupa ndogo	choo·pa n·doh·goh

163

There are different types of home-made brews in East Africa, depending on the region, but the most common ones are made of maize, millet or banana. Local brews are usually drunk from a shared plastic pot called *lita* lee·ta, though you can agree to pour from the pot into glasses. When joining a group of people drinking *pombe* pohm·bay (alcoholic drink) the accepted practice is to promptly order another litre which then gets added to the pot. If you're tempted to partake in drinking local brews, be aware of the health risks that are often associated with the consumption of some of them.

Can I have a glass, please?
Naomba bilauri. na·ohm·ba bee·la·oo·ree

mbege	m·*bay*·gay	banana beer
pombe	pohm·bay	alcoholic beverage
pombe	pohm·bay	home-made brew
ya kienyeji	ya kee·ay·*nyay*·jee	
konyagi	koh·*nya*·gee	local distilled spirit

a bottle/glass	chupa/glasi	choo·pa/gla·see
of ... wine	ya mvinyo ...	ya m·vee·nyoh ...
dessert	tamu	ta·moo
red	mwekundu	mway·koon·doo
rosé	pinki	peen·kee
sparkling	yenye	yay·nyay
	mapovu	ma·poh·voo
white	mweupe	mway·oo·pay
a shot of ...	toti ya ...	toh·tee ya ...
gin	gini	gee·nee
rum	rumi	roo·mee
tequila	tekila	tay·kee·la
vodka	vodka	vohd·ka
whisky	wiski	wee·skee

drinking up

Cheers!
Heri!   hay·ree

This is hitting the spot.
Inatosheka.   ee·na·toh·*shay*·ka

I feel fantastic!
Nasikia nzuri sana!   na·see·*kee*·a n·*zoo*·ree *sa*·na

I think I've had one too many.
Nafikiri   na·fee·*kee*·ree
nimekunywa   nee·may·*koony*·wa
moja mno.   *moh*·ja m·noh

I'm feeling drunk.
Nimelewa.   nee·may·*lay*·wa

I feel ill.
    Nasikia mgonjwa.   na·see·*kee*·a m·*gohn*·jwa

Where's the toilet?
    Choo kiko wapi?   choh *kee*·koh *wa*·pee

I'm tired, I'd better go home.
    Nimechoka, nirudi   nee·may·*choh*·ka nee·*roo*·dee
    nyumbani.   nyoom·*ba*·nee

Can you call a taxi for me?
    Niitie teksi.   nee·ee·*tee*·ay tayk·see

I don't think you should drive.
    Sidhani ni salama kwa   see·*dha*·nee nee sa·*la*·ma kwa
    wewe kuendesha.   *way*·way koo·ayn·*day*·sha

dining East African style

Being invited to share a meal with East Africans at home is a treat not to be turned down, but be prepared for some customs that are different from what you might be used to.

Before eating, a bowl and a pitcher of water are often passed around for washing hands. The usual procedure is to hold your hands over the bowl while your host pours water over them. Sometimes soap is provided, as is a towel for drying off.

The centre of the meal itself is usually *ugali* oo·*ga*·lee (a staple made from maize or cassava flour) which is normally taken with the right hand from a communal pot, rolled into a small ball with the fingers, dipped into some sort of sauce and eaten. Food is never handled or eaten with the left hand.

At the end of the meal, try to avoid being the one who takes the last handful from the communal bowl, as this may leave your hosts worrying they haven't provided enough. After the meal, the water and wash basin are brought around again so that everyone can wash their hands.

Sharing a meal with others forms the basis for social life in East Africa, but don't be surprised if conversation stops while the food is being eaten.

buying food

kununua chakula

What's the local speciality?
Chakula cha kienyeji
gani ni maalum sana?
cha·*koo*·la cha kee·ay·*nyay*·jee
ga·nee nee *ma*·loom *sa*·na

What's that?
Hicho ni nini?
hee·choh nee *nee*·nee

Can I taste it?
Naomba nionje.
na·*ohm*·ba nee·*ohn*·jay

How much is a kilo of (mangoes)?
Kilo ya (maembe)
ni bei gani?
kee·loh ya (ma·*aym*·bay)
nee bay *ga*·nee

Can I have a bag, please?
Nipe mfuko.
nee·pay m·*foo*·koh

food stuff

cooked	*kupikwa*	koo·*pee*·kwa
cured	*kutiwa na chumvi*	koo·*tee*·wa na *choom*·vee
	na kukaushwa	na koo·ka·*oo*·shwa
dried	*kukaushwa*	koo·ka·*oo*·shwa
fresh	*mbichi*	m·*bee*·chee
frozen	*kugandishwa*	koo·gan·*dee*·shwa
	katika barafu	ka·*tee*·ka ba·*ra*·foo
smoked	*kukaushwa*	koo·ka·*oo*·shwa
	na moshi	na *moh*·shee
raw	*mbichi*	m·*bee*·chee

167

I'd like ...	Nataka ...	na·ta·ka ...
(200) grams	gramu	gra·moo
	(mia mbili)	(mee·a m·bee·lee)
a dozen	kumi na mbili	koo·mee na m·bee·lee
half a kilo	nusu kilo	noo·soo kee·loh
a kilo	kilo moja	kee·loh moh·ja
(two) kilos	kilo (mbili)	kee·loh (m·bee·lee)
a bottle	chupa	choo·pa
a jar	chupa ndogo	choo·pa n·doh·goh
a piece	kipande	kee·pan·day
(three) pieces	vipande	vee·pan·day
	(vitatu)	(vee·ta·too)
(six) slices	slaisi (sita)	sla·ee·see (see·ta)
(just) a little	kidogo (tu)	kee·doh·goh (too)
more	zaidi	za·ee·dee
some ...	kiasi ...	kee·a·see ...
this/that one	hiki/hicho	hee·kee/hee·choh

Less.	Punguza.	poon·*goo*·za
A bit more.	Ongeza kidogo.	ohn·*gay*·za kee·*doh*·goh
Enough.	Bas.	bas

Do you have ...?	Kuna ...?	*koo*·na...
anything	rahisi	ra·*hee*·see
cheaper	zaidi	za·*ee*·dee
other kinds	aina	a·*ee*·na
	nyingine	nyeen·*gee*·nay

Where's the ... section?	... iko wapi?	... *ee*·koh wa·pee
dairy	Ma ziwa	ma·*zee*·wa
fish	Samaki	sa·*ma*·kee
frozen goods	Vyakula	vya·*koo*·la
	vilivyo-	vee·lee·vyo·
	gandishwa	gan·*dee*·shwa
	katika barafu	ka·*tee*·ka ba·*ra*·foo
fruit and vegetables	Matunda	ma·*toon*·da
	na mboga	na m·*boh*·ga
meat	Nyama	*nya*·ma
poultry	Kuku	*koo*·koo

listen for ...

Nikusaidie?	
nee·koo·sa·ee·*de*·ay	**Can I help you?**
Unataka nini?	
oo·na·*ta*·ka nee·nee	**What would you like?**
Kiasi gani?	
kee·*a*·see *ga*·nee	**How much? (quantity)**
Kitu kingine?	
kee·too keen·*gee*·nay	**Anything else?**
Hamna/Hakuna.	
ham·na/ha·*koo*·na	**There isn't any.**

self-catering

cooking utensils

Could I please	*Naomba*	na·*ohm*·ba
borrow a ...?	*kuazima ...*	koo·a·*zee*·ma ...
I need a ...	*Nahitaji ...*	na·hee·*ta*·jee ...
chopping board	*bao la kukatia*	*ba*·oh la koo·ka·*tee*·a
frying pan	*kikaango*	kee·ka·*an*·goh
knife	*kisu*	*kee*·soo
meat cleaver	*kisu kikubwa*	*kee*·soo kee·*koob*·wa
	cha nyama	cha *nya*·ma
saucepan	*sufuria*	soo·foo·*ree*·a

For more cooking implements, see the **dictionary**.

vegetarian & special meals
kutokula nyama na milo maalum

ordering food

kuagiza chakula

Is there a ...	*Kuna hoteli*	koo·na hoh·*tay*·lee
restaurant	*ya chakula ...*	ya cha·*koo*·la ...
near here?	*hapa karibuni?*	*ha*·pa ka·ree·*boo*·nee
Do you have	*Mna chakula ...?*	*m*·na cha·*koo*·la ...
... food?		
halal	*halali*	ha·*la*·lee
vegetarian	*bila nyama*	*bee*·la *nya*·ma
I don't eat ...	*Sili ...*	*see*·lee ...
butter	*siagi*	see·*a*·gee
eggs	*mayai*	ma·*ya*·ee
fish	*samaki*	sa·*ma*·kee
fish stock	*supu ya*	*soo*·poo ya
	samaki	sa·*ma*·kee
meat stock	*supu ya nyama*	*soo*·poo ya *nya*·ma
oil	*mafuta*	ma·*foo*·ta
pork	*nyama*	*nya*·ma
	nguruwe	n·goo·*roo*·way
poultry	*kuku*	*koo*·koo
red meat	*nyama*	*nya*·ma
Is this ...?	*Hiki ...?*	*hee*·kee ...
decaffeinated	*ni bila kafini*	nee *bee*·la ka·*fee*·nee
low-fat	*ni chenye*	nee *chay*·nyay
	mafuta	ma·*foo*·ta
	machache	ma·*cha*·chay
low in	*ni chenye*	nee *chay*·nyay
sugar	*sukari*	soo·*ka*·ree
	kidogo tu	kee·*doh*·goh too
salt-free	*bila chumvi*	*bee*·la *choom*·vee

vegetarian & special meals

Is it cooked in/with ...?
  Kinapikwa na ...? kee·na·*pee*·kwa na ...

Could you prepare a meal without ...?
  Unaweza kuandaa oo·na·*way*·za koo·an·*da*
  mlo bila ...? m·loh *bee*·la ...

special diets & allergies

vyakula maalum na mzio

I'm on a special diet.
  Nakula vyakula na·*koo*·la vya·*koo*·la
  maalum tu. *ma*·loom too

I'm vegetarian.
  Mimi ni mlaji wa *mee*·mee nee m·*la*·jee wa
  mboga za majani tu. m·*boh*·ga za ma·*ja*·nee too

I'm vegan.
  Mimi ni mtu asiyetumia *mee*·mee nee a·see·yay·too·*mee*·a
  aina yoyote ya a·*ee*·na yoh·*yoh*·tay
  mazao ya mnyama. ma·*za*·oh ya m·*nya*·ma

I'm (a) ...	*Mimi ni ...*	*mee*·mee nee ...
Buddhist	*Mbudisti*	m·boo·*dee*·stee
Hindu	*Mhindu*	m·*heen*·doo
Jewish	*Myahudi*	m·ya·*hoo*·dee
Muslim	*Mwislamu*	mwee·*sla*·moo

I'm allergic to ...	*Nina mzio wa ...*	*nee*·na m·*zee*·oh wa ...
dairy	*mazao ya*	ma·*za*·oh ya
produce	*maziwa*	ma·*zee*·wa
eggs	*mayai*	ma·*ya*·ee
gelatine	*jelatini*	jay·la·*tee*·nee
honey	*asali*	a·*sa*·lee
MSG	*msg*	aym·*ays*·gee
nuts	*kokwa*	*koh*·kwa
peanuts	*karanga*	ka·*ran*·ga
seafood	*vyakula kutoka*	vya·*koo*·la koo·*toh*·ka
	baharini	ba·ha·*ree*·nee
shellfish	*kombe*	*kohm*·bay

This miniguide to Swahili cuisine lists dishes and ingredients in Swahili alphabetical order. It's designed to help you get the most out of your gastronomic experience by providing you with food terms that you may see on the menu. For certain dishes we've marked the region or city where they're most popular.

A

achari a·cha·ree
  pickles · chutney · relish
aiskrimu a·ee·skree·moo ice cream
alizeti a·lee·zay·tee sunflower seeds
asali a·sa·lee honey

B

balungi ba·loon·gee grapefruit
bamia ba·mee·a okra
barafu ba·ra·foo ice
baridi ba·ree·dee cold ⓐ
bata ba·ta duck
  — **mdogo** m·doh·goh duckling
bekoni bay·koh·nee bacon
bia bee·a beer
  — **baridi** ba·ree·dee cold
  — **ya moto** ya moh·toh warm
biriani bee·ree·a·nee Indian & Pakistani-
  inspired dish – a mixture of rice & spices,
  usually with meat or beans
biringani bee·reen·ga·nee
  eggplant · aubergine
biskuti bees·koo·tee biscuit · cookie
blue bandi bloo ban·dee margarine
boha boh·ha sugar cane **pombe**
bokuboku boh·koo·boh·koo festive dish
  with a pasty texture made from cooked
  ground wheat & meat cooked in spices,
  served over fried onion (Zanzibar)
brokoli broh·koh·lee broccoli
buni boo·nee coffee beans
busi boo·see barley **pombe**

C

chai cha·ee tea
  — **masala** ma·sa·la spiced sweet tea
  (often with cardamom)
  — **tangawizi** tan·ga·wee·zee
  tea flavoured with ginger
  — **ya asubuhi** ya a·soo·boo·hee
  breakfast
chakula cha·koo·la food
  — **cha jioni** cha jee·oh·nee dinner
  — **cha kichina** cha kee·chee·na
  Chinese food
  — **cha kihindi** cha kee·heen·dee
  Indian food
  — **kikuu** kee·koo main courses
  — **cha mchana** cha m·cha·na lunch
  — **kutoka bahari** koo·toh·ka ba·ha·ree
  seafood
chang'aa chang·a home-brewed
  firewater – not recommended for health
  reasons
chapati cha·pa·tee round bread cooked
  like a pancake – you tear off pieces to
  pick up other food
chaza cha·za oyster
chenja chayn·ja drink made by soaking
  uncooked rice in water with sugar
chenye viungo chay·nyay vee·oon·goh
  spicy
chenza chayn·za mandarin
chewa chay·wa rock cod
chipsi chee·psee deep-fried potatoes
  (chips or French fries) – commonly used
  to bulk up a meal
  —**mayai** ma·ya·ee greasy omelette
  made with chips – very popular fast food

chizi *chee-zee (cottage) cheese (also known as* **jibini**)
chumvi *choom-vee salt*
chungwa *choon-gwa orange*

D

dafu *da-foo coconut (green)*
dagaa *da-ga freshwater sardines fried & eaten whole*
dalasini *da-la-see-nee cinnamon*
dengu *dayn-goo lentils*

E

embe *aym-bay mango*
— **mafuta** *ma-foo-ta avocado*

G

gini *gee-nee gin*
giligilani *gee-lee-gee-la-nee coriander seeds*
glukos *gloo-kohs plain sweet biscuits*
gogwe *gohg-way tree tomato*
gongo *gohn-goh illegal distilled cashew nut drink*

H

halua *hal-oo-a Turkish delight*
heringi *hay-reen-gee herring*

I

iliki *ee-lee-ke cardamom*
irio *ee-ree-oh potato, cabbage & beans mashed together (also known as* **kienyeji**)

J

jibini *jee-bee-nee see* **chizi**
jodari *joh-da-ree tuna*
jusi *joo-see juice*
— **ya makwaju** *ya ma-kwa-joo tamarind juice*

— **ya mananasi** *ya ma-na-na-see pineapple juice*
— **ya pasheni** *ya pa-shay-nee passion fruit juice*

K

kaa *ka crab*
kababu *ka-ba-boo small kebabs – a popular snack food*
kabichi *ka-bee-chee cabbage*
kahawa *ka-ha-wa coffee*
— **baridi yenye barafu** *ba-ree-dee yay-nyay ba-ra-foo iced coffee*
— **ya maziwa** *ya ma-zee-wa white coffee*
— **ya rangi** *ya ran-gee black coffee*
kamba *kam-ba crayfish*
kambakoche *kam-ba-koh-chay rock lobster*
kande *kan-day stew made with beans & whole kernels of maize*
kangara *kan-ga-ra maize & honey* **pombe**
kapile *ka-pee-lay cooked food sold in the market*
karafuu *ka-ra-foo clove (the spice)*
karanga *ka-ran-ga peanut*
karoti *ka-roh-tee carrot*
kasezi bong *ka-say-zee bong undistilled Ugandan millet-based alcohol (not recommended for health reasons)*
keki *kay-kee cake*
kiamsha hamu *kee-am-sha ha-moo appetisers*
kiazi (ulaya) *kee-a-zee (oo-la-ya) (European) potato*
— **kikuu** *kee-koo yam potato*
— **kitamu** *kee-ta-moo sweet potato*
kienyeji *kee-ay-nyay-jee see* **irio**
kima *kee-ma mincemeat*
kimbo *keem-boh cooking fat (brand name)*
kisibiti *kee-see-bee-tee cumin*
kisutuo *kee-soo-too-oh food received as a thank you for helping someone*
kitindamlo *kee-teen-da-m-loh dessert*
kitumbuo *kee-toom-boo-oh deep-fried rice bread*

kitunguu kee-toon-*goo* onion
— **saumu** sa-*oo*-moo garlic
klub soda kloob *soh*-da soda water
koko *koh*-koh cocoa
kokteli kohk-*tay*-lee cocktail
kokwa koh-*kwa* nut
komoni *koh*-moh-nee local millet beer
konyagi koh-*nya*-gee general name for
locally produced liquor • local gin-like
spirit
korosho koh-*roh*-shoh cashew nut – often
sold roasted as a street food
kuku *koo*-koo chicken
— **choma** *cho*-ma roast chicken
kunde *koon*-day cowpea (tropical pea)
kupikwa katika majani koo-*peek*-wa
ka-*tee*-ka ma-*ja*-nee baked in leaves
kwaju *kwa*-joo tamarind

L

lager la-*gayr* lager beer
limau lee-*ma*-oo lemon
lozi *loh*-zee almond

M

maandazi man-*da*-zee semisweet
deep-fried doughnut-like pastry, often
containing coconut milk & sometimes
spiced – popular snack food
mabuyu ma-*boo*-yoo
sweet & sour baobab seeds
madafu ma-*da*-foo
fresh juice of a green coconut
mafuta ma-*foo*-ta oil
maharagwe ma-ha-*rag*-way red kidney
beans (often cooked with coconut)
mahindi ma-*heen*-dee
corn • maize • roast corn cobs
maji *ma*-jee water
— **ya dafu** ya *da*-foo coconut milk
— **ya madini** ya ma-*dee*-nee mineral
water
— **ya machungwa** ya ma-*choon*-gwa
orange juice
— **ya ndimu** ya n-*dee*-moo lime juice
makaroni ma-ka-*roh*-nee see **spageti**

manjano man-*ja*-noh turmeric
mastafeli ma-sta-*fay*-lee soursop
matapa ma-*ta*-pa cassava leaves cooked
in peanut sauce often served with
prawns (Mozambique)
matoke ma-*toh*-kay green bananas or
plantains boiled, steamed or mashed &
eaten as a staple
mayai ma-*ya*-ee eggs (also called **yai**)
— **yaliyochemshwa**
ya-lee-yoh-*chem*-shwa hard-boiled eggs
— **yaliyokaangwa**
ya-lee-yo-ka-*ang*-wa fried eggs
— **yaliyovurugwa**
ya-lee-yo-voo-*roog*-wa scrambled eggs
maziwa ma-*zee*-wa milk
— **ganda** *gan*-da yoghurt
— **ya unga** ya *oon*-ga powdered milk
maziwalala ma-zee-wa-*la*-la 'sleeping
milk' – yoghurt-like fermented milk
mbege m-*bay*-gay banana beer
mbichi m-*bee*-chee raw
mbivu m-*bee*-voo ripe
mboga m-*boh*-ga vegetable • vegetables
or relish served as a side dish with **ugali**
mchaichai m-cha-ee-*cha*-ee lemongrass
mchele m-*chay*-lay uncooked white rice
mchicha m-*chee*-cha spinach – sometimes
cooked with onion & tomato
mchuzi m-*choo*-zee sauce (often spicy)
eaten with **ugali**, containing either fish,
meat, beans or spinach • any sauce •
curry
— **wa nyama** wa *nya*-ma beef stew –
in Zanzibar, can be a curry with lemon
juice & spices including turmeric
— **wa nyanya** wa *nya*-nya
tomato sauce
— **wa pilipili hoho**
wa pee-lee-*pee*-lee *hoh*-hoh chilli sauce
mgiligilani m-gee-lee-gee-*la*-nee
fresh coriander leaves
miche ya mianzi *mee*-chay ya mee-*an*-zee
bamboo shoots
mishikaki mee-shee-*ka*-kee meat on
a skewer grilled until crisp – popular
roadside snack served with salt &
possibly chilli

mkate m·ka·tay bread
— **mayai** ma·ya·ee
'egg bread' – dough wrapped around
minced meat & fried egg
— **wa mayai** wa ma·ya·ee mixture of
eggs, ground meat, onion & spices fried
until brown and eaten hot (popular on
the East African Coast)
— **wa ngano asilia** wa n·ga·noh
a·see·lee·a wholemeal bread
mkizi m·kee·zee grey mullet
mlenda m·layn·da green sticky vegetable
similar to okra
mnofu m·noh·foo beefsteak (also known
as **steki**)
mpishi m·pee·shee flavoured cooking fat
(brand name) · cook (chef)
mtama m·ta·ma sorghum · millet (often
cooked into a gruel as a breakfast food)
mtande m·tan·day food hung to dry
mtindi m·teen·dee cultured milk product
similar to yoghurt · cream (usually skim
from boiled milk)
mtori m·toh·ree banana soup
muhogo moo·hoh·goh cassava · grilled
cassava topped with chilli sauce
(a roadside snack)
muwa moo·wa sugar cane
mvinyo m·vee·nyoh wine
— **mwekundu** mway·koon·doo
red wine
— **mwenye povu** mway·nyay poh·voo
sparkling wine
— **mweupe** mway·oo·pay white wine

N

nanasi na·na·see pineapple
nazi na·zee coconut (ripe)
ndimu n·dee·moo lime
ndizi n·dee·zee banana
— **ko kastad** koh ka·stad custard made
from sliced bananas & chopped peanuts,
spiced with cloves, cinnamon & nutmeg
(Zanzibar)
— **ya kupika** ya koo·pee·ka plantain
nduwalo n·doo·wa·loh sailfish
ngisi n·gee·see squid
njegere n·jay·gay·ray pigeon pea

nusu noo·soo half portion
nyama nya·ma meat
— **choma** choh·ma grilled meat – often
goat meat – cooked over a charcoal
pit & sold in bite-sized pieces
— **mamba** mam·ba crocodile meat
— **mbuni** m·boo·nee ostrich meat
— **mbuzi** m·boo·zee
goat meat · mutton
— **ng'ombe** ng·ohm·bay beef
— **nguruwe** n·goo·roo·way
pork – not widely available as many of
the Swahili-speaking areas are Muslim
— **punda milia** poon·da mee·lee·a
zebra meat
— **swala** swa·la impala meat
— **twiga** twee·ga giraffe meat
— **ya mkebe** ya m·kay·bay tinned meat
— **ya kopo** ya koh·poh tinned meat
— **ya wanyama pori** ya wa·nya·ma
poh·ree game meat – may be legally
farmed or illegally poached
nyanya nya·nya tomato
— **ya mkebe** ya m·kay·bay
tomato paste

O

oluwombo o·loo·wohm·boh dish made
from meat or even peanuts mixed with
mushrooms (Uganda)
omlet ohm·layt omelette

P

papa pa·pa shark
papai pa·pa·ee papaya · pawpaw
parachichi pa·ra·chee·chee avocado
pasheni pa·shay·nee passion fruit
pera pay·ra guava
peremende pay·ray·mayn·day sweet ⓝ
pilau pee·la·oo rice, vegetables & meat
cooked in a seasoned broth
pilipili pee·lee·pee·lee pepper
— **hoho** hoh·hoh
hot pepper · chilli · chilli sauce
— **manga** man·ga
black pepper · black peppercorn
— **mbichi** m·bee·chee green pepper

pipi *pee·pee* candy
piripiri *pee·ree·pee·ree* very hot sauce made from chilli pepper & lemon juice, eaten with meat, fish & shellfish
pojo *poh·joh* mung beans
pombe *pohm·bay* popular home-made beer-like brew made from maize, millet, banana, or other local produce
    — **kali** *ka·lee* spirits
popkon *pohp·kohn* popcorn
posho *poh·shoh* see ugali
pweza *pway·za* octopus

R

rasiberi *ra·see·bay·ree* raspberry
rojorojo *roh·joh·roh·joh* viscous food (especially sauce)
rubisi *roo·bee·see* banana wine
rumi *roo·mee* rum

S

saladi *sa·la·dee* lettuce • salad
samaki *sa·ma·kee* fish
    — **ya kupaka** *ya koo·pa·ka* fish cooked in a spicy coconut sauce
    — **ya kuwonga** *ya koo·wohn·ga* fish croquettes (Zanzibar)
    — **ya mkebe/kopo** *ya m·kay·bay/koh·poh* tinned sardines
sambusa *sam·boo·sa* mixture of meat, onion, vegetables & spices fried in a triangular-shaped pastry & eaten as a snack (also known as **samosa**)
samosa *sa·moh·sa* see **sambusa**
sandwichi *sand·wee·chee* sandwich
shampeni *sham·pay·nee* champagne
shayiri *sha·yee·ree* barley • oats
siagi *see·a·gee* butter
siki *see·kee* vinegar
simsim *seem·seem* sesame seeds • sesame candy (Zanzibar)
slaisi *sla·ee·see* slice (see also **tosti**)
soda *soh·da* soft drink
sorpotel *sohr·poh·tayl* stew of beef & pork flavoured with a rich spice mix (Zanzibar)
soseji ya nyama nguruwe *soh·say·jee ya nya·ma n·goo·roo·way* pork sausage

spageti *spa·gay·tee* spaghetti (see also **makaroni**)
stauti *sta·oo·tee* stout beer
steki *stay·kee* see **mnofu**
stroberi *stroh·bay·ree* strawberry
sukari *soo·ka·ree* sugar
sukuma wiki *soo·koo·ma wee·kee* mixture of basic greens (eg spinach) often served with meat dishes
supu *soo·poo* soup • broth (sometimes spicy) made from pieces of chicken, meat or fish
    — **ya kuku** *ya koo·koo* chicken soup with onion, cabbage, tomato & celery

T

tangawizi *tan·ga·wee·zee* ginger
tembo *taym·boh* palm wine
tende *tayn·day* date
tikiti (maji) *tee·kee·tee (ma·jee)* melon • watermelon
tilapia *tee·la·pee·a* tilapia (Nile perch)
tofaa *toh·fa* apple
topetope *toh·pay·toh·pay* cherimoya • custard apple
tosti *toh·stee* slice of bread (often toasted), also known as **slaisi**
tunda *toon·da* fruit

U

ubwabwa *oo·bwa·bwa* rice cooked with coconut
ugali *oo·ga·lee* traditional dish made by mixing maize and/or cassava flour in hot water until it becomes like a stiff porridge & eaten by rolling it in the hand to form a small ball which is then dipped in sauce before eating (also known as **posho** in Uganda)
uji *oo·jee* thin sweet porridge
ulanzi *oo·lan·zee* bamboo juice **pombe**
umanga *oo·man·ga* plain food (without relish)
unga wa kahawa wa moja kwa moja *oon·ga wa ka·ha·wa wa moh·ja kwa moh·ja* instant coffee

unga wa mahindi *oon*-ga wa ma-*heen*-dee *maize/corn meal*
unga wa pilipili hoho *oon*-ga wa pee-lee-*pee*-lee *hoh*-hoh *chilli powder*
unga wa viazi vikuu *oon*-ga va vee-*a*-zee vee-*ku*-u *yam flour*
uraka oo-*ra*-ka *brewed cashew nut drink*
utumbo wa nyama oo-*toom*-boh wa *nya*-ma *offal • intestines*

V

vinginevyo veen-gee-*nay*-vyo *side dishes*
vinywaji veeny-*wa*-jee *drinks*
vitambua vee-tam-*boo*-a *small cakes made with rice flour*

W

wanzuki wan-*zoo*-kee *honey beer*
wali *wa*-lee *cooked rice (available with a variety of meats or sauces)*
  — maharagwe ma-ha-*ra*-gway *cooked rice and beans*
waragi wa-*ra*-gee *millet-based alcohol (Uganda)*

Y

yai *see* **mayai**
ya kuchemshwa ya koo-*chaym*-shwa *boiled*
ya kuchomwa ya koo-*choh*-mwa *broiled • grilled*
ya kuiva kidogo ya koo-*ee*-va kee-*doh*-goh *rare (meat)*
ya kuiva kubisa/sana ya koo-*ee*-va koo-*bee*-sa/*sa*-na *well-done*
ya kuiva wastani ya koo-*ee*-va wa-*sta*-nee *medium (meat)*
ya kukaanga ya koo-ka-*a*-nga *fried*
ya kuoka ya koo-*oh*-ka *roasted*
ya kuokwa ya koo-*ok*-wa *baked*
ya kupikwa ya koo-*peek*-wa *cooked • heated*

Z

zabibu za-*bee*-boo *grapes*
  — nyeupe zilizokaushwa nyay-*oo*-pay zee-lee-zoh-ka-*oo*-shwa *sultanas*
zabibubata za-bee-boo-*ba*-ta *cape gooseberries (Kenya)*

emergencies

dharura

Careful!	*Angalia!*	an·ga·*lee*·a
Help!	*Saidia!*	sa·ee·*dee*·a
Stop!	*Simama!*	see·*ma*·ma
Go away!	*Toka!*	*toh*·ka
Thief!	*Mwizi!*	*mwee*·zee
Fire!	*Moto!*	*moh*·toh
Watch out!	*Angalia!*	an·ga·*lee*·a

Leave me alone!
  Niache! — nee·*a*·chay

I won't give you any money!
  Sitakupa hela! — see·ta·*koo*·pa *hay*·la

It's an emergency.
  Ni dharura. — nee dha·*roo*·a

There's been an accident.
  Ajali imetokea. — a·*ja*·lee ee·may·toh·*kay*·a

Call the police.
  Waite polisi. — wa·*ee*·tay poh·*lee*·see

Call a doctor.
  Mwite daktari. — m·*wee*·tay dak·*ta*·ree

Call an ambulance.
  Ita gari la hospitali. — *ee*·ta *ga*·ree la ho·spee·*ta*·lee

signs		
Dharura	dha·*roo*·ra	**Emergency Department**
Hospitali	hoh·spee·*ta*·lee	**Hospital**
Polisi	poh·*lee*·see	**Police**

essentials

179

Could you please help?
Saidia, tafadhali. sa·ee·*dee*·a ta·fa·*dha*·lee

Can I use your phone?
Naomba kutumia na·*ohm*·ba koo·too·*mee*·a
simu yako. *see*·moo *ya*·koh

I'm lost.
Nimejipotea. nee·may·jee·poh·*tay*·a

Where are the toilets?
Vyoo viko wapi? vyoh *vee*·ko *wa*·pee

Is it safe ...?	*Ni salama ...?*	nee sa·*la*·ma ...
at night	*usikuni*	oo·see·*koo*·nee
for gay people	*kwa wasenge*	kwa wa·*sayn*·gay
for travellers	*kwa watalii*	kwa wa·ta·*lee*
for women	*kwa wanawake*	kwa wa·na·*wa*·kay
on your own	*kuwa pekee*	*koo*·wa pay·*kay*

police

Where's the police station?
Kituo cha polisi kee·*too*·oh cha poh·*lee*·see
kiko wapi? *kee*·koh *wa*·pee

I want to report an offence.
Nataka kutoa na·*ta*·ka koo·*toh*·a
taarifa ya jinai. ta·*ree*·fa ya jee·*na*·ee

Can I see your police identification card?
Nionyeshe kadi nee·oh·*nyay*·shay *ka*·dee
ya kitambulisho ya kee·tam·boo·*lee*·shoh
ya polisi. ya poh·*lee*·see

It was him/her.
Alikuwa yeye. a·lee·*koo*·wa *yay*·yay

I have insurance.
Nina bima. *nee*·na *bee*·ma

My (backpack) was stolen.
(Shanta) iliibwa. (*shan*·ta) ee·lee·ee·*bwa*

I've been …		
assaulted	*Nilishambuliwa.*	nee·lee·sham·boo·*lee*·wa
mugged	*Nilivamiwa.*	nee·lee·va·*mee*·wa
raped	*Nilibakwa.*	nee·lee·*ba*·kwa
robbed	*Niliibiwa.*	nee·lee·ee·*bee*·wa

He/She tried to … me.	*Alijaribu …*	a·lee·ja·*ree*·boo …
assault	*kunishambulia*	koo·nee·sham·boo·*lee*·a
rape	*kunibaka*	koo·nee·*ba*·ka
rob	*kuniibia*	koo·nee·ee·*bee*·a
trick	*kunidanganya*	koo·nee·dan·*ga*·nya

I've lost my …	*Nilipoteza …*	nee·lee·poh·*tay*·za …
bags	*mizigo yangu*	mee·*zee*·goh *yan*·goo
car	*gari langu*	*ga*·ree *lan*·goo
credit card	*kadi ya benki*	*ka*·dee ya *bayn*·kee
money	*pesa yangu*	*pay*·sa *yan*·goo
passport	*pasipoti yangu*	pa·see·*poh*·tee *yan*·goo

What am I accused of?
Nashtakiwa na nini? na·shta·*kee*·wa na *nee*·nee

I'm sorry.
Nasikia majuto. na·see·*kee*·a ma·*joo*·toh

I didn't realise I was doing anything wrong.
Nilikuwa sielewi nee·lee·*koo*·wa see·ay·*lay*·wee
kwamba nilifanya *kwam*·ba nee·lee·*fa*·nya
kosa lolote. *koh*·sa loh·*loh*·tay

I didn't do it.
Sikuifanya. see·koo·ee·*fa*·nya

Can I pay an on-the-spot fine?
Naweza kulipa faini na·*way*·za koo·*lee*·pa fa·*ee*·nee
hapa hapa? *ha*·pa *ha*·pa

Can I make a phone call?
Naweza kutumia simu? na·*way*·za koo·too·*mee*·a *see*·moo

I want to contact my embassy/consulate.
Nataka kuwasiliana na·*ta*·ka koo·wa·see·lee·*a*·na
na ubalozi wangu. na oo·ba·*loh*·zee *wan*·goo

Can I have a lawyer (who speaks English)?

Naomba mwanasheria   na·*ohm*·ba mwa·na·*shay*·*ree*·a
(anayesema Kiingereza).   (a·na·yay·*say*·ma kee·een·gay·*ray*·za)

This drug is for personal use.

Dawa hili ni kwa   *da*·wa *hee*·lee nee kwa
matumizi yangu   ma·too·*mee*·zee *yan*·goo
mwenyewe.   mway·*nyay*·way

I have a prescription for this drug.

Nina agizo la daktari   *nee*·na a·*gee*·zoh la dak·*ta*·ree
kwa dawa hili.   kwa *da*·wa *hee*·lee

the police may say ...

Unashitakiwa na ...	oo·na·shee·ta·*kee*·wa na ...	**You're charged with ...**
Anashitakiwa na ...	a·na·shee·ta·*kee*·wa na ...	**He/She is charged with ...**
kubaki baada ya visa kuisha	koo·*ba*·kee ba·*a*·da ya *vee*·sa koo·*ee*·sha	**overstaying your visa**
kuiba dukani	koo·*ee*·ba doo·*ka*·nee	**shoplifting**
kutokuwa na visa	koo·toh·*koo*·wa na *vee*·sa	**not having a visa**
kuvuruka amani	koo·voo·*roo*·ka a·*ma*·nee	**disturbing the peace**
kuwa na (kitu kinyume cha sheria)	*koo*·wa na (*kee*·too kee·*nyoo*·may cha shay·*ree*·ya)	**possession (of illegal substances)**
shambulio	sham·boo·*lee*·oh	**assault**

Ni faini ya kuegesha gari.
  nee fa·*ee*·nee ya   **It's a parking fine.**
  koo·ay·*gay*·sha *ga*·ree
Ni faini ya kwenda mwendo kubwa mno.
  nee fa·*ee*·nee ya *kwayn*·da   **It's a speeding fine.**
  mwayn·do *koob*·wa m·noh

doctor

daktari

Where's the	*... hapo karibuni*	*... ha·*poh ka·ree·*boo·*nee
nearest ...?	*iko wapi?*	ee·koh wa·pee
dentist	*Daktari wa meno*	dak·*ta·*ree wa *may·*noh
doctor	*Daktari*	dak·*ta·*ree
emergency department	*Wadi ya dharura*	wa·dee ya dha·*roo·*ra
hospital	*Hospitali*	hoh·spee·*ta·*lee
medical centre	*Kituo cha afya*	kee·*too·*oh cha *af·*ya
(night)	*Duka la madawa*	*doo·*ka la ma·*da·*wa
pharmacist	*(la saa za manane)*	(la sa za ma·*na·*nay)
optometrist	*Daktari wa macho*	dak·*ta·*ree wa *ma·*choh
rural clinic	*Kliniki*	klee·*nee·*kee

I need a doctor (who speaks English).
Nahitaji daktari   na·hee·*ta·*jee dak·*ta·*ree
(anayesema   (a·na·yay·*say·*ma
Kiingereza).   kee·een·gay·*ray·*za)

Could I see a female doctor?
Inawezekana nione   ee·na·way·zay·*ka·*na nee·*oh·*nay
daktari mwanamke?   dak·*ta·*ree mwa·*nam·*kay

Could the doctor come here?
Daktari anaweza   dak·*ta·*ree a·na·*way·*za
kuja hapa?   *koo·*ja ha·pa

Is there an after-hours emergency number?
Kuna simu ya dharura   *koo·*na *see·*moo ya dha·*roo·*ra
kupiga baada ya   koo·*pee·*ga ba·*a·*da ya
saa za kazi?   sa za *ka·*zee

I've run out of my medication.
Dawa langu limekwisha.   *da·*wa *lan·*goo lee·may·*kwee·*sha

This is my usual medicine.
Hili ni dawa langu   hee·lee nee *da*·wa *lan*·goo
la kawaida.   la ka·wa·*ee*·da

My child weighs (20 kilos).
Mtoto wangu ana uzito   m·*toh*·toh *wan*·goo *a*·na oo·*zee*·toh
wa (kilo ishirini).   wa (*kee*·loh ee·shee·*ree*·nee)

What's the correct dosage?
Niambie kipimo halisi?   nee·am·*bee*·ay kee·*pee*·moh ha·*lee*·see

I don't want a blood transfusion.
Sitaki damu kutoka   see·*ta*·kee *da*·moo koo·*toh*·ka
mtu mwengine.   m·too mwayn·*gee*·nay

Please use a new syringe.
Tumia sindano mpya.   too·*mee*·a seen·*da*·noh m·pya

I have my own syringe.
Nina sindano yangu.   *nee*·na seen·*da*·noh *yan*·goo

---

the doctor may say ...

Kuna shida gani? *koo*·na *shee*·da *ga*·nee	**What's the problem?**
Una maumivu wapi? oo·na ma·oo·*mee*·voo *wa*·pee	**Where does it hurt?**
Una homa? oo·na *hoh*·ma	**Do you have a temperature?**
Umekuwa hivyo kwa muda gani? oo·may·*koo*·wa *heev*·yoh kwa *moo*·da *ga*·nee	**How long have you been like this?**
Imetokea kabla? ee·may·toh·*kay*·a *ka*·bla	**Have you had this before?**
Umekunywa maji yasiyo salama? oo·may·*koony*·wa *ma*·jee ya·*see*·yoh sa·*la*·ma	**Have you drunk any unsafe water?**
Umekula chakula kisicho salama? oo·may·*koo*·la cha·*koo*·la kee·*see*·choh sa·*la*·ma	**Have you eaten any unsafe food?**

the doctor may say ...

Wewe hufanya mapenzi?
way·way hoo·*fa*·nya
ma·*payn*·zee
Are you sexually active?

Umewahi kufanya mapenzi bila kinga?
oo·may·*wa*·hee koo·*fa*·nya
ma·*payn*·zee bee·la *keen*·ga
**Have you had
unprotected sex?**

Unakunywa?
oo·na·*koony*·wa
Do you drink?

Unavuta sigara?
oo·na·*voo*·ta see·*ga*·ra
Do you smoke?

Unatumia madawa ya kulevya?
oo·na·too·*mee*·a ma·*da*·wa
ya koo·*lay*·vya
Do you take drugs?

Una mzio wa kitu chochote?
oo·na m·*zee*·oh wa *kee*·too
choh·*choh*·tay
**Are you allergic
to anything?**

Unatumia dawa lolote?
oo·na·too·*mee*·a *da*·wa
loh·*loh*·tay
Are you on medication?

Unasafiri kwa muda gani?
oo·na·sa·*fee*·ree kwa
moo·da *ga*·nee
**How long are you
travelling for?**

Inabidi ulazwe hospitalini.
ee·na·*bee*·dee oo·*laz*·way
hoh·spee·ta·*lee*·nee
**You need to be
admitted to hospital.**

Inatakiwa daktari akuangalie ukifika nyumbani.
ee·na·ta·*kee*·wa dak·*ta*·ree
a·koo·an·ga·*lee*·ay oo·kee·*fee*·ka
nyoom·*ba*·nee
**You should have it
checked when you
go home.**

Afadhali urudi kwenu kwa matibabu.
a·fa·*dha*·lee oo·*roo*·dee
kway·noo kwa ma·tee·*ba*·boo
**You should return
home for treatment.**

Wewe huwaza magonjwa yasiyoonekana.
way·way hoo·*wa*·za ma·*gohn*·jwa
ya·see·yoh·oh·nay·*ka*·na
You're a hypochondriac.

health

I'm vaccinated	Nimechanjwa	nee·may·chan·jwa
against ...	kwa ...	kwa ...
hepatitis	uvimbe wa	oo·veem·bay wa
A/B/C	ini A/B/C	ee·nee a/bay/say
meningitis	homa ya uti	hoh·ma ya oo·tee
	wa mgongo	wa m·gohn·goh
rabies	kichaa cha mbwa	kee·cha cha m·bwa
tetanus	pepopunda	pay·poh·poon·da
typhoid	homa ya	hoh·ma ya
	matumbo	ma·toom·boh
yellow fever	homa ya manjano	hoh·ma ya man·ja·noh

I need new ...	Nahitaji ... mpya.	na·hee·ta·jee ... m·pya
contact lenses	lenzi mboni	layn·zee m·boh·nee
glasses	miwani	mee·wa·nee

My prescription is …
Agizo la daktari ni …   a·gee·zoh la dak·ta·ree nee …

Can I have a receipt for my insurance?
Niandikie risiti kwa   nee·an·dee·kee·ay ree·see·tee kwa
kampuni yangu ya bima.   kam·poo·nee yan·goo ya bee·ma

symptoms & conditions

I'm sick.
Mimi ni mgonjwa.   mee·mee nee m·gohn·jwa

My friend is (very) sick.
Rafiki yangu ni   ra·fee·kee yan·goo nee
mgonjwa (sana).   m·gohn·jwa (sa·na)

My child is (very) sick.
Mwanangu ni   mwa·nan·goo nee
mgonjwa (sana).   m·gohn·jwa (sa·na)

He/She is having a/an …

allergic reaction	*Ana matatizo ya mzio.*	*a*·na ma·ta·*tee*·zoh ya m·*zee*·oh
asthma attack	*Anashambuliwa na pumu.*	a·na·sham·boo·*lee*·wa na *poo*·moo
baby	*Anajifungua.*	a·na·jee·foon·*goo*·a
epileptic fit	*Anashambuliwa na kifafa.*	a·na·sham·boo·*lee*·wa na kee·*fa*·fa
heart attack	*Ameshambuliwa na maradhi ya moyo.*	a·may·sham·boo·*lee*·wa na ma·*ra*·dhee ya *moh*·yoh

I've been …

injured	*Nimejeruhiwa.*	nee·may·jay·roo·*hee*·wa
vomiting	*Nimekuwa natapika.*	nee·may·*koo*·wa na·ta·*pee*·ka

I feel …   *Nasikia …*   na·see·*kee*·a …

anxious	*wasiwasi*	wa·see·*wa*·see
better	*afadhali*	a·fa·*dha*·lee
depressed	*huzuni*	hoo·*zoo*·nee
dizzy	*kizunguzungu*	kee·zoon·goo·zoon·goo
hot and cold	*joto na baridi*	*joh*·toh na ba·*ree*·dee
nauseous	*kichefuchefu*	kee·chay·foo·*chay*·foo
shivery	*mitetemeko*	mee·tay·lay·*may*·koh
strange	*siyo kawaida*	*see*·yoh ka·wa·*ee*·da
weak	*hafifu*	ha·*fee*·foo
worse	*mbaya zaidi*	m·*ba*·ya za·*ee*·dee

It hurts here.
Inauma hapa.   ee·na·*oo*·ma *ha*·pa

I'm dehydrated.
Nimekausha maji.   nee·may·ka·*oo*·sha *ma*·jee

I can't sleep.
Siwezi kulala.   see·*way*·zee koo·*la*·la

I think it's the medication I'm on.
Nadhani ni dawa ninalomeza.   na·*dha*·nee nee *da*·wa nee·na·loh·*may*·za

I'm on medication for …
  Ninameza dawa kwa …   nee·na·*may*·za *da*·wa kwa …

He/She is on medication for …
  Anameza dawa kwa …   a·na·*may*·za *da*·wa kwa …

I have (a/an) …
  Nina …   *nee*·na …

He/She has (a/an) …
  Ana …   *a*·na …

AIDS	*ukimwi*	oo·*keem*·wee
amoebic	*ugonjwa*	oo·*gohn*·jwa
dysentery	*wa amoeba*	wa a·moh·*ay*·ba
asthma	*pumu*	*poo*·moo
bedbugs	*kunguni*	koon·*goo*·nee
bilharzia	*kichocho*	kee·*choh*·choh
cholera	*kipindupindu*	kee·peen·doo·*peen*·doo
cold n	*mafua*	ma·*foo*·a
constipation	*hali ya*	*ha*·lee ya
	kufunga choo	koo·*foon*·ga cho
cough	*kikohozi*	kee·koh·*hoh*·zee
diabetes	*kisukari*	kee·soo·*ka*·ree
diarrhoea	*kuhara*	koo·*ha*·ra
fever	*homa*	*hoh*·ma
headache	*maumivu ya*	ma·oo·*mee*·voo ya
	kichwa	*kee*·chwa
HIV	*VVU*	vee·vee·*yoo*
malaria	*malaria*	ma·*la*·ree·a
meningitis	*homa ya uti*	*hoh*·ma ya oo·tee
	wa mgongo	wa m·*gohn*·goh
nausea	*kichefuchefu*	kee·chay·foo·*chay*·foo
pain	*maumivu*	ma·oo·*mee*·voo
runny nose	*pua yenye*	*poo*·a *yay*·nyay
	makamasi	ma·ka·*ma*·see
sore throat	*koo lenye*	koh *lay*·nyay
	maumivu	ma·oo·*mee*·voo
intestinal worms	*minyoo*	mee·*nyoh*
typhoid	*homa ya*	*hoh*·ma ya
	matumbo	ma·*toom*·boh

women's health

(I think) I'm pregnant.
(Nafikiri) mimi ni   (na·fee·*kee*·ree) *mee*·mee nee
mja mzito.   *m*·ja m·*zee*·toh

I'm on the pill.
Natumia vidonge vya   na·too·*mee*·a vee·*dohn*·gay vya
uzazi wa mpango.   oo·*za*·zee wa m·*pan*·goh

I haven't had my period for (six) weeks.
Sijaingia mwezini   see·ja·een·*gee*·a mway·*zee*·nee
kwa wiki (sita).   kwa *wee*·kee (*see*·ta)

I've noticed a lump here.
Nimegundua   nee·may·goon·*doo*·a
uvimbe hapa.   oo·*veem*·bee *ha*·pa

Do you have something for (period pain)?
Una dawa kwa   oo·na *da*·wa kwa
(maumivu ya   (ma·oo·*mee*·voo ya
mwezini)?   mway·*zee*·nee)

---

the doctor may say ...

Ulipopata hedhi ilikuwa lini?
oo·lee·poh·*pa*·ta *hay*·dhee
ee·lee·*koo*·wa *lee*·nee
When did you last have your period?

Umepata hedhi?
oo·may·*pa*·ta *hay*·dhee
Are you menstruating?

Unatumia uzazi wa mpango?
oo·na·too·*mee*·a oo·*za*·zee
wa m·*pan*·goh
Are you using contraception?

Wewe ni mja mzito?
way·way nee *m*·ja m·*zee*·toh
Are you pregnant?

Wewe ni mja mzito.
way·way nee *m*·ja m·*zee*·toh
You're pregnant.

I have a ...	Nina ...	nee·na ...
urinary tract infection	ambukizo la mfumo wa mkojo	am·boo·kee·zoh la m·foo·moh wa m·koh·joh
yeast infection	ambukizo la hamira	am·boo·kee·zoh la ha·mee·ra
I need ...	Nahitaji ...	na·hee·ta·jee ...
a pregnancy test	kupima kama mimi ni mja mzito	koo·pee·ma ka·ma mee·mee nee m·ja m·zee·toh
contraception	uzuiaji mimba	oo·zoo·ee·a·jee meem·ba
the morning-after pill	kidonge cha kuzuia mimba kumeza baada ya mahusiano	kee·dohn·gay cha koo·zoo·ee·a meem·ba koo·may·za ba·a·da ya ma·hoo·see·a·noh

allergies

mzio

I'm allergic to ...	Nina mzio wa ...	nee·na m·zee·oh wa ...
He/She is allergic to ...	Ana mzio wa ...	a·na m·zee·oh wa ...
antibiotics	viuavija-sumu	vee·oo·a·vee·ja·soo·moo
anti-inflammatories	madawa ya kupunguza uvimbe	ma·da·wa ya koo·poon·goo·za oo·veem·bee
aspirin	aspirini	as·pee·ree·nee
bees	nyuki	nyoo·kee
penicillin	penisilini	pay·nee·see·lee·nee
pollen	chavua	cha·voo·a
sulphur-based drugs	madawa yenye sulfa ndani	ma·da·wa yay·nyay sool·fa n·da·nee

I have a skin allergy.
Nina mzio wa ngozi.   nee·na m·zee·oh wa n·goh·zee

inhaler	*kivutia pumzi*	kee·voo·*tee*·a *poom*·zee
injection	*sindano*	seen·*da*·noh
antimalarials	*madawa kuzuia*	ma·*da*·wa koo·zoo·*ee*·a
	malaria	ma·*la*·ree·a

For food-related allergies, see **vegetarian & special meals**, page 172.

alternative treatments

matibabu mengine

I don't use (Western medicine).
Situmii (uganga   see·too·*mee* (oo·*gan*·ga
wa Ulaya).   wa oo·*la*·ya)

Can I see someone who practices acupuncture?
Naomba kuona   na·*ohm*·ba koo·oh·na
mtaalamu wa tiba ya   m·ta·*la*·moo wa *tee*·ba ya
kuchoma sindano.   koo·*choh*·ma seen·*da*·noh

Can I see someone who practices naturopathy?
Naomba kuona   na·*ohm*·ba koo·oh·na
mtaalamu wa   m·ta·*la*·moo wa
matibabu asilia.   ma·tee·*ba*·boo a·see·*lee*·a

better safe than sorry

Here are a few terms you might need to know while you're in East Africa, just to be on the safe side:

(DEET) insect repellent
dawa la kufukuza   *da*·wa la koo·foo·*koo*·za
wadudu (aina ya dit)   wa·*doo*·doo (a·*ee*·na ya deet)
(permethrin) insect repellent
dawa la kufukuza   *da*·wa la koo·foo·*koo*·za
wadudu (aina ya   wa·*doo*·doo (a·*ee*·na ya
permethrin)   payr·*may*·threen)
water purification tablets
vidonge vya   vee·*dohn*·gay vya
kusafisha maji   koo·sa·*fee*·sha *ma*·jee

parts of the body

My ... hurts.
   ... yangu inauma.   *... yan·goo ee·na·oo·ma*

I can't move my ...
   Siwezi kuhamisha   *see·way·zee koo·ha·mee·sha*
   ... yangu.   *... yan·goo*

I have a cramp in my ...
   Nina mkakamao   *nee·na m·ka·ka·ma·oh*
   kwenye ... yangu.   *kway·nyay ... yan·goo*

My ... is swollen.
   ... yangu imevimba.   *... yan·goo ee·may·veem·ba*

eye
jicho
jee·choh

nose
pua
poo·a

mouth
mdomo
m·doh·moh

ear
sikio
see·kee·oh

head
kichwa
kee·chwa

arm/hand
mkono
m·koh·noh

chest
kifua
kee·foo·a

stomach
tumbo
toom·boh

bottom
matako
ma·ta·koh

foot/leg
mguu
m·goo

pharmacist

I need something for (a headache).
Nahitaji dawa kwa   na·hee·*ta*·jee *da*·wa kwa
(maumivu ya kichwa).   (ma·oo·*mee*·voo ya *kee*·chwa)

Do I need a prescription for …?
Inabidi niwe na   ee·na·*bee*·dee *nee*·way na
agizo la daktari kwa …?   a·*gee*·zoh la dak·*ta*·ree kwa …

I have a prescription.
Nina agizo la daktari.   *nee*·na a·*gee*·zoh la dak·*ta*·ree

How many times a day?
Mara ngapi kwa siku?   *ma*·ra n·*ga*·pee kwa *see*·koo

Will it make me drowsy?
Itanisinzisha?   ee·ta·nee·seen·*zee*·sha

antiseptic n	*dawa ya*	*da*·wa ya
	kusafisha jeraha	koo·sa·*fee*·sha jay·*ra*·ha
condoms	*kondom*	*kohn*·dohm
contraceptives	*kingamimba*	keen·ga·*meem*·ba
iodine	*iodini*	ee·oh·*dee*·nee
painkillers	*viondoa*	vee·ohn·*doh*·a
	maumivu	ma·oo·*mee*·voo
rehydration	*dawa ya*	*da*·wa ya
salts	*kuongeza*	koo·ohn·*gay*·za
	maji mwilini	*ma*·jee mwee·*lee*·nee

the pharmacist may say …

Mara mbili kwa siku (pamoja na chakula).
   ma·ra m·*bee*·lee   **Twice a day (with food).**
   kwa *see*·koo (pa·*moh*·ja na
   cha·*koo*·la)

Umewahi kumeza hili?
   oo·may·*wa*·hee   **Have you taken this before?**
   koo·*may*·za *hee*·lee

Ni lazima umalize kosi.
   nee *la*·zee·ma   **You must complete**
   oo·ma·*lee*·zay koh·see   **the course.**

dentist

I have a ...	Nina ...	nee·na ...
broken	jino	jee·noh
tooth	lililovunjika	lee·lee·loh·voon·jee·ka
cavity	kutokoka	koo·toh·koh·ka
	kwa jino	kwa jee·noh
toothache	maumivu	ma·oo·mee·voo
	ya jino	ya jee·noh
I need (a/an) ...	Nahitaji ...	na·hee·ta·jee ...
anaesthetic	ganzi	gan·zee
filling	kijazio	kee·ja·zee·oh

I've lost a filling.
Nimepoteza kijazio.   nee·may·poh·tay·za kee·ja·zee·oh

My gums hurt.
Ufizi unaniumiza.   oo·fee·zee oo·na·nee·oo·mee·za

I don't want it extracted.
Sitaki ung'oaji.   see·ta·kee oong·oh·a·jee

---

the dentist may say ...

Fumbua sana. foom·boo·a sa·na	**Open wide.**
Haitauma hata kidogo. ha·ee·ta·oo·ma ha·ta kee·doh·goh	**This won't hurt a bit.**
Tafuna na kamata. ta·foo·na na ka·ma·ta	**Bite down on this.**
Usihame. oo·see·ha·may	**Don't move.**
Sukutua! soo·koo·too·a	**Rinse!**
Rejea, sijamaliza. ray·jay·a see·ja·ma·lee·za	**Come back, I haven't finished.**

What is sustainable travel and responsible tourism?

Being a responsible tourist in East Africa means acknowledging that travel inevitably impacts on the host communities and environment you visit. When you travel, you're not only embracing the diversity of this big, wide, wonderful world – you're adding your footprints to those left by some of the 700-million-plus people who travel internationally each year. This runaway juggernaut affects wilderness, native species and traditional cultures. The goal is to make the impact as positive as possible by giving back to local communities and acting to minimise negative outcomes. In doing so, you're helping to make your steps lighter, greener and friendlier.

How can travel to East Africa have a positive effect on local industries and wildlife?

A region of stunning geography, all-night partying and wondrous architecture, East Africa is also the ultimate destination to observe the 'Big Five' (elephant, rhinoceros, leopard, lion and Cape buffalo) in their natural habitat. However, with the global inequities of wealth distribution so pronounced in East Africa, it's particularly important to ensure that your travel enjoyment is not at the expense of locals and their environment.

safari

195

At one level, the impact of tourism can be positive – it can provide an incentive for locals to preserve environments and wildlife by generating employment, while enabling them to maintain their traditional lifestyles. However, the negative impacts of tourism can be substantial and contribute to the gradual erosion of traditional life. You can try to keep your impact as low as possible by following these tips:

• Support local enterprise. Use locally owned hotels and restaurants and buy souvenirs directly from the tradespeople and craftspeople who make them.
• Don't buy items made from natural materials such as ivory, skins and shells.
• Choose safari and trekking operators that treat local communities as equal partners, and that are committed to protecting local ecosystems.
• Question any so-called ecotourism operators about what they're really doing to protect the environment and the people who live there.
• Instead of giving cash, food or medicines to locals, make a donation to a recognised project such as a health centre or school.
• Try to get a balanced view of life in developing countries, and focus on the strong points of local culture.
• Resist the local tendency to be indifferent to littering. On treks, in parks or when camping, carry out your litter and leave areas cleaner than you found them.
• In order to help minimise land degradation, keep to the tracks when walking or when on safari, or encourage your driver to do so.

What are the main safari regions in East Africa?

East Africa has a clutch of popular parks showcasing some of the greatest wildlife spectacles on earth. Highlights are the magnificent Serengeti–Masai Mara ecosystem; the wildlife-packed Ngorongoro Crater and Tarangire National Park in Tanzania; Parc National de Volcans, Rwanda's original Gorillas in the Mist backdrop; and the hippo-, crocodile- and elephant-filled Murchison Falls and Budongo Central Forest Reserve with its chimpanzees and dense forest, in Uganda.

buffalo	mbogo	m·*boh*·goh
elephant	ndovu/tembo	n·*doh*·voo/*teym*·boh
leopard	chui	*choo*·ee
lion	simba	*seem*·baa
rhinoceros	kifaru	kee·*faa*·roo

For more on East African wildlife, see the box **local plants & animals** on page 152.

I'd like to visit a native-style tourist station.

Ningependa kufikia	neen·gey·*peyn*·daa koo·*fee*·kaa
kwenye kituo cha	kweyn·yey kee·*too*·oh chaa
kitalii cha kienyeji.	kee·taa·*lee* chaa kee·eyn·*yey*·jee

Are there any local-style guesthouses in the park?

Kuna nyumba za	koo·naa nyoom·baa zaa
wageni za kienyeji	waa·*gey*·nee zaa kee·eyn·*yey*·jee
ndani ya hifadhi?	n·*daa*·nee yaa hee·*faa*·dhee

Are there fair working standards at this park?

Kuna viwango vya	koo·naa vee·*waan*·goh vyaa
kazi za kistaarabu	kaa·zee zaa kee·staa·*raa*·boo
ndani ya hifadhi?	n·*daa*·nee yaa hee·*faa*·dhee

Is your business involved in tourism activities that protect the environment?

Biashara yako	bee·aa·*shaa*·raa *yaa*·koh
inajihusisha na	ee·naa·jee·hoo·*see*·shaa naa
shughuli za kitalii	shoo·*goo*·lee zaa kee·taa·*lee*
kuhifadhi	koo·hee·*faa*·dhee
mazingira?	maa·zeen·*gee*·raa

I'd like to hire a local guide.

Nataka kuajiri	naa·*taa*·kaa koo·aa·*jee*·ree
kiongozi kutoka	kee·ohn·*goh*·zee koo·*toh*·kaa
hapo jirani.	haa·poh jee·*raa*·nee

I'd like to go somewhere off the beaten track.

Nataka kuenda	naa·*taa*·kaa koo·*eyn*·daa
mahali ambapo	maa·*haa*·lee aam·*baa*·poh
siyo kawaida	*see*·yoh kaa·waa·*ee*·daa
kwa watalii.	kwaa waa·taa·*lee*

Is it safe to walk around this section of the park?

Ni salama	nee saa·*laa*·maa
nikitembea kwa	nee·kee·teym·*bey*·aa kwaa
miguu katika	mee·*goo* kaa·*tee*·kaa
sehemu hii ya	sey·*hey*·moo hee yaa
hifadhi?	hee·*faa*·dhee

Do you have information about the preservation of wildlife at this park?

Je, unazo taarifa	jey oo·*naa*·zoh taa·*ree*·faa
zinazohusiana	zee·naa·zoh·hoo·see·*aa*·naa
na utunzaji wa	naa oo·toon·*zaa*·jee waa
wanyama pori	waan·*yaa*·maa poh·ree
ndani ya hifadhi hii?	n·*daa*·nee yaa hee·*faa*·dhee hee

Do you have any endangered species at this park?

Je, unao viumbe	jey oo·*naa*·oh vee·*oom*·bey
walioko hatarini	waa·lee·*oh*·koh haa·taa·*ree*·nee
katika hifadhi hii?	kaa·*tee*·kaa hee·*faa*·dhee hee

Do you have the Big Five animals at this park?

Je, unao wanyama	jey oo·*naa*·oh waan·*yaa*·maa
wakuu watano katika	waa·*koo* waa·*taa*·noh kaa·*tee*·kaa
hifadhi hii?	hee·*faa*·dhee hii

Can you recommend a company that organises safaris?

Unaweza	oo·naa·*wey*·zaa
kupendekeza	koo·peyn·dey·*key*·zaa
kampuni ya safari	kaam·*poo*·nee yaa saa·*faa*·ree
kwa miguu?	kwaa mee·*goo*

For more practical phrases, see also **tours/safaris**, page 97, and **outdoors**, page 147.

Verbs are shown in the dictionary in their root forms, with a hyphen in front. To express a series of functions in a sentence, the verb can have several prefixes, infixes and suffixes. Some adjectives will also have a hyphen in front as they take different prefixes depending on certain characteristics of the thing being described. For more details on verbs and adjectives, see the **phrasebuilder**. You'll also find words marked as adjective ⓐ, noun ⓝ, verb ⓥ, singular sg or plural pl where necessary. A Swahili dictionary is also available online at www.kamusiproject.org.

A

aboard *chomboni* chohm·*boh*·nee
abortion *kutoa mimba*
  koo·*toh*·a meem·ba
about *kuhusu* koo·*hoo*·soo
above *juu ya* joo ya
abroad *nchi za nje* n·chee za n·jay
accident *ajali* a·*ja*·lee
accommodation *malazi* ma·*la*·zee
account (bank) *akaunti* a·ka·*oon*·tee
across *ng'ambo* ng·*am*·boh
activist *mhamisishaji*
  m·ha·mee·see·*sha*·jee
actor *mwigizaji* mwee·gee·*za*·jee
acupuncture
  tiba ya kuchoma na sindano
  tee·ba ya koo·*choh*·ma na seen·*da*·noh
adaptor *adapta* a·*dap*·ta
address *anwani* an·*wa*·nee
administration *usimamizi*
  oo·see·ma·*mee*·zee
admission (price) *bei ya kuingia*
  bay ya koo·een·*gee*·a
admit *-laza* ·*la*·za
adult ⓝ *mtu mzima* m·too m·*zee*·ma
advertisement *tangazo* tan·*ga*·zoh
advice *ushauri* oo·sha·*oo*·ree
aeroplane *ndege* n·*day*·gay
Africa *Afrika* a·*free*·ka
after *baada ya* ba·*a*·da ya
afternoon *mchana* m·*cha*·na
aftershave *losheni baada ya kunyoa*
  ndevu loh·*shay*·nee ba·*a*·da ya
  koo·*nyoh*·a n·*day*·voo
again *tena* *tay*·na
age *umri* *oom*·ree

agree *-kubali* ·koo·*ba*·lee
agriculture *kilimo* kee·*lee*·moh
ahead *mbele* m·*bay*·lay
AIDS *ukimwi* oo·*keem*·wee
air (outside) *hewa* *hay*·wa
air (in a tyre) *upepo* oo·*pay*·poh
air-conditioned *kwenye a/c*
  kway·nyay ay·*see*
air conditioning *a/c* ay·*see*
airline *kampuni ya ndege*
  kam·*poo*·nee ya n·*day*·gay
airmail *barua kwa ndege*
  ba·*roo*·a kwa n·*day*·gay
airplane *ndege* n·*day*·gay
airport *uwanja wa ndege*
  oo·*wan*·ja wa n·*day*·gay
airport tax *kodi ya uwanja wa ndege*
  koh·dee ya oo·*wan*·ja wa n·*day*·gay
aisle (on plane) *njia* n·*jee*·a
alarm clock *saa yenye kengele*
  sa *yay*·nyay kayn·*gay*·lay
alcohol *kilevi* kee·*lay*·vee
alcoholic drink *pombe* *pohm*·bay
all *zote* *zoh*·tay
allergy *mzio* m·*zee*·oh
almond *lozi* loh·*zee*
almost *karibu na* ka·*ree*·boo na
alone *pekee* pay·*kay*
already *tayari* ta·*ya*·ree
also *pia* *pee*·a
altar *madhahabu* ma·dha·*ha*·boo
altitude *kimo* *kee*·moh
always *daima* da·*ee*·ma
ambassador *balozi* ba·*loh*·zee
ambulance *gari la hospitali*
  ga·ree la hoh·spee·*ta*·lee
America *Marekani* ma·ray·*ka*·nee

American football *futbol ya kimarekani*
foot-bohl ya kee-ma-ray-*ka*-nee
anaemia *upungufu wa damu*
oo-poon-*goo*-foo wa *da*-moo
anarchist *mshabiki wa utawala huria*
m-sha-*bee*-kee wa oo-ta-*wa*-la hoo-*ree*-a
ancient *ya kale* ya *ka*-lay
and *na* na
angry *mwenye hasira*
mway-nyay ha-*see*-ra
animal *mnyama* m-*nya*-ma
ankle *kiwiko cha mguu*
kee-*wee*-koh cha m-*goo*
another *nyingine* nyeen-*gee*-nay
answer *jibu* jee-*boo*
ant *sungusungu* soon-goo-*soon*-goo
antelope *palahala* pa-la-*ha*-la
antibiotic *kiuavijasumu*
kee-oo-a-vee-ja-*soo*-moo
antinuclear *dhidi ya nyuklia*
dhee-dee ya nyoo-klee-a
antique ⓝ *ya zamani* ya za-*ma*-nee
antiseptic ⓝ *dawa ya kusafisha jeraha*
da-wa ya koo-sa-*fee*-sha jay-*ra*-ha
any *yoyote* yoh-*yoh*-tay
apartment *fleti* flay-tee
appendix (body) *kibole* kee-*boh*-lay
apple *tofaa* to-*fa*
appointment *miadi* mee-*a*-dee
April *mwezi wa nne* mway-zee wa n-nay
archaeological *ya elimu kale*
ya ay-*lee*-moo ka-*lay*
architect *msanifu wa majengo*
m-sa-*nee*-foo wa ma-*jayn*-goh
architecture *ujenzi* oo-*jayn*-zee
argue -*bisha* *bee*-sha
arm *mkono* m-*koh*-noh
aromatherapy *tiba ya harufu*
tee-ba ya ha-*roo*-foo
arrest -*kamata* -ka-*ma*-ta
arrivals *wanaofika* wa-na-oh-*fee*-ka
arrive -*fika* -*fee*-ka
art *sanaa* sa-*na*
art gallery *nyumba ya sanaa*
nyoom-ba ya sa-*na*
artist *msanii* m-sa-*nee*
ashtray *chombo cha majivu*
chohm-boh cha ma-*jee*-voo
Asia *Asia* a-*see*-a
ask (a question) -*uliza* -oo-*lee*-za
ask (for something) -*omba* -*ohm*-ba
aspirin *aspirini* a-spee-*ree*-nee
asthma *pumu* poo-moo

at *kwenye* kway-nyay
athletics *michezo ya riadha*
mee-*chay*-zoh ya ree-*a*-dha
atmosphere *hewa* hay-wa
aubergine *biringani* bee-reen-*ga*-nee
August *mwezi wa nane*
mway-zee wa *na*-nay
aunt *shangazi* shan-*ga*-zee
Australia *Australia* a-oo-*stra*-lee-a
automated teller machine (ATM)
mashine ya kutolea pesa
ma-*shee*-nay ya koo-toh-*lay*-a *pay*-sa
autumn *kipindi cha baridi kidogo*
kee-*peen*-dee cha ba-*ree*-dee
kee-*doh*-goh
avenue *barabara* ba-ra-*ba*-ra
avocado *embe mafuta* aym-bay ma-*foo*-ta
awful *mbaya sana* m-*ba*-ya *sa*-na

B

B&W (film) *nyeusi na nyeupe*
nyay-*oo*-see na nyay-*oo*-pay
baboon *nyani* nya-nee
baby *mtoto mchanga*
m-*toh*-toh m-*chan*-ga
baby food *chakula cha mtoto mchanga*
cha-*koo*-la cha m-toh-toh m-*chan*-ga
baby powder *pauda kwa mtoto*
pa-*oo*-da kwa m-*toh*-toh
babysitter *yaya* ya-ya
back (body) *mgongo* m-*gohn*-goh
back (position) *nyuma* nyoo-ma
backpack *shanta* shan-ta
bacon *bekoni* bay-*koh*-nee
bad *mbaya* m-*ba*-ya
bag *mfuko* m-*foo*-koh
baggage *mizigo* mee-*zee*-goh
baggage allowance *uzito usiolipiwa*
oo-*zee*-toh oo-see-oh-lee-*pee*-wa
baggage claim *sehemu ya
kuchukulia mizigo* say-*hay*-moo ya
koo-choo-koo-*lee*-a mee-*zee*-goh
bakery *duka la mkate* doo-ka la m-*ka*-tay
balance (account) *urari* oo-*ra*-ree
balcony *ubaraza* oo-ba-*ra*-za
ball *mpira* m-*pee*-ra
ballet *ngoma ya kuigiza hadithi*
n-*goh*-ma ya koo-ee-*gee*-za ha-*dee*-thee
banana *ndizi* n-*dee*-zee
band (music) *kikundi* kee-*koon*-dee
bandage *plasta* pla-sta

Band-Aid *elasto* ay·*la*·stoh
bank *benki* bayn·kee
bank account *akaunti ya benki*
  a·ka·*oon*·tee ya *bayn*·kee
banknote *noti* noh·tee
baptism *ubatizo* oo·ba·*tee*·zoh
bar *baa* ba
bar work *kazi kwenye baa*
  ka·zee kway·nyay ba
barber *kinyozi* kee·*nyoh*·zee
basket *kikapu* kee·*ka*·poo
basketball *mpira wa kikapu*
  m·*pee*·ra wa kee·*ka*·poo
bath *bafu* ba·foo
bathing suit *nguo za kuogelea*
  n·goo·oh za koo·oh·gay·*lay*·a
bathroom (for bathing) *bafuni*
  ba·*foo*·nee
bathroom (toilet) *choo* choh
battery *betri* bay·tree
be -*wa* ·wa
beach *ufukwe* oo·*fook*·way
beach volleyball *mpira wa wavu ufukoni*
  m·*pee*·ra wa wa·voo oo·foo·*koh*·nee
beans *maharagwe* ma·ha·*rag*·way
beansprouts *miche ya maharagwe*
  mee·chay ya ma·ha·*rag*·way
beautiful *ya kupendeza*
  ya koo·payn·*day*·za
beauty salon *saloni* sa·*loh*·nee
because *kwa sababu* kwa sa·*ba*·boo
bed *kitanda* kee·*tan*·da
bed linen *shuka* shoo·ka
bedding *shuka na tandiko*
  shoo·ka na tan·*dee*·koh
bedroom *chumba cha kulala*
  choom·ba cha koo·*la*·la
bee *nyuki* nyoo·kee
beef *nyama ng'ombe* nya·ma ng·*ohm*·bay
beer *bia* bee·a
beetroot *kiazisukari* kee·a·zee·soo·*ka*·ree
before *kabla* ka·bla
beggar *mwombaji* mwohm·*ba*·jee
behind *nyuma* nyoo·ma
Belgium *Ubelgiji* oo·bayl·*gee*·jee
below *chini* chee·nee
beside *jirani* jee·*ra*·nee
best *nzuri kabisa* n·zoo·ree ka·*bee*·sa
bet *dau* da·oo
better *afadhali* a·fa·*dha*·lee
between *katikati* ka·tee·*ka*·tee
Bible *Biblia* beeb·*lee*·a
bicycle *baisikeli* ba·ee·see·*kay*·lee

big *kubwa* koob·wa
bigger *kubwa zaidi* koob·wa za·*ee*·dee
biggest *kubwa kabisa* koob·wa ka·*bee*·sa
bike *baisikeli* ba·ee·see·*kay*·lee
bike chain *mnyororo wa baisikeli*
  m·nyoh·*roh*·roh wa ba·ee·see·*kay*·lee
bike lock *kufuli ya baisikeli*
  koo·*foo*·lee ya ba·ee·see·*kay*·lee
bike path *njia ya baisikeli*
  n·*jee*·a ya ba·ee·see·*kay*·lee
bike shop *duka la baisikeli*
  doo·ka la ba·ee·see·*kay*·lee
bill (restaurant etc) *bili* bee·lee
binoculars *darubini* da·roo·*bee*·nee
bird *ndege* n·*day*·gay
birth certificate *cheti cha kuzaliwa*
  chay·tee cha koo·za·*lee*·wa
birthday *sikukuu ya kuzaliwa*
  see·koo·koo ya koo·za·*lee*·wa
biscuit *biskuti* bee·skoo·tee
bite (dog, insect etc) ⓝ *uma* oo·ma
bitter *chungu* choon·goo
black *nyeusi* nyay·oo·see
bladder *kibofu* kee·boh·foo
blanket *blanketi* blan·*kay*·tee
blind *kipofu* kee·poh·foo
blister *lengelenge* layn·gay·*layn*·gay
blockage *kizuizi* kee·zoo·ee·zee
blood *damu* da·moo
blood group *aina ya damu*
  a·*ee*·na ya da·moo
blood pressure *shinikizo la damu*
  shee·nee·*kee*·zoh la da·moo
blood test *kipimo cha damu*
  kee·*pee*·moh cha da·moo
blue *buluu* boo·loo
board (a plane, ship etc) -*panda* ·*pan*·da
boarding house *nyumba ya wageni*
  nyoom·ba ya wa·*gay*·nee
boarding pass *pasi ya kupanda ndege*
  pa·see ya koo·*pan*·da n·*day*·gay
boat *boti* boh·tee
body *mwili* mwee·lee
boiled *ya kuchemshwa*
  ya koo·*chaym*·shwa
bone *mfupa* m·foo·pa
book ⓝ *kitabu* kee·*ta*·boo
book ⓥ -*fanya buking* ·fa·nya boo·keeng
booked out *hakuna nafasi*
  ha·koo·na na·*fa*·see
bookshop *duka la vitabu*
  doo·ka la vee·*ta*·boo
boots (footwear) *mabuti* ma·*boo*·tee

border *mpaka* m·*pa*·ka
bored -*choshwa* ·*choh*·shwa
boring *ya kuchosha* ya koo·*choh*·sha
borrow -*kopa* ·*koh*·pa
botanic garden *bustani ya kibotania*
   boo·*sta*·nee ya ·kee·boh·ta·*nee*·a
both *mbili* m·*bee*·lee
bottle *chupa* choo·pa
bottle opener *kifungua chupa*
   kee·foon·*goo*·a choo·pa
bottle shop *duka la pombe kali*
   doo·ka la ·*pohm*·bay ka·lee
bottom (body) *matako* ma·*ta*·koh
bottom (position) *chini* chee·nee
bowl *bakuli* ba·*koo*·lee
box *sanduku* san·*doo*·koo
boxer shorts *chupi* choo·pee
boxing *ndondi* n·*dohn*·dee
boy *mvulana* m·voo·*la*·na
boyfriend *mpenzi* m·*payn*·zee
bra *sidiria* see·dee·*ree*·a
brakes *breki* bray·kee
brandy *brandi* bran·dee
brave *shupavu* shoo·*pa*·voo
bread *mkate* m·*ka*·tay
bread rolls *skonzi* skohn·zee
break -*vunja* ·*voon*·ja
break down -*vunjika* ·voon·*jee*·ka
breakfast *chai ya asubuhi*
   cha·ee ya a·soo·boo·hee
breast (body) *titi* tee·tee
breast-feed -*nyonyesha* ·nyoh·*nyay*·sha
breathe -*pumua* ·poo·*moo*·a
bribe -*toa rushwa* ·toh·a roosh·wa
bridge *daraja* da·*ra*·ja
briefcase *mkoba* m·*koh*·ba
bring -*leta* ·*lay*·ta
brochure *kijitabu* kee·jee·*ta*·boo
broken *ya kuvunjika* ya koo·voon·*jee*·ka
broken down *ya kuharibika*
   ya koo·ha·ree·*bee*·ka
bronchitis *mkamba* m·*kam*·ba
brother *kaka* ka·ka
brown *kahawia* ka·ha·*wee*·a
bruise *jeraha* jay·*ra*·ha
brush *burashi* boo·*ra*·shee
bucket *ndoo* n·doh
Buddhist *Mbudisti* m·boo·*dee*·stee
budget *bajeti* ba·jay·tee
buffalo *nyati* nya·tee
buffet *meza kujihudumia*
   may·za koo·jee·hoo·doo·*mee*·a
bug *mdudu* m·*doo*·doo

build -*jenga* ·*jayn*·ga
builder *mjenzi* m·*jayn*·zee
building *jengo* jayn·goh
burn ⓝ *jeraha la moto*
   jay·*ra*·ha la moh·toh
burnt *ya kuchomwa* ya koo·*chohm*·wa
Burundi *Burundi* boo·roon·dee
bus (city) *daladala/matatu* Tan/Ken
   da·la·*da*·la/ma·*ta*·too
bus (intercity) *basi* ba·see
bus station *stendi ya basi*
   stayn·dee ya ba·see
bus stop *kituo cha basi*
   kee·*too*·oh cha ba·see
business *biashara* bee·a·*sha*·ra
business class *daraja la wafanyabiashara*
   da·*ra*·ja la wa·fa·nya·bee·a·*sha*·ra
business person *mfanyabiashara*
   m·fa·nya·bee·a·*sha*·ra
business trip *safari kwa biashara*
   sa·*fa*·ree kwa bee·a·*sha*·ra
busker *mwimbaji barabarani*
   mweem·*ba*·jee ba·ra·ba·*ra*·nee
busy (person) *mwenye shughuli nyingi*
   mway·nyay shoo·*goo*·lee nyeen·gee
but *lakini* la·kee·nee
butcher *bucha* boo·cha
butcher's shop *bucha* boo·cha
butter *siagi* see·*a*·gee
butterfly *kipepeo* kee·pay·*pay*·oh
button *kifungo* kee·*foon*·goh
buy -*nunua* ·noo·*noo*·a

C

cabbage *kabichi* ka·*bee*·chee
café *mgahawa* m·ga·*ha*·wa
cake *keki* kay·kee
cake shop *duka la keki* doo·ka la ·*kay*·kee
calculator *kikokotoo* kee·koh·koh·*toh*·oh
calendar *kalenda* ka·*layn*·da
call -*ita* ·ee·ta
camel *ngamia* n·ga·*mee*·a
camera *kemra* kaym·ra
camera shop *duka la kemra*
   doo·ka la kaym·ra
camp -*piga kambi* ·*pee*·ga kam·bee
camp site *kiwanja cha kupigia kambi*
   kee·*wan*·ja cha kuu·pee·*gee*·a kam·bee
camping ground
   uwanja wa kupigia kambi
   oo·*wan*·ja cha kuu·pee·*gee*·a kam·bee

camping store *duka la vifaa vya kambi* doo·ka la vee·*fa* vya *kam*·bee
can (be able) *-weza* ·*way*·za
can (have permission) *-ruhusiwa* roo·hoo·*see*·wa
can (tin) *mkebe/kopo* m·*kay*·bay/*koh*·poh
can opener *opena ya kopo* oh·*pay*·na ya *koh*·poh
Canada *Kanada* ka·na·da
cancel *-futa* ·*foo*·ta
cancer *kansa* kan·sa
candle *mshumaa* m·shoo·*ma*
candy *pipi* pee·pee
cantaloupe *tikiti maji ndogo la rangi ya machungwa* tee·*kee*·tee ma·jee n·doh·goh la *ran*·gee ya ma·*choon*·gwa
capsicum *pilipili hoho* pee·lee·pee·lee hoh·hoh
car *gari* ga·ree
car hire *kukodi gari* koo·koh·dee ga·ree
car owner's title *huki ya kisheria ya mmiliki wa gari* ha·kee ya kee·shay·*ree*·a ya m·mee·*lee*·kee wa ga·ree
car park *sehemu ya kuegeshea magari* say·*hay*·moo ya koo·ay·gay·*shay*·a ma·ga·ree
car registration *usajili wa gari* oo·sa·jee·lee wa ga·ree
caravan *lori la wasafiri* loh·ree la wa·sa·*fee*·ree
cardiac arrest *kusimama kwa mapigo ya moyo* koo·see·*ma*·ma kwa ma·*pee*·goh ya *moh*·yoh
cards (playing) *karata* ka·*ra*·ta
care (for someone) *-tunza* ·*toon*·za
carpenter *seremala* say·ray·*ma*·la
carrot *karoti* ka·roh·tee
carry *-beba* ·*bay*·ba
carton *katoni* ka·toh·nee
cash (n) *fedha* fay·dha
cash register *rejista* ray·*gee*·sta
cash (a cheque) *-lipwa fedha kwa kutoa hundi* ·*leep*·wa fay·dha kwa koo·*toh*·a hoon·dee
cashew *korosho* koh·roh·shoh
cashier *keshia* kay·*shee*·a
casino *kasino* ka·see·noh
cassette *kanda* kan·da
castle *husuni* hoo·soo·nee
casual work *kibarua* kee·ba·*roo*·a
cat *paka* pa·ka
cathedral *kanisa kuu* ka·*nee*·sa koo
Catholic (denomination) *Romani* roh·*ma*·nee

Catholic (person) *Mkatoliki* m·ka·toh·*lee*·kee
cauliflower *koliflawa* koh·lee·*fla*·wa
cave *pango* pan·goh
CD *CD* see·dee
CD-ROM *cd-rom* see·dee·rohm
celebration *sherehe* shay·*ray*·hay
cell phone *simu ya mkononi* see·moo ya m·koh·*noh*·nee
cemetery *makaburini* ma·ka·boo·*ree*·nee
cent *senti* sayn·tee
centimetre *sentimita* sayn·tee·*mee*·ta
Central Africa *Afrika ya Kati* a·*free*·ka ya ka·tee
centre *katikati* ka·tee·*ka*·tee
ceramics *ufinyanzi* oo·fee·*nyan*·zee
cereal *nafaka* na·*fa*·ka
certificate *cheti* chay·tee
chain *mnyororo* m·nyoh·*roh*·roh
chair *kiti* kee·tee
championships *mashindano ya ubingwa* ma·sheen·*da*·noh ya oo·*been*·gwa
chance *nafasi* na·*fa*·see
change (coins) *sarafu* sa·ra·too
change (money) *-badilisha hela* ·ba·dee·*lee*·sha hay·la
changing room (in shop) *chumba cha kubadilisha nguo* choom·ba cha koo·ba·dee·*lee*·sha n·goo·oh
charming *mwenye haiba* mway·nyay ha·*ee*·ba
cheap *rahisi* ra·hee·see
cheat (n) *mdanganyi* m·dan·ga·*nyee*
check (banking) *hundi* hoon·dee
check (bill) *bili* bee·lee
check *-kagua* ·ka·goo·a
check-in (desk) *mapokezi* ma·poh·*kay*·zee
checkpoint *kituo cha ukaguzi* kee·*too*·oh cha oo·ka·*goo*·zee
cheese *jibini* jee·bee·nee
cheetah *duma* doo·ma
chef *mpishi* m·*pee*·shee
chemist (pharmacy) *duka la dawa* doo·ka la *da*·wa
chemist (person) *mfamasia* m·fa·ma·*see*·a
cheque (banking) *hundi* hoon·dee
cheque (bill) *bili* bee·lee
cherry *cheri* chay·ree
chess *sataranji* sa·ta·*ran*·jee
chessboard *ubao wa sataranji* oo·*ba*·oh wa sa·ta·*ran*·jee
chest (body) *kufua* koo·*foo*·a

chewing gum mpira m·pee·ra
chicken kuku koo·koo
chicken pox tetekuwanga
tay·tay·koo·wan·ga
child mtoto m·toh·toh
child seat kiti cha mtoto
kee·tee cha m·toh·toh
childminding ulezi wa mtoto
oo·lay·zee wa m·toh·toh
children watoto wa·toh·toh
chilli pilipili hoho pee·lee·pee·lee hoh·hoh
chilli sauce mchuzi wa pilipili hoho
m·choo·zee wa pee·lee·pee·lee hoh·hoh
China China chee·na
chiropractor tabibu wa maungo
ta·bee·boo wa ma·oon·goh
choose -chagua ·cha·goo·a
chopping board bao la kukatia
ba·oh la koo·ka·tee·a
Christian Mkristo m·kree·stoh
Christian name jina la kwanza
jee·na la kwan·za
Christmas Krismasi krees·ma·see
church kanisa ka·nee·sa
cigar biri bee·ree
cigarette sigara see·ga·ra
cigarette lighter kiwashio kee·wa·shee·oh
cinema sinema see·nay·ma
circus sarakasi sa·ra·ka·see
citizenship uraia oo·ra·ee·a
city mji m·jee
city centre katikati ya mji
ka·tee·ka·tee ya m·jee
civil rights haki za binadamu
ha·kee za been·a·da·moo
class (category) tabaka ta·ba·ka
class system mfumo wa matabaka
m·foo·moh wa ma·ta·ba·ka
classical ya jadi ya ja·dee
clay udongo oo·dohn·goh
clean ⓐ safi sa·fee
clean -safisha ·sa·fee·sha
cleaning usafi oo·sa·fee
client mteja m·tay·ja
cliff mwamba mwam·ba
climb -panda ·pan·da
cloakroom chumba cha makoti
choom·ba cha ma·koh·tee
clock saa sa
close -funga ·foon·ga
closed ya kufungwa ya koo·foon·gwa
clothesline kamba ya kukausha nguo
kam·ba ya koo·ka·oo·sha n·goo·oh

clothing nguo n·goo·oh
clothing store duka la nguo
doo·ka la n·goo·oh
cloud wingu ween·goo
cloudy kuna mawingu
koo·na ma·ween·goo
clutch (car) klachi kla·chee
coach (bus) basi ba·see
coast pwani pwa·nee
coat koti koh·tee
cobra koboko koh·boh·koh
cocaine kokeini koh·kay·ee·nee
cockroach mende mayn·day
cocoa kakao ka·ka·oh
coconut nazi na·zee
coffee kahawa ka·ha·wa
coins sarafu sa·ra·foo
cold ⓐ baridi ba·ree·dee
cold (illness) ugonjwa oo·gon·jwa
colleague mwenzi wangu
mwayn·zee wan·goo
collect call gharama kwa mpigiwa simu
gha·ra·ma kwa m·pee·gee·wa see·moo
college chuo choo·oh
colour rangi ran·gee
comb chanuo cha·noo·oh
come -ja ·ja
comedy ya kuchekesha ya koo·chay·kay·sha
comfortable ya starehe ya sta·ray·hay
commission kamisheni ka·mee·shay·nee
communications (profession)
mawasiliano ma·wa·see·lee·a·noh
communion komunyo koh·moo·nyoh
(The) Comoros Islands Visiwa vya Komoros
vee·see·wa vya koh·moh·rohs
companion mwenzi mwayn·zee
company kampuni kam·poo·nee
compass dira dee·ra
complaint lalamiko la·la·mee·koh
complimentary (free) bure boo·ray
computer kompyuta kohm·pyoo·ta
computer game
mchezo kwenye kompyuta
m·chay·zoh kway·nyay kom·pyoo·ta
concert onyesho la muziki
oh·nyay·shoh la moo·zee·kee
concussion mshtuko wa ubongo
m·shtoo·koh wa oo·bohn·goh
conditioner (hair)
dawa la kuboresha nywele
da·wa la koo·boh·ray·sha nyway·lay
condom kondom kohn·dohm
conference (big) mikutano
mee·koo·ta·noh

conference (small) *mkutano*
m·koo·*ta*·noh
confession *ungamo* oon·*ga*·moh
confirm (a booking) *-hakikisha*
·ha·kee·*kee*·sha
congratulations *hongera* hohn·*gay*·ra
conjunctivitis *uvimbe wa mboni*
oo·*veem*·bay wa m·*boh*·nee
connection *kiungo* kee·*oon*·goh
conservative *muhafidhina*
moo·ha·fee·*dhee*·na
constipation *uyabisi wa tumbo*
oo·ya·*bee*·see wa *toom*·boh
consulate *ubalozi mdogo*
oo·ba·*loh*·zee m·*doh*·goh
contact lenses *lenzi mboni*
layn·zee m·*boh*·nee
contact lenses solution
myeyuko wa lenzi mboni
m·yay·*yoo*·koh wa *layn*·zee m·*boh*·nee
contraceptives *kingamimba*
keen·ga·*meem*·ba
contract *mkataba* m·ka·*ta*·ba
convenience store
duka la bidhaa mbalimbali
doo·ka la bee·*dha* m·ba·lee·m·*ba*·lee
convent *jumuiya ya masista*
joo·moo·*ee*·ya ya ma·*see*·sta
cook ⓝ *mpishi* m·*pee*·shee
cook ⓥ *-pika* ·*pee*·ka
cookie *biskuti* bee·*skoo*·tee
cooking *kupika* koo·*pee*·ka
cool (temperature) *ya baridi*
ya ba·*ree*·dee
copper *shaba* *sha*·ba
corkscrew *kizibuo* kee·zee·*boo*·oh
corn *mahindi* ma·*heen*·dee
corner *kona* *koh*·na
corrupt *ya kula rushwa* ya koo·la *roosh*·wa
cost *gharama* ga·*ra*·ma
cotton *pamba* *pam*·ba
cotton balls *mafusha ya pamba* pl
ma·*foo*·sha ya *pam*·ba
cotton buds *vijiti vya pamba safi* pl
vee·*jee*·tee vya *pam*·ba *sa*·fee
cough *kikohozi* kee·koh·*hoh*·zee
cough medicine *dawa la kukohoa*
da·wa la koo·koh·*hoh*·a
count *-hesabu* ·hay·*sa*·boo
counter (at bar) *kaunta* ka·*oon*·ta
country *nchi* n·*chee*
countryside *nyika* *nyee*·ka
coupon *kuponi* koo·*pohn*·ee

courgette *mumunye ya kula*
moo·*moo*·nyay ya *koo*·la
court (legal) *mahakama* ma·ha·*ka*·ma
court (tennis) *kiwanja* kee·*wan*·ja
cover charge *bei ya kuingia*
bay ya koo·een·*gee*·a
cow *ng'ombe* ng·*ohm*·bay
cracker (biscuit) *mkate mkavu*
m·*ka*·tay m·*ka*·voo
crafts *vitu vya sanaa* vee·too vya sa·*na*
crash *mgongano* m·gohn·*ga*·noh
crazy *mwenye kichaa* mway·nyay kee·*cha*
cream *mtindi* m·*teen*·dee
credit *mkopo* m·*koh*·poh
credit card *kadi ya benki*
ka·dee ya *bayn*·kee
crocodile *mamba* *mam*·ba
crop *zao* *za*·oh
cross (religious) *msalaba* m·sa·*la*·ba
crowded *ya kujazana* ya koo·ja·*za*·na
cucumber *tango* *tan*·goh
cup *kikombe* kee·*kohm*·bay
cupboard *kabati* ka·ba·*tee*
currency exchange *kubadilisha hela*
koo·ba·dee·*lee*·sha *hay*·la
current (electricity) *mkondo* m·*kohn*·doh
curry *bizari* bee·*za*·ree
custom (tradition) *mila* *mee*·la
customs *forodha* foh·*roh*·dha
cut *-kata* ·*ka*·ta
cutlery *visu* *vee*·soo
CV *maelezo binafsi ya ujuzi*
ma·ay·*lay*·zoh bee·*naf*·see ya oo·*joo*·zee
cycle *-panda baisikeli*
·*pan*·da ba·ee·see·*kay*·lee
cycling *kupanda baisikeli*
koo·*pan*·da ba·ee·see·*kay*·lee
cyclist *mpanda baisikeli*
m·*pan*·da ba·ee·see·*kay*·lee
cystitis *kuvimba kibofu*
koo·*veem*·ba kee·*boh*·foo

D

dad *baba* *ba*·ba
daily *kila siku* kee·la *see*·koo
dance *-cheza densi* ·*chay*·za dayn·see
dancing *densi* dayn·see
dangerous *hatari* ha·*ta*·ree
dark (at night) *giza* *gee*·za
dark (of colour) *nyeusi* nyay·*oo*·see
date (appointment) *miadi* mee·*a*·dee

date (fruit) *tende* tayn·day
date (day) *tarehe* ta·*ray*·hay
date (a person) -*wa marafiki*
·wa ma·ra·*fee*·kee
date of birth *tarehe ya kuzaliwa*
ta·*ray*·hay ya koo·za·*lee*·wa
daughter *binti* been·tee
dawn *kucha* koo·cha
day *siku* see·koo
(the) day after tomorrow *kesho kutwa*
kay·shoh koot·wa
(the) day before yesterday *juzi* joo·zee
dead *amekufa* a·may·koo·fa
deaf *ziwi* zee·wee
December *mwezi wa kumi na mbili*
mway·zee wa koo·mee na m·*bee*·lee
decide -*amua* ·a·*moo*·a
deep -*refu* ·*ray*·foo
deforestation *kuharibu misitu*
koo·ha·*ree*·boo mee·*see*·too
degrees (temperature) *nyuzi* nyoo·zee
delay *ucheleweshaji*
oo·chay·lay·way·*sha*·jee
deliver -*fikisha* ·fee·kee·sha
democracy *demokrasia*
day·moh·*kra*·see·a
demonstration (protest) *maandamano*
ma·an·da·*ma*·noh
Denmark *Denmarki* dayn·*mar*·kee
dental floss *uzi wa meno*
oo·zee wa *may*·noh
dentist *daktari wa meno*
dak·*ta*·ree wa *may*·noh
deodorant *diodorani* dee·oh·doh·*ra*·ne
depart -*ondoka* ·ohn·*doh*·ka
department store *duka lenye vitu vingi*
doo·ka *lay*·nyay vee·too veen·gee
departure *kuondoka* koo·ohn·*doh*·ka
departure gate *mlango wa kuondoka*
m·*lan*·goh wa koo·ohn·*doh*·ka
deposit (bank) *amana* a·*ma*·na
desert *jangwa* jan·gwa
design *rasimu* ra·*see*·moo
dessert *kitindamlo* kee·teen·da·m·loh
destination *kifiko* kee·*fee*·koh
details *vipengele* vee·payn·*gay*·lay
diabetes *kisukari* kee·soo·*ka*·ree
dial tone *mlio wa simu*
m·*lee*·oh wa *see*·moo
diaper *nepi* nay·pee
diaphragm (contraceptive) *kiwambo
cha kizuia mimba* kee·*wam*·boh cha
kee·zoo·*ee*·a *meem*·ba

diarrhoea *kuhara* koo·*ha*·ra
diary *kitabu cha kumbukumbu*
kee·*ta*·boo cha koom·boo·*koom*·boo
dice *dadu* da·doo
dictionary *kamusi* ka·*moo*·see
die -*fa* ·fa
diet ⓝ *mlo* m·loh
different *tofauti* to·fa·oo·tee
difficult *vigumu* vee·*goo*·moo
digital *dijiti* dee·*jee*·tee
dining car *bogi la kulia chakula*
boh·gee la koo·*lee*·a cha·*koo*·la
dinner *chakula cha jioni*
cha·*koo*·la cha jee·*oh*·nee
direct *moja kwa moja* moh·ja kwa *moh*·ja
direct dial *kupiga simu moja kwa moja*
koo·*pee*·ga see·moo moh·ja kwa *moh*·ja
direction *uelekeo* oo·ay·lay·*kay*·oh
director *mkurugenzi* m·koo·roo·*gayn*·zee
dirty *chafu* cha·foo
disabled *wasiojiweza*
wa·see·oh·jee·*way*·za
disco *disko* dees·koh
discount *punguzo* poon·*goo*·zoh
discrimination *ubaguzi* oo·ba·*goo*·zee
disease *maradhi* ma·ra·dhee
dish *chakula* cha·*koo*·la
disk *diski* dee·skee
disk (floppy) *disketi* dees·*kay*·tee
diving *kuzamia* koo·za·*mee*·a
diving equipment *vifaa vya kuzamia*
vee·fa vya koo·za·*mee*·a
divorced *kutalikiwa* koo·ta·lee·*kee*·wa
dizziness *kizunguzungu*
kee·zoon·goo·*zoon*·goo
do -*fanya* ·*fa*·nya
doctor *daktari* dak·*ta*·ree
documentary (film) *filamu ya hali halisi*
fee·la·moo ya ha·lee ha·lee·see
dog *mbwa* m·bwa
dole *posho* poh·shoh
doll *mwanasesere* mwa·na·say·*say*·ray
dollar *dola* doh·la
door *mlango* m·*lan*·goh
dope (drugs) *madawa ya kulevya*
ma·*da*·wa ya koo·*lay*·vya
double *mbilimbili* m·bee·lee·m·*bee*·lee
double bed *kitanda cha watu wawili*
kee·*tan*·da cha wa·too wa·*wee*·lee
double room *chumba cha watu wawili*
choom·ba cha wa·too wa·*wee*·lee
down *chini* chee·nee
downhill *kwa kuteremka*
kwa koo·tay·*raym*·ka

dozen *kumi na mbili*
koo·mee na m-*bee*-lee
drama *hadithi kama riwaya*
ha-*dee*-thee ka-ma ree-*wa*-ya
dream *ndoto* n-*doh*-toh
dress *vazi* va-zee
dried *ya kukaushwa* ya koo-ka-*oosh*-wa
dried fruit *matunda yaliyokaushwa*
ma-*toon*-da ya-lee-yoh-ka-*oosh*-wa
drink ⓝ *kinywaji* kee-*nywa*-jee
drink -*nywa* -nywa
drink (alcoholic) ⓝ *pombe* pohm-bay
drive -*endesha* -ayn-*day*-sha
drivers license *leseni ya kuendesha gari*
lay-*say*-nee ya koo-ayn-*day*-sha *ga*-ree
drug *dawa* da-wa
drug addiction *utegemezi wa madawa ya kulevya* oo-tay-gay-*may*-zee wa ma-*da*-wa ya koo-*lay*-vya
drug dealer *mwuzaji wa madawa ya kulevya* mwoo-za-jee wa ma-*da*-wa ya koo-*lay*-vya
drug trafficking
kuuza madawa ya kulevya
koo-oo-za ma-*da*-wa ya koo-*lay*-vya
drug user *mtumiaji wa madawa ya kulevya* m-too-mee-*a*-jee wa ma-*da*-wa ya koo-*luy*-vya
(illegal) drugs *madawa (ya kulevya)*
ma-*da*-wa (ya koo-*lay*-vya)
drum *ngoma* n-*goh*-ma
(be) drunk -*lewa* -*lay*-wa
dry -*kausha* -ka-oo-sha
dry ⓐ *kavu* ka-voo
duck *bata* ba-ta
dummy (pacifier) *nyonyo bandia*
nyoh-nyoh ban-*dee*-a
DVD *dvd* dee-vee-*dee*

E

each *kila* kee-la
ear *sikio* see-*kee*-oh
early *mapema* ma-*pay*-ma
earn -*pata* -pa-ta
earplugs *vizibo vya masikio*
vee-zee-boh vya ma-see-*kee*-oh
earrings *herini* hay-ree-nee
Earth *Dunia* doo-nee-a
earthquake *tetemeko la ardhi*
tay-tay-*may*-koh la ar-dhee
east *masikari* ma-sha-*ree*-kee

East Africa *Afrika ya Mashariki*
a-*free*-ka ya ma-sha-*ree*-kee
Easter *Pasaka* pa-*sa*-ka
easy *rahisi* ra-hee-see
eat -*la* -la
economy class *daraja la tatu*
da-*ra*-ja la *ta*-too
ecstasy (drug) *ekstasi* ayk-sta-see
eczema *ukurutu* oo-koo-roo-too
education *elimu* ay-lee-moo
egg *yai* ya-ee
eggplant *biringani* bee-reen-*ga*-nee
election *uchaguzi* oo-cha-goo-zee
electrical store *duka la bidhaa za umeme*
doo-ka la bee-*dha*-za oo-*may*-may
electricity *umeme* oo-*may*-may
elephant *ndovu/tembo*
n-*doh*-voo/*taym*-boh
elevator *lifti* leef-tee
email *barua pepe* ba-*roo*-a *pay*-pay
embarrassment *aibu* a-ee-boo
embassy *ubalozi* oo-ba-*loh*-zee
emergency *dharura* dha-*roo*-ra
emotional *mwenye hisia*
rnway-nyay hee-*see*-a
employee *mfanyakazi* m-fa-nya-*ka*-zce
employer *mwajiri* mwa-*jee*-ree
empty *tupu* too-poo
end *mwisho* mwee-shoh
endangered species *spishi zilizo hatarini*
spee-shee zee-*lee*-zoh ha-ta-*ree*-nee
(I'm) engaged *nimechumbiwa*
nee-may-choom-*bee*-wa
engagement (to be married)
uchumba oo-*choom*-ba
engine *injini* een-*jee*-nee
engineer *mhandisi* m-han-*dee*-see
engineering *uhandisi* oo-han-*dee*-see
England *Uingereza* oo-een-gay-*ray*-za
English (language) *Kiingereza*
kee-een-gay-*ray*-za
enjoy oneself -*furahia* -foo-ra-*hee*-a
enough *ya kutosha* ya koo-*toh*-sha
enter -*ingia* -een-*gee*-a
entertainment guide
mwongozo wa burudani
mwohn-*goh*-zoh wa boo-roo-*da*-nee
entry (access) *mwingilio* mween-gee-*lee*-oh
envelope *bahasha* ba-ha-sha
environment *mazingira* ma-zeen-*gee*-ra
epilepsy *kifafa* kee-*fa*-fa
equal opportunity *fursa sawa* foor-sa *sa*-wa
equality *usawa* oo-*sa*-wa

equipment *vifaa* vee-*fa*

escalator *eskaleta* ays-ka-*lay*-ta

estate agency *wakala wa shamba* wa-*ka*-la wa *sham*-ba

Ethiopia *Uhabeshi* oo-ha-*bay*-shee

euro *euro* ay-oo-roh

Europe *Ulaya* oo-*la*-ya

euthanasia *eutanasia* ay-oo-ta-*na*-see-a

evening *jioni* jee-oh-nee

every *kila* *kee*-la

everyone *wote* *woh*-tay

everything *kila kitu* *kee*-la *kee*-too

exactly *kamili* ka-*mee*-lee

example *mfano* m-*fa*-noh

excellent *barabara* ba-*ra*-ba-ra

excess baggage *mizigo ziada* mee-*zee*-goh zee-*a*-da

exchange -*badilisha* -ba-dee-*lee*-sha

exchange rate *kiwango cha kubadilishia fedha* kee-*wan*-goh cha koo-ba-dee-*lee*-shee-a *fay*-dha

excluded *ya kuachwa* ya koo-*ach*-wa

exhaust (car) *mchemuo* m-chay-*moo*-oh

exhibition *maonyesho* ma-oh-*nyay*-shoh

exit *kutoka* koo-*toh*-ka

expensive *ghali* *ga*-lee

experience *uzoefu* oo-zoh-*ay*-foo

exploitation *utumiaji* oo-too-mee-*a*-jee

express ⓐ *ekspres* ayk-*sprays*

express mail *barua ya haraka* ba-*roo*-a ya ha-*ra*-ka

extension (visa) *uongezaji wa visa* oo-ohn-gay-*za*-jee wa *vee*-sa

eye *jicho* jee-*choh*

eye drops *matone ya macho* ma-*toh*-nay ya ma-choh

eyes *macho* ma-choh

F

fabric *kitambaa* kee-tam-*ba*

face (body) *uso* oo-soh

face cloth *kitambaa cha mkono* kee-tam-*ba* cha m-*koh*-noh

factory *kiwanda* kee-*wan*-da

factory worker *mfanyakazi wa kiwandani* m-fa-nya-*ka*-zee wa kee-wan-*da*-nee

fall (autumn) *kipindi cha baridi kidogo* kee-*peen*-dee cha ba-*ree*-dee kee-*doh*-goh

fall (down) -*anguka* -an-*goo*-ka

family *familia* fa-mee-*lee*-a

family name *jina la familia* *jee*-na la fa-mee-*lee*-a

famous *maarufu* ma-a-*roo*-foo

fan (machine) *feni* fay-nee

fan (sport, etc) *mshabiki* m-sha-*bee*-kee

fanbelt *mkanda wa feni* m-*kan*-da wa *fay*-nee

far *mbali* m-*ba*-lee

fare *nauli* na-oo-lee

farm *shamba* *sham*-ba

farmer *mkulima* m-koo-*lee*-ma

fashion *mtindo* m-*teen*-doh

fast *ya kasi* ya *ka*-see

fat ⓐ *nene* nay-nay

father *baba* *ba*-ba

father-in-law *babamkwe* ba-ba-*m*-kway

(someone's) fault *kosa* *koh*-sa

faulty *yenye kosa* yay-nyay *koh*-sa

fax machine *faksi* *fak*-see

February *mwezi wa pili* *mway*-zee wa *pee*-lee

feed -*lisha* -*lee*-sha

feel (touch) -*hisi* -*hee*-see

feeling (physical) *hisia* hee-*see*-a

feelings *hisia* hee-*see*-a

female *ya kike* ya *kee*-kay

fence *wigo* *wee*-goh

ferry *kivuko* kee-*voo*-koh

festival *tamasha* ta-*ma*-sha

fever *homa* *hoh*-ma

few *chache* cha-chay

fiancé *mchumba* m-*choom*-ba

fiancée *mchumba* m-*choom*-ba

fiction *uzushi* oo-*zoo*-shee

fig *tini* *tee*-nee

fight *pigano* pee-*ga*-noh

fill -*jaza* -*ja*-za

fillet *sarara* sa-*ra*-ra

film (cinema) *filamu* fee-*la*-moo

film (for camera) *mkanda wa picha* m-*kan*-da wa *pee*-cha

film speed *mwendo wa mkanda* *mwayn*-doh wa m-*kan*-da

filtered *ya chujwa* ya *chooj*-wa

find -*gundua* -goon-*doo*-a

fine ⓝ *faini* fa-*ee*-nee

fine ⓐ *nzuri* n-*zoo*-ree

finger *kidole* kee-*doh*-lay

finish ⓝ *mwisho* *mwee*-shoh

finish -*maliza* -ma-*lee*-za

Finland *Ufini* oo-*fee*-nee

fire *moto* *moh*-toh

firewood *kuni* koo·nee
first *ya kwanza* ya kwan·za
first class *daraja ya kwanza* da·ra·ja la kwan·za
first-aid kit *kisanduku cha huduma ya kwanza* kee·san·doo·koo cha hoo·doo·ma ya kwan·za
first name *jina la kwanza* jee·na la kwan·za
fish *samaki* sa·ma·kee
fishing *uvuvi* oo·voo·vee
fish shop *duka la samaki* doo·ka la sa·ma·kee
flag *bendera* bayn·day·ra
flamingo *heroe* hay·roh·ay
flashlight (torch) *tochi* toh·chee
flat ⓝ *fleti* flay·tee
flat ⓐ *tambalale* tam·ba·la·lay
flea *kiroboto* kee·roh·boh·toh
fleamarket *mnada* m·na·da
flight (of a bird) *mruko* m·roo·koh
flight (plane) *ndeye* n·day·gay
flood *mafuriko* ma·foo·ree·koh
floor *sakafu* sa·ka·foo
floor (storey) *ghorofa* go·ro·fa
florist *duka la maua* doo·ka la ma·oo·a
flour *unga* oon·ga
flower *ua* oo·a
flu *fluu* floo
fly *-ruka* ·roo·ka
fog *ukungu* oo·koon·goo
follow *-fuata* foo·a·ta
food *chakula* cha·koo·la
food supplies *akiba za chakula* a·kee·ba za cha·koo·la
food vendor *mwuzaji wa chakula* mwoo·za·jee wa cha·koo·la
foot *mguu* m·goo
football (soccer) *soka* soh·ka
footpath *njia ya miguu* n·jee·a ya mee·goo
foreign *ya kigeni* ya kee·gay·nee
forest *msitu* m·see·too
forever *milele* mee·lay·lay
forget *-sahau* ·sa·ha·oo
forgive *-samehe* ·sa·may·hay
fork *uma* oo·ma
fortnight *wiki mbili* wee·kee m·bee·lee
fortune teller *mtabiri* m·ta·bee·ree
foul (sport) *faulo* fa·oo·loh
foyer *sebule* say·boo·lay
fragile *ya kuvunjika kirahisi* ya koo·voon·jee·ka kee·ra·hee·see

France *Ufaransa* oo·fa·ran·sa
free (available) *kupatikana* koo·pa·tee·ka·na
free (gratis) *bure* boo·ray
free (not bound) *huru* hoo·roo
freeze *-ganda* ·gan·da
fresh *bichi* bee·chee
Friday *Ijumaa* ee·joo·ma
fridge *friji* free·jee
fried *ya kukaangwa* ya koo·ka·an·gwa
friend *rafiki* ra·fee·kee
from *kutoka* koo·toh·ka
frost *sakitu* sa·kee·too
frozen *ya kugandwa* ya koo·gan·dwa
fruit *tunda* toon·da
fry *-kaanga* ·ka·an·ga
frying pan *kikaango* kee·ka·an·goh
full *ya kujaa* ya koo·ja
full-time *ya muda kamili* ya moo·da ka·mee·lee
fun *burudani* boo·roo·da·nee
funeral *kilio* kee·lee·oh
funny *ya kuchekesha* ya koo·chay·kay·sha
furniture *fenicha* fay·nee·cha
future ⓝ *mbeleni* m·bay·lay·nee

G

game (sport) *mchezo* m·chay·zoh
game park *hifadhi ya wanyama* hee·fa·dhee ya wa·nya·ma
garage *gereji* gay·ray·jee
garbage *takataka* ta·ka·ta·ka
garbage can *pipa la taka* pee·pee la ta·ka
garden *bustani* boo·sta·nee
gardener *mtunza bustani* m·toon·za boo·sta·nee
gardening *kilimo cha bustani* kee·lee·moh cha boo·sta·nee
garlic *kitunguu saumu* kee·toon·goo sa·oo·moo
gas (for cooking) *mafuta ya taa* ma·foo·ta ya ta
gas (petrol) *mafuta* ma·foo·ta
gas cartridge *mtungi wa gesi* m·toon·gee wa gay·see
gate (airport, etc) *mlango* m·lan·goh
gauze *shashi* sha·shee
gay *msenge* m·sayn·gay
gazelle *swala* swa·la
Germany *Ujerumani* oo·jay·roo·ma·nee
get *-pata* ·pa·ta

get off (a train, etc) -shuka ·shoo·ka
gift zawadi za·wa·dee
gig (musical) onyesho oh·nyay·shoh
giraffe twiga twee·ga
girl msichana m·see·cha·na
girlfriend mpenzi m·payn·zee
give -pa ·pa
given name jina la kwanza
   jee·na la kwan·za
glandular fever homa ya matezi
   hoh·ma ya ma·tay·zee
glass (drinking) glesi glay·see
glasses (spectacles) miwani mee·wa·nee
gloves maglavu ma·gla·voo
glue gundi goon·dee
go -enda ·ayn·da
go out -enda nje ·ayn·da n·jay
go out with -rafikiana ·ra·fee·kee·a·na
go shopping -enda dukani
   ·ayn·da doo·ka·nee
goal goli goh·lee
goalkeeper kipa kee·pa
goat mbuzi m·boo·zee
God Mungu moon·goo
goggles (swimming) miwani ya kuogelea
   mee·wa·nee ya koo·oh·gay·lay·a
gold dhahabu dha·ha·boo
golf ball mpira wa gofu
   m·pee·ra wa goh·foo
golf course uwanja wa gofu
   oo·wan·ja wa goh·foo
good nzuri n·zoo·ree
government serikali say·ree·ka·lee
gram gramu gra·moo
grandchild mjukuu m·joo·koo
grandfather babu ba·boo
grandmother bibi bee·bee
grapefruit balungi ba·loon·gee
grapes zabibu za·bee·boo
grass nyasi nya·see
grateful mwenye shukrani
   mway·nyay shook·ra·nee
grave kaburi ka·boo·ree
gray kijivu kee·jee·voo
great (fantastic) nzuri sana
   n·zoo·ree sa·na
green kijani kee·ja·nee
greengrocer duka la mboga
   doo·ka la m·boh·ga
grey kijivu kee·jee·voo
groceries vyakula vya·koo·la
groundnut karanga ka·ran·ga
grow -mea ·may·a

guarantee dhamana dha·ma·na
guess -buni ·boo·nee
guesthouse gesti gay·stee
guide (audio) mwongozo wa sauti
   mwohn·goh·zoh (wa sa·oo·tee)
guide (person) kiongozi kee·ohn·goh·zee
guide dog mbwa wa kuongoza
   m·bwa wa koo·ohn·goh·za
guidebook kitabu cha mwongozo
   kee·ta·boo cha mwohn·goh·zoh
guided tour safari yenye kiongozi
   sa·fa·ree yay·nyay kee·ohn·goh·zee
guilty mwenye hatia mway·nyay ha·tee·a
guitar zeze zay·zay
gum mpira m·pee·ra
gun bunduki boon·doo·kee
gym (fitness room) ukumbi oo·koom·bee
gymnastics sarakasi sa·ra·ka·see
gynaecologist daktari wa akina mama
   dak·ta·ree wa a·kee·na ma·ma

H

hair nywele nyway·lay
hairbrush burashi ya nywele
   boo·ra·shee ya nyway·lay
haircut kukata nywele
   koo·ka·ta nyway·lay
hairdresser msusi m·soo·see
halal halali ha·la·lee
half nusu noo·soo
hallucination wazimu wa·zee·moo
ham nyama nguruwe
   nya·ma n·goo·roo·way
hammer nyundo nyoon·doh
hammock machela ma·chay·la
hand mkono m·koh·noh
handbag mkoba m·koh·ba
handball mpira wa mikono
   m·pee·ra wa mee·koh·noh
handicrafts kazi ya mikono
   ka·zee ya mee·koh·noh
handkerchief kitambaa cha mkono
   kee·tam·ba cha m·koh·noh
handlebars usukani pl oo·soo·ka·nee
handmade kutengenezwa kwa mkono
   koo·tayn·gay·nayz·wa kwa m·koh·noh
handsome mrembo m·raym·boh
happy mwenye furaha
   mway·nyay foo·ra·ha
harassment usumbufu oo·soom·boo·foo
harbour bandari ban·da·ree

hard (not soft) *ngumu* n·*goo*·moo
hard-boiled egg *yai lililochemshwa*
  ya·ee lee·lee·loh·*chaym*·shwa
hardware store *duka la vifaa vya ujenzi*
  doo·ka la vee·*fa* vya oo·*jayn*·zee
hash *bangi ban·gee*
hat *kofia* koh·*fee*·a
have *-wa na* ·wa na
have a cold *-wa mgonjwa*
  ·wa m·*gohn*·jwa
have fun *-furahia* ·foo·ra·*hee*·a
hawker *mchuuzi* m·choo·oo·zee
hay fever *homa ya mzio*
  hoh·ma ya m·zee·oh
he *yeye* yay·yay
head *kichwa* keech·wa
headache *maumivu ya kichwa*
  ma·oo·*mee*·voo ya *keech*·wa
headlights *taa za mbele* ta za m·*bay*·lay
health *afya* af·ya
hear *-sikia* ·see·*kee*·a
hearing aid *chombo cha kusaidia kusikia*
  chohm·boh cha koo·sa·ee·*dee*·a
  koo·see·*kee*·a
heart *moyo* moh·*yoh*
heart attack *kushambuliwa na maradhi*
  ya moyo koo·sham·boo·lee·wa na
  ma·*ra*·dhee ya *moh*·yoh
heart condition *ugonjwa wa moyo*
  oo·*gohn*·jwa wa *moh*·yoh
heat *joto* joh·*toh*
heated *ya moto* ya *moh*·toh
heater *kipasha moto* kee·*pa*·sha *moh*·toh
heating *joto* joh·toh
heavy *nzito* n·*zee*·toh
helmet *helmeti* hayl·*may*·tee
help ⓝ *msaada* m·sa·*a*·da
help *-saidia* ·sa·ee·*dee*·a
hepatitis *uvimbi wa ini*
  oo·*veem*·bee wa ee·nee
her (ownership) *yake* ya·kay
herbs *mboga za majani*
  m·*boh*·ga za ma·*ja*·nee
herbalist *mganga wa madawa ya*
  kienyeji m·*gan*·ga wa ma·*da*·wa ya
  kee·*ay*·*nyay*·jee
here *hapa* ha·pa
heroin *heroini* hay·roh·*ee*·nee
high *juu* joo
high school *shule ya msingi*
  shoo·lay ya m·*seen*·gee
highchair *kiti juu cha mtoto*
  kee·tee joo cha m·*toh*·toh

highway *barabara* ba·ra·*ba*·ra
hike *-tembea porini*
  ·*taym*·*bay*·a poh·*ree*·nee
hiking *kutembea porini*
  kou·taym·*bay*·a poh·*ree*·nee
hiking boots *mabuti ya kutembea*
  porini ma·*boo*·tee ya koo·taym·*bay*·a
  poh·*ree*·nee
hiking route *njia ya kutembea porini*
  n·*jee*·a ya koo·taym·*bay*·a poh·*ree*·nee
hill *mlima* m·*lee*·ma
Hindu *Mhindu* m·*heen*·doo
hippopotamus *kiboko* kee·*boh*·koh
hire *-kodi* ·*koh*·dee
his *yake* ya·kay
historical *ya kihistoria*
  ya kee·hee·stoh·*ree*·a
history *historia* hee·stoh·*ree*·a
hitchhike *-omba lifti* ·ohm·ba *leef*·tee
HIV *VVU* vee·vee·*yno*
holiday *sikukuu* see·koo·*koo*
holidays *likizo* lee·kee·zoh
home *nyumbani* nyoom·*ba*·nee
home brew *pombe ya kienyeji*
  pohm·bay ya kee·*ay*·*nyay*·jee
homeless *bila nyumba* bee·la nyoom·ha
homemaker *mke anayekaa nyumbani*
  m·kay a·na·*yay*·*ka* nyoom·*ba*·nee
homosexual *msenge* m·*sayn*·gay
honey *asali* a·*sa*·lee
honeymoon *fungu* foon·*ga*·tay
hoodlum *mhuni* m·*hoo*·nee
horn *honi* hoh·nee
horoscope *falaki* fa·*la*·kee
horse *farasi* fa·*ra*·see
horse riding *kupanda farasi*
  koo·*pan*·da fa·*ra*·see
hospital *hospitali* hoh·spee·*ta*·lee
hospitality *ukarimu* oo·ka·*ree*·moo
hot *joto* joh·toh
hot water *maji ya moto*
  ma·jee ya *moh*·toh
hotel *gesti* gay·stee
hour *saa* sa
house *nyumba* nyoom·ba
housework *kazi ya nyumbani*
  ka·zee ya nyum·*ba*·nee
how *namna* nam·na
how much *kiasi gani* kee·*a*·see *ga*·nee
hug *-kumbatia* ·koom·ba·*tee*·a
huge *kubwa sana* koob·wa *sa*·na
human resources *uwezo wa watu*
  oo·*way*·zoh wa *wa*·too

human rights *haki za binadamu*
ha·kee za be·na·*da*·moo
humanities *sayansi za jamii*
sa·*yan*·see za ja·*mee*
hundred *mia* mee·a
hunger *njaa* n·*ja*
hunting *uwindaji* oo·ween·*da*·jee
hurt *-uma* ·oo·ma
husband *mume* moo·may
hyena *fisi* fee·see

I

I *mimi* mee·mee
ice *barafu* ba·*ra*·foo
ice axe *kishota cha kukatia barafu*
kee·*shoh*·ta cha koo·ka·*tee*·a ba·*ra*·foo
ice cream *aiskrimu* a·ee·skree·moo
ice hockey *hoki ya barafuni*
hoh·kee ya ba·ra·foo·nee
identification card (ID) *kitambulisho*
kee·tam·boo·*lee*·shoh
idiot *mjinga* m·jeen·ga
if *kama* ka·ma
ill *mgonjwa* m·gohn·jwa
immigration *uhamiaji* oo·ha·mee·*a*·jee
impala *swalapala* swa·la·*pa*·la
important *muhimu* moo·*hee*·moo
impossible *haiwezekani*
ha·ee·way·zay·*ka*·nee
in *katika* ka·*tee*·ka
in a hurry *kwa haraka* kwa ha·*ra*·ka
in front of *mbele ya* m·*bay*·lay ya
included *ndani yake* n·*da*·nee ya·kay
income tax *kodi ya mapato*
koh·dee ya ma·*pa*·toh
India *Uhindi* oo·heen·dee
Indian Ocean *Bahari Hindi*
ba·*ha*·ree heen·dee
indicator *kionyeshi* kee·oh·*nyay*·shee
indigestion *kuvimbiwa* koo·veem·*bee*·wa
indoor *ndani* n·*da*·nee
industry *kiwanda* kee·*wan*·da
infection *ambukizo* am·boo·kee·zoh
inflammation *uvimbe* oo·veem·bay
influenza *fluu* floo
information *taarifa* ta·a·*ree*·fa
ingredient *kiambato* kee·am·*ba*·toh
inject *-choma sindano* ·*choh*·ma seen·*da*·noh
injection *dawa la sindano*
da·wa la seen·*da*·noh
injury *jeraha* jay·*ra*·ha
inner tube *tyubu* tyoo·boo

innocent *asiye na hatia* a·*see*·yay na ha·*tee*·a
inside *ndani* n·*da*·nee
instructor *mwalimu* mwa·*lee*·moo
insurance *bima* bee·ma
interesting *ya kuvutia* ya koo·voo·*tee*·a
intermission *mapumziko*
ma·poom·zee·koh
international *ya kimataifa*
ya kee·ma·ta·*ee*·fa
Internet *mtandao wa kompyuta*
m·tan·*da*·oh wa kohm·*pyoo*·ta
Internet café *intanet kafe*
een·ta·*nayt* ka·*fay*
interpreter *mkalimani* m·ka·lee·*ma*·nee
interview *mahojiano* ma·hoh·jee·*a*·noh
invite *-karibisha* ·ka·ree·*bee*·sha
Ireland *Irelandi* ee·ray·*layn*·dee
iron (for clothes) *pasi* pa·see
island *kisiwa* kee·*see*·wa
Israel *Israeli* ees·ra·*ay*·lee
it *hii* hee
IT *teknolojia ya maarifa*
tayk·noh·loh·*jee*·a ya ma·a·*ree*·fa
Italy *Italia* ee·*ta*·lee·a
itch *mwasho* mwa·shoh
itemised *kuandikwa kitu kimoja kimoja*
koo·an·*deek*·wa kee·too kee·*moh*·ja
kee·*moh*·jah
itinerary *ratiba ya safari*
ra·*tee*·ba ya sa·*fa*·ree
IUD *kitanzi cha kuzuia kuzaa*
kee·*tan*·zee cha koo·zoo·*ee*·a koo·*za*

J

jacket *jaketi* ja·*kay*·tee
jail *gereza* gay·*ray*·za
jam *jamu* ja·moo
January *mwezi wa kwanza*
mway·zee wa *kwan*·za
Japan *Japani* ja·*pa*·nee
jar *chupa* choo·pa
jaw *taya* ta·ya
jealous *mwenye wivu*
mway·nyay wee·voo
jeans *jinzi* jeen·zee
jeep *jipi* jee·pee
jet lag *kizunguzungu cha saa*
kutokana na kusafiri kwa ndege
kee·zoon·goo·*zoon*·goo cha sa
koo·toh·*ka*·na na koo·sa·*fee*·ree kwa
n·*day*·gay

jewellery *vipuli* vee·poo·lee
jewellery store *duka la vipuli*
doo·ka la vee·poo·lee
Jewish *Myahudi* m·ya·hoo·dee
job *kazi* ka·zee
jogging *kukimbia taratibu*
koo·keem·bee·a ta·ra·tee·boo
joke *soga* soh·ga
journalist *mwandishi wa habari*
mwan·dee·shee wa ha·ba·ree
journey *safari* sa·fa·ree
judge *hakimu* ha·kee·moo
juice *jusi* joo·see
July *mwezi wa saba* mway·zee wa sa·ba
jump *-ruka* ·roo·ka
jumper (sweater) *sweta* sway·ta
jumper leads *kebo za kuwashia*
kay·boh za koo·wa·shee·a
June *mwezi wa sita* mway·zee wa see·ta

K

Kenya *Kenya* kayn·ya
ketchup *mchuzi wa nyanya*
m·choo·zee wa nya·nya
key *ufunguo* oo·foon·goo·oh
keyboard *kichapishi* kee·cha·pee·shee
kick *-piga teke* ·pee·ga tay·kay
kidney *figo* fee·goh
kilogram *kilo* kee·loh
kilometre *kilomita* kee·loh·mee·ta
kind (nice) *mkarimu* m·ka·ree·moo
kindergarten *chekechea* chay·kay·chay·a
king *mfalme* m·fal·may
kiosk *kioski* kee·oh·skee
kiss ⓝ *busu* boo·soo
kiss *-busu* ·boo·soo
kitchen *jiko* jee·koh
knee *goti* goh·tee
knife *kisu* kee·soo
know *-jua* ·joo·a
kosher *halali* ha·la·lee

L

labourer *mfanyakazi* m·fa·nya·ka·zee
laces *kamba za viatu* kam·ba za vee·a·too
lake *ziwa* zee·wa
lamb *mwanakondoo* mwa·na·kohn·doh
land *ardhi* ar·dhee
landlady/landlord *mwenye nyumba*
mway·nyay nyoom·ba

language *lugha* loo·gha
laptop *kompyuta ya kubeba*
kohm·pyoo·ta ya koo·bay·ba
large *kubwa* koob·wa
last (previous) *ya kabla* ya kab·la
last (final) *ya mwisho* ya mwee·shoh
last week *wiki iliyopita*
wee·kee ee·lee·yoh·pee·ta
late *ya kuchelewa* ya koo·chay·lay·wa
later *baadaye* ba·a·da·yay
laugh *-cheka* ·chay·ka
launderette *dobi* doh·bee
laundry (clothes) *nguo kufua*
n·goo·oh koo·foo·a
laundry (place) *udobi* oo·doh·bee
laundry (room) *chumba cha dobi*
choom·ba cha doh·bee
law *sheria* shay·ree·a
lawyer *mwanasheria* mwa·na·shay·ree·a
laxative *dawa la kuendesha*
da·wa la koo·ayn·day·sha
lazy *mvivu* m·vee·voo
leader *kiongozi* kee·ohn·goh·zee
leaf *jani* ja·nee
learn *-jifunza* ·jee·foon·za
leather *ngozi* n·goh·zee
lecturer *mhadhiri* m·ha·dhee·ree
ledge *mwamba* mwam·ba
left (direction) *kushoto* koo·shoh·toh
left luggage *mizigo iliyowekwa*
mee·zee·goh ee·lee·yoh·wayk·wa
left-luggage office *chumba cha kuwekea
mizigo* choom·ba cha koo·way·kay·a
mee·zee·goh
left-wing *mrengo wa kushoto*
m·rayn·goh wa koo·shoh·toh
leg *mguu* m·goo
legal *halali* ha·la·lee
legislation *sheria* shay·ree·a
legume *kundekunde* koon·day·koon·day
lemon *limau* lee·ma·oo
lemonade *maji ya limau*
ma·jee ya lee·ma·oo
leopard *chui* choo·ee
lens (eye) *mboni* m·boh·nee
lentil *dengu* dayn·goo
lesbian *msagaji* m·sa·ga·jee
less *chache* cha·chay
letter (mail) *barua* ba·roo·a
lettuce *saladi* sa·la·dee
liar *mwongo* mwohn·goh
library *maktaba* mak·ta·ba
lice *chawa* cha·wa

license *laiseni* la·ee·*say*·nee
licence plate number *namba ya gari* nam·ba ya *ga*·ree
lie (not stand) *-lala* ·*la*·la
life *maisha* ma·ee·sha
life jacket *jaketi la kuokolea* ja·*kay*·tee la koo·oh·koh·*lay*·a
lift (elevator) *lifti* *leef*·tee
light (brightness) *mwanga* mwan·ga
light (lamp) *taa* ta
light (colour) *nyeupe* nyay·oo·pay
light (not heavy) *nyepesi* nyay·*pay*·see
light bulb *balbu ya taa* bal·boo ya ta
light meter *kipima mwanga* kee·*pee*·ma mwan·ga
lighter (match) *kibiriti* kee·bee·*ree*·tee
lighter (cigarette) *kiwashio* kee·wa·*shee*·oh
like *-penda* ·*payn*·da
lime (fruit) *ndimu* n·*dee*·moo
linen (material) *kitani* kee·*ta*·nee
linen (sheets etc) *mashuka* ma·*shoo*·ka
lion *simba* *seem*·ba
lip balm *dawa la midomo* *da*·wa la mee·*doh*·moh
lips *midomo* mee·*doh*·moh
lipstick *rangi ya mdomo* ran·gee ya m·*doh*·moh
liquor store *duka la pombe* *doo*·ka la *pohm*·bay
listen *-sikiliza* ·see·kee·*lee*·za
little (not much) *chache* cha·chay
little (small) *-dogo* ·*doh*·goh
live (somewhere) *-ishi* ·ee·shee
liver *ini* ee·nee
lizard *mjusi* m·*joo*·see
local ⓐ *ya kienyeji* ya kee·ayn·*nyay*·jee
lock ⓝ *kufuli* koo·*foo*·lee
lock *-funga kwa ufunguo* ·*foon*·ga kwa oo·foon·*goo*·oh
locked *ya kufungwa* ya koo·*foon*·gwa
lollies *pipi* *pee*·pee
long *ndefu* n·*day*·foo
look *-angalia* ·an·ga·*lee*·a
look after *-tunza* ·*toon*·za
look for *-tafuta* ·ta·*foo*·ta
lookout *lindo* *leen*·doh
loose *kejekeje* kay·jay·kay·jay
loose change *pesa kichele* *pay*·sa kee·*chay*·lay
lose *-potea* ·poh·*tay*·a
lost *ya kupotezwa* ya koo·poh·*tayz*·wa

lost property office *chumba cha mali ya kuokota* choom·ba cha ma·lee ya koo·oh·koh·ta
(a) lot *nyingi* nyeen·gee
loud ⓝ *kwa sauti* kwa sa·oo·tee
love ⓝ *upendo* oo·payn·doh
love ⓥ *-penda* ·*payn*·da
lover *mpenzi* m·*payn*·zee
low *chini* *chee*·nee
lubricant *kilainishio* kee·la·ee·nee·shee·oh
luck *bahati* ba·*ha*·tee
lucky *mwenye bahati* mway·nyay ba·*ha*·tee
luggage *mizigo* mee·zee·goh
luggage locker *sanduku la kuhifadhia mizigo* san·doo·koo la koo·hee·fa·dhee·a mee·zee·goh
luggage tag *tiketi ya mzigo* tee·*kay*·tee ya m·zee·goh
lump *uvimbe* oo·*veem*·bay
lunch *chakula cha mchana* cha·koo·la cha m·cha·na
lung *pafu* pa·foo
luxury *anasa* a·na·sa

M

machine *mashine* ma·*shee*·nay
Madagascar *Madagascar* ma·da·*ga*·skar
magazine *gazeti* ga·*zay*·tee
mail (letters) *barua* ba·*roo*·a
mail (postal system) *posta* poh·sta
mailbox *sanduku la posta* san·doo·koo la *poh*·sta
main *-kuu* ·koo
main road *barabara kuu* ba·ra·*ba*·ra koo
make *-tengeneza* ·tayn·gay·*nay*·za
make-up *kipodozi* kee·poh·*doh*·zee
malaria *malaria* ma·*la*·ree·a
Malawi *Malawi* ma·*la*·wee
man *mwanamume* mwa·na·*moo*·may
manager (restaurant, hotel) *meneja* may·*nay*·ja
manager (sales, sports) *mkurugenzi* m·koo·roo·*gayn*·zee
mandarin *chenza* *chayn*·za
mango *embe* aym·bay
manual worker *mfanyakazi wa kutumia mikono* m·fa·nya·*ka*·zee wa koo·too·*mee*·a mee·*koh*·noh
many *nyingi* nyeen·gee

map *ramani* ra·ma·nee
March *mwezi wa tatu*
mway·zee wa ta·too
margarine *blue bandi* bloo·ban·dee
marijuana *bangi* ban·gee
marital status *hadhi ya kindoa*
ha·dhee ya kee·n·doh·a
market *soko* soh·koh
marmalade *jamu ya machungwa*
ja·moo ya ma·choon·gwa
marriage *ndoa* n·doh·a
(I'm) married (man) *nimeoa*
nee·may·oh·a
(I'm) married (woman) *nimeolewa*
nee·may·oh·lay·wa
marry (man) *-oa* ·oh·a
marry (woman) *-olewa* ·oh·lay·wa
martial arts *mieleka* mee·ay·lay·ka
mass (Catholic) *misa* mee·sa
massage *kuchuliwa* koo·choo·lee·wa
masseur/masseuse *mchuaji* m·choo·a·jee
mat *mkeka* m·kay·ka
match (sports) *mechi* may·chee
matches (for lighting) *vibiriti*
vee·bee·ree·tee
mattress *godolo* goh·doh·loh
May *mwezi wa tano* mway·zee wa ta·noh
maybe *labda* lab·da
mayonnaise *mayonezi* ma·yoh·nay·zee
mayor *mwenyekiti* mway·nyay·kee·tee
me *mimi* mee·mee
meal *mlo* m·loh
measles *surua* soo·roo·a
meat *nyama* nya·ma
mechanic *fundi* foon·dee
media *vyombo vya habari*
vyohm·boh vya ha·ba·ree
medicine (study, profession) *udaktari*
oo·dak·ta·ree
medicine (medication) *dawa* da·wa
meditation *kutaamali* koo·ta·a·ma·lee
meet *-kuta* ·koo·ta
melon *tikiti maji* tee·kee·tee ma·jee
member *mwanachama* mwa·na·cha·ma
menstruation *hedhi* hay·dhee
menu *menyu* may·nyoo
message *ujumbe* oo·joom·bay
metal ⓝ *metali* may·ta·lee
metre *mita* mee·ta
microwave (oven) *joko la mikrowevu*
joh·koh la mee·kroh·way·voo
midday (noon) *saa sita mchana*
sa see·ta m·cha·na

midnight *saa sita usiku*
sa see·ta oo·see·koo
migraine *kipandauso* kee·pan·da·oo·soh
military ⓝ *jeshi* jay·shee
military service *kutumikia jeshi*
koo·too·mee·kee·a ja·shee
milk *maziwa* ma·zee·wa
millimetre *milimita* mee·lee·mee·ta
million *milioni* mee·lee·oh·nee
mince *nyama ya kusaga*
nya·ma ya koo·sa·ga
mineral water *maji ya madini*
ma·jee ya ma·dee·nee
minute *dakika* da·kee·ka
mirror *kioo* kee·oh
miscarriage *kuharibu mimba*
koo·ha·ree·boo meem·ba
Miss *Bibi* bee·bee
miss (feel absence of) *-kosa* ·koh·sa
mistake *kosa* koh·sa
mix *-changanyika* ·chan·ga·nyee·ka
mobile phone *simu ya mkononi*
see·moo ya m·koh·noh·nee
modem *modemu* moh·day·moo
modern *ya kisasa* ya kee·sa·sa
moisturiser *krimu ya kulainisha ngozi*
kree·moo ya koo·la·ee·nee·sha n·goh·zee
monastery *nyumba ya utawa wa*
wanaume nyoom·ba ya oo·ta·wa wa
wa·na·oo·may
Monday *Jumatatu* joo·ma·ta·too
money *pesa* pay·sa
monk *mtawa* m·ta·wa
monkey *tumbili* toom·bee·lee
month *mwezi* mway·zee
monument *mnara* m·na·ra
moon *mwezi* mway·zee
more *zaidi* za·ee·dee
morning *asubuhi* a·soo·boo·hee
morning sickness *kichefuchefu cha*
asubuhi kee·chay·foo·chay·foo cha
a·soo·boo·hee
mosque *msikiti* m·see·kee·tee
mosquito *mbu* m·boo
mosquito net *chandarua* chan·da·roo·a
motel *gesti* gay·stee
mother *mama* ma·ma
mother-in-law *mamamkwe*
ma·ma·m·kway
motorbike *pikipiki* pee·kee·pee·kee
motorboat *motaboti* moh·ta·boh·tee
motorcycle *pikipiki* pee·kee·pee·kee
motorway *barabara* ba·ra·ba·ra

mountain *mlima* m-*lee*-ma
mountain bike *baisikeli kwenye gia*
  ba-ee-see-*kay*-lee *kway*-nyay *gee*-a
mountain path *njia ya kupanda mlimani*
  n-*jee*-a ya koo-*pan*-da m-lee-*ma*-nee
mountain range *safu ya milima*
  sa-foo ya mee-*lee*-ma
mountaineering *kupanda milima*
  koo-*pan*-da mee-*lee*-ma
mouse *panya* pa-nya
mouth *mdomo* m-*doh*-moh
movie *filamu* fee-*la*-moo
Mozambique *Msumbiji* m-soom-*bee*-jee
Mr *Bwana* bwa-na
Mrs *Bi* bee
Ms (Miss) *Bibi* bee-bee
mud *matope* ma-*toh*-pay
mum *mama* ma-ma
mumps *machumbwichumbwi*
  ma-choom-bwee-*choom*-bwee
murder ⓝ *mauaji* ma-oo-*a*-jee
murder ⓥ *-ua* -oo-a
muscle *musuli* moo-*soo*-lee
museum *makumbusho*
  ma-koom-*boo*-shoh
mushroom *uyoga* oo-*yoh*-ga
music *muziki* moo-*zee*-kee
music shop *duka la muziki*
  doo-ka la moo-zee-kee
musician *mwanamuziki*
  mwa-na-moo-*zee*-kee
Muslim *Mwislamu* mwee-*sla*-moo
mussel *kome* koh-may
mustard *mastadi* ma-*sta*-dee
mute *bubu* boo-boo
my *yangu* yan-goo

N

nail clippers *mkasi wa kucha*
  m-*ka*-see wa koo-cha
name *jina* jee-na
napkin *kitambaa cha mkono*
  kee-tam-*ba* cha m-*koh*-noh
nappy *nepi* nay-pee
nappy rash *upele wa nepi*
  oo-*pay*-lay wa nay-pee
national park *hifadhi ya wanyama*
  hee-*fa*-dhee ya wa-*nya*-ma
nationality *raia* ra-ee-a
nature *hali asili* ha-le a-*see*-lee
naturopathy *matibabu asilia*
  ma-tee-*ba*-boo a-see-*lee*-a

nausea *kichefuchefu*
  kee-chay-foo-*chay*-foo
near *karibu* ka-*ree*-boo
nearby *hapo karibu* ha-poh ka-ree-boo-nee
nearest *karibu zaidi* ka-*ree*-boo za-ee-dee
necessary *lazima* la-*zee*-ma
necklace *mkufu* m-koo-foo
need *-hitaji* -hee-*ta*-jee
needle (sewing) *sindano (ya kushonea)*
  seen-*da*-noh (ya koo-shoh-*nay*-a)
needle (syringe) *sindano (ya dawa)*
  seen-*da*-noh (ya da-wa)
negative ⓐ *ya kukana* ya koo-*ka*-na
neither *wala* wa-la
net *neti* nay-tee
Netherlands *Uholanzi* oo-hoh-*lan*-zee
never *kamwe* kam-way
new *mpya* m-pya
New Year's Day *Siku ya Mwaka Mpya*
  see-koo ya *mwa*-ka m-pya
New Year's Eve *Mkesha wa Mwaka Mpya*
  m-*kay*-sha wa *mwa*-ka m-pya
news *habari* ha-*ba*-ree
newsstand *duka la magazeti*
  doo-ka la ma-ga-*zay*-tee
newsagency *shirika la habari*
  shee-*ree*-ka la ha-*ba*-ree
newspaper *gazeti* ga-*zay*-tee
newspaper vendor *mwuzaji wa magazeti*
  mwoo-*za*-jee wa ma-ga-*zay*-tee
next *ijayo* ee-*ja*-yoh
next (month) (mwezi) *ujao*
  (*mway*-zee) oo-*ja*-oh
next to *kando ya* kan-doh ya
nice *mwema* mway-ma
nickname *jina la utani* jee-na la oo-*ta*-nee
night *usiku* oo-*see*-koo
night out *usiku nje* oo-*see*-koo n-jay
nightclub *klabu ya usiku*
  kla-boo ya oo-*see*-koo
no *hapana* ha-*pa*-na
no vacancy *hakuna nafasi*
  ha-*koo*-na na-*fa*-see
noisy *yenye kelele* yay-nyay kay-*lay*-lay
none *hakuna* ha-koo-na
nonsmoking *hakuna sigara*
  ha-*koo*-na see-*ga*-ra
noodles *tambi* tam-bee
noon *saa sita mchana* sa *see*-ta m-*cha*-na
north *kaskazini* kas-ka-*zee*-nee
North Africa *Afrika ya Kaskazini*
  a-*free*-ka ya ka-ska-zee-nee

Norway *Norwei* nohr·*way*·ee
nose *pua* poo·a
not *hapana* ha·*pa*·na
not yet *bado* ba·doh
notebook *daftari* daf·*ta*·ree
nothing *hakuna kitu* ha·koo·na kee·too
November *mwezi wa kumi na moja*
    mway·zee wa koo·mee na moh·ja
now *sasa* sa·sa
nuclear energy *nishati ya nyuklia*
    nee·sha·tee ya nyook·lee·a
nuclear testing *majaribio ya nyuklia*
    ma·ja·ree·*bee*·oh ya nyook·lee·a
nuclear waste *takataka za nyuklia*
    ta·ka·ta·ka za nyook·lee·a
number *namba* nam·ba
numberplate *kipande cha namba ya gari*
    kee·*pan*·day cha nam·ba ya *ga*·ree
nun *sista* see·sta
nurse *mwuguzi* mwoo·goo·zee
nut *kokwa* kohk·wa

O

ocean *bahari* ba·*ha*·ree
October *mwezi wa kumi*
    mway·zee wa koo·mee
off (spoiled) *mbaya* m·*ba*·ya
office *ofisi* oh·*fee*·see
office worker *mfanyakazi ofisini*
    m·fa·nya·*ka*·zee o·fee·*see*·nee
often *mara nyingi* ma·ra nyeen·gee
oil *mafuta* ma·foo·ta
old ⓐ *ya zamani* ya za·*ma*·nee
old person ⓝ *mzee* m·*zay*
olive *zaituni* za·ee·*too*·nee
olive oil *mafuta ya zaituni*
    ma·foo·ta ya za·ee·*too*·nee
Olympic Games *Michezo ya Olimpiki*
    mee·*chay*·zoh ya oh·leem·*pee*·kee
omelette *omlet* ohm·*layt*
on *juu ya* joo ya
on time *kuwahi* koo·*wa*·hee
once *mara moja* ma·ra moh·ja
one *moja* moh·ja
one-way ticket *tiketi ya kwenda tu*
    tee·*kay*·tee ya kwayn·da too
onion *kitunguu* kee·toon·goo
only *tu* too
open ⓥ *-fungua* ·foon·goo·a
open ⓐ *wazi* wa·zee
opening hours *masaa ya kufunguliwa*
    ma·*sa* ya koo·foon·goo·*lee*·wa

opera *opera* oh·*pay*·ra
opera house *jumba la opera*
    joom·ba la oh·*pay*·ra
operation (medical) *operesheni*
    oh·pay·ray·*shay*·nee
operator *opareta* oh·pa·*ray*·ta
opinion *maoni* ma·*oh*·nee
opposite *kinyume* kee·*nyoo*·may
optometrist *daktari wa macho*
    dak·*ta*·ree wa *ma*·choh
or *au* a·oo
orange (fruit) *chungwa* choon·gwa
orange (colour) *rangi ya machungwa*
    ran·gee ya ma·choon·gwa
orange juice *maji ya machungwa*
    ma·jee ya ma·*choon*·gwa
orchestra *okestra* oh·*kay*·stra
order ⓝ *agizo* a·gee·zoh
order ⓥ *-agiza* ·a·gee·za
ordinary *kawaida* ka·wa·ee·da
orgasm *mshushio* m·shoo·*shee*·oh
original *ya awali* ya a·wa·lee
oryx *choroa* choh·*roh*·a
ostrich *mbuni* m·boo·nee
other *nyingine* nyeen·*gee*·nay
our *yetu* yay·too
out of order *imevunjika*
    ee·may·voon·*jee*·ka
outside *nje* n·jay
ovarian cyst *uvimbe wa ovari*
    oo·*veem*·bay wa oh·*va*·ree
ovary *ovari* oh·*va*·ree
oven *joko* joh·koh
overcoat *kabuti* ka·*boo*·tee
overdose *dozi kubwa mno ya dawa*
    doh·zee koob·wa m·noh ya *da*·wa
overnight *kwa usiku mmoja*
    kwa oo·*see*·koo m·*moh*·ja
overseas *nchi za nje* n·chee za n·jay
owe *-wa na deni* ·wa na *day*·nee
owner *mwenye* mway·nyay
oxygen *oksijeni* ohk·see·*jay*·nee
oyster *chaza* cha·za
ozone layer *tabaka la hewa ya ozoni*
    ta·*ba*·ka la *hay*·wa ya oh·*zoh*·nee

P

pacemaker *kirekebisho moyo*
    kee·ray·kay·*bee*·shoh moh·yoh
pacifier (dummy) *nyonyo bandia*
    nyoh·nyoh ban·*dee*·a
package *furushi* foo·*roo*·shee

packet (general) *pakiti* pa·kee·tee
padlock *kufuli* koo·foo·lee
page *ukurasa* oo·koo·ra·sa
pain *maumivu* ma·oo·mee·voo
painful *ya kuumiza* ya koo·oo·mee·za
painkiller *kiondoa maumivu*
kee·ohn·doh·a ma·oo·mee·voo
painter *msanii wa rangi*
m·sa·nee wa ran·gee
painting (a work) *picha* pee·cha
painting (the art)
sanaa ya uchoraji wa rangi
sa·na ya oo·choh·ra·jee wa ran·gee
pair (couple) *wawili wawili*
wa·wee·lee wa·wee·lee
palace *jumba* joom·ba
pan *kikaango* kee·ka·an·goh
pants (trousers) *suruali* soo·roo·a·lee
panty liners *kibandiko cha chupi* pl
kee·ban·dee·koh cha choo·pee
paper *karatasi* ka·ra·ta·see
paperwork *kazi ya ukarani*
ka·zee ya oo·ka·ra·nee
paraplegic *kilema* kee·lay·ma
parcel *kifurushi* kee·foo·roo·shee
parents *wazazi* wa·za·zee
park ⓝ *hifadhi* hee·fa·dhee
park (a car) *-egesha* ·ay·gay·sha
parliament *bunge* boon·gay
part (component) *sehemu* say·hay·moo
part-time *kibarua* kee·ba·roo·a
party (night out) *sherehe* shay·ray·hay
party (politics) *chama* cha·ma
pass *-pita* ·pee·ta
passenger *abiria* a·bee·ree·a
passionfruit *pasheni* pa·shay·nee
passport *pasipoti* pa·see·poh·tee
passport number *namba ya pasipoti*
nam·ba ya pa·see·poh·tee
past ⓝ *zamani* za·ma·nee
pasta *tambi* tam·bee
pastry *kitobosha* kee·toh·boh·sha
path *njia* n·jee·a
pay *-lipa* ·lee·pa
payment *malipo* ma·lee·poh
pea *njegere* n·jay·gay·ray
peace *amani* a·ma·nee
peach *pichi* pee·chee
peak (mountain) *kilele* kee·lay·lay
peanut *karanga* ka·ran·ga
pear *pea* pay·a
pedal *pedeli* pay·day·lee
pedestrian *mtembezi* m·taym·bay·zee

pen (ballpoint) *kalamu* ka·la·moo
pencil *pensili* payn·see·lee
penis *mboo* m·boh
penknife *kisu cha mfukoni*
kee·soo cha m·foo·koh·nee
pensioner *mzee* m·zay
people *watu* wa·too
pepper *pilipili* pee·lee·pee·lee
pepper (bell) *pilipili mbichi*
pee·lee·pee·lee m·bee·chee
per (day) *kwa* kwa
per cent *asilimia* a·see·lee·mee·a
perfect *kamili* ka·mee·lee
performance *onyesho* oh·nyay·shoh
perfume *marashi* ma·ra·shee
period pain *maumivu ya mwezini*
ma·oo·mee·voo ya mway·zee·nee
permission *ruhusa* roo·hoo·sa
permit *kibali* kee·ba·lee
person *mtu* m·too
petition *ombi* ohm·bee
petrol *mafuta* ma·foo·ta
petrol station *kituo cha mafuta*
kee·too·oh cha ma·foo·ta
pharmacist *mfamasia* m·fa·ma·see·a
pharmacy *duka la dawa* doo·ka la da·wa
phone book *kitabu cha namba za simu*
kee·ta·boo cha nam·ba za see·moo
phone box *kibanda cha simu*
kee·ban·da cha see·moo
phonecard *kadi ya simu za vibandani*
ka·dee ya see·moo za vee·ban·da·nee
photo *picha* pee·cha
photographer *mpigapicha*
m·pee·ga·pee·cha
photography *upigaji picha*
oo·pee·ga·jee pee·cha
phrasebook *kitabu cha misemo*
kee·ta·boo cha mee·say·moh
pickaxe *sururu* soo·roo·roo
pickles *achari* a·cha·ree
picnic *mandari* man·da·ree
pie *pai* pa·ee
piece *kipande* kee·pan·day
pig *nguruwe* n·goo·roo·way
pill *kidonge* kee·dohn·gay
(the) pill *kidonge cha kuzuia mimba*
kee·dohn·gay cha koo·zoo·ee·a
meem·ba
pillow *mto* m·toh
pillowcase *foronya* foh·roh·nya
pineapple *nanasi* na·na·see
pink *pinki* peen·kee

place *mahali* ma·ha·lee
place of birth *mahali pa kuzaliwa*
ma·ha·lee pa koo·za·lee·wa
plane *ndege* n·day·gay
planet *sayari* sa·ya·ree
plant *mmea* m·may·a
plastic *plastiki* pla·stee·kee
plate *sahani* sa·ha·nee
plateau *uwanda wa juu* oo·wan·da wa joo
platform *jukwaa* joo·kwa
play (in theatre) *mchezo wa kuigiza*
m·chay·zoh wa koo·ee·gee·za
play cards *-cheza karata* ·chay·za ka·ra·ta
play guitar *-cheza gitaa* ·chay·za gee·taa
plug (bath) *kizibo* kee·zee·boh
plug (electricity) *plagi* pla·gee
plum *plamu* pla·moo
poached (game) *ujangili* oo·jan·gee·lee
pocket *mfuko* m·foo·koh
pocket knife *kisu cha mfukoni*
kee·soo cha m·foo·koh·nee
poetry *shairi* pl sha·ee·ree
point ⓝ *nukta* nook·ta
point ⓥ *-elekeza* ·ay·lay·kay·za
poisonous *yenye sumu* yay·nyay soo·moo
police *polisi* poh·lee·see
police officer *polisi* poh·lee·see
police station *kituo cha polisi*
kee·too·oh cha poh·lee·see
policy *sera* say·ra
politician *mwanasiasa* mwa·na·see·a·sa
politics *siasa* see·a·sa
pollen *chavua* cha·voo·a
pollution *uchafuzi* oo·cha·foo·zee
pool (game) *biliadi* bee·lee·a·dee
pool (swimming) *bwawa* bwa·wa
poor *maskini* mas·kee·nee
popular *ya kupendwa* ya koo·payn·dwa
pork *nyama nguruwe*
nya·ma n·goo·roo·way
port (sea) *bandari* ban·da·ree
positive *ya hakika* ya ha·kee·ka
possible *ya kuwezekana*
ya koo·way·zay·ka·na
postage *stempu* staym·poo
postcard *postikadi* poh·stee·ka·dee
post code *simbo ya posta*
seem·boh ya poh·sta
poster *bango* ban·goh
post office *posta* poh·sta
pot (ceramics) *chungu* choon·goo
pot (dope) *bangi* ban·gee
potato *kiazi* kee·a·zee

pottery *vyombo vya udongo*
vyohm·boh vya oo·dohn·goh
pound (money, weight) *paundi*
pa·oon·dee
poverty *umaskini* oo·ma·skee·nee
powder *poda* poh·da
power *nguvu* n·goo·voo
prawn *kamba* kam·ba
pray *-sali* ·sa·lee
prayer *sala* sa·la
prefer *-pendelea* ·payn·day·lay·a
pregnancy test kit *upimaji mimba*
oo·pee·ma·jee meem·ba
pregnant *mjamzito* m·ja·m·zee·toh
premenstrual tension *zingizi*
zeen·gee·zee
prepare *-andaa* ·an·da
prescription *agizo la daktari*
a·gee·zoh la dak·ta·ree
present (gift) *zawadi* za·wa·dee
present (time) *sasa* sa·sa
president *rais* ra·ees
pressure *shinikizo* shee·nee·kee·zoh
pretty *ya kupendeza* ya koo·payn·day·za
price *bei* bay
priest *padri* pa·dree
prime minister *waziri mkuu*
wa·zee·ree m·koo
printer (computer) *printa* preen·ta
prison *gereza* gay·ray·za
prisoner *mfungwa* m·foon·gwa
private *binafsi* bee·naf·see
profit *faida* fa·ee·da
program *mradi* m·ra·dee
projector *projekta* proh·jayk·ta
promise *-ahidi* ·a·hee·dee
prostitute *malaya* ma·la·ya
protect *-kinga* ·keen·ga
protected species *spishi zilizo hifadhiwa*
spee·shee zee·lee·zoh hee·fa·dhee·wa
protest ⓝ *maandamano*
ma·an·da·ma·noh
protest ⓥ *-pinga* ·peen·ga
provisions *maakuli* ma·a·koo·lee
prune *plamu kavu* pla·moo ka·voo
pub (bar) *baa* ba
public relations *uhusiano wa jamii*
oo·hoo·see·a·noh wa ja·mee
public telephone *simu ya mtaani*
see·moo ya m·ta·nee
public toilet *choo cha hadhara*
choh cha ha·dha·ra
pull *-vuta* ·voo·ta

pump ⓝ *pampu* pam·poo
pumpkin *boga* boh·ga
puncture *pancha* pan·cha
pure *halisi* ha·lee·see
purple *zambarau* zam·ba·ra·oo
purse *mkoba* m·koh·ba
push -*sukuma* ·soo·koo·ma
put -*weka* ·way·ka

Q

qualifications *sifa za kielimu*
    see·fa za kee·ay·lee·moo
quality *sifa* see·fa
quarantine *karantini* ka·ran·tee·nee
quarter *robo* roh·boh
queen *malkia* mal·kee·a
question *swali* swa·lee
queue *mstari* m·sta·ree
quick *nyepesi* nyay·pay·see
quiet -*tulivu* ·too·lee·voo
quit -*acha* ·a·cha

R

rabbit *sungura* soon·goo·ra
race (sport) *shindano* sheen·da·noh
racetrack *uwanja wa mbio*
    oo·wan·ja wa m·bee·oh
racing bike *baisikeli ya mashindano*
    ba·ee·see·kay·lee ya ma·sheen·da·noh
racism *ubaguzi wa rangi*
    oo·ba·goo·zee wa ran·gee
racquet *raketi* ra·kay·tee
radiator *kinururishi* kee·noo·roo·ree·shee
radio *redio* ray·dee·oh
radish *figili* fee·gee·lee
railway station *stesheni ya treni*
    stay·shay·nee ya tray·nee
rain *mvua* m·voo·a
raincoat *koti la mvua* koh·tee la m·voo·a
raisin *zabibu kavu* za·bee·boo ka·voo
rally (public meeting) *mkutano wa*
    hadhara m·koo·ta·noh wa ha·dha·ra
rape ⓝ *ubakaji* oo·ba·ka·jee
rape ⓥ -*baka* ·ba·ka
rare (food) *ya kuiva kidogo*
    ya koo·ee·va kee·doh·goh
rare (uncommon) *nadra* na·dra
rash *upele* oo·pay·lay
rat *panya* pa·nya
raw -*bichi* ·bee·chee

razor *wembe* waym·bay
razor blade *wembe* waym·bay
read -*soma* ·soh·ma
reading *somo* soh·moh
ready *tayari* ta·ya·ree
real estate agent *wakala wa maeneo*
    wa·ka·la wa ma·ay·nay·oh
rear (location) *nyuma* nyoo·ma
reason (explanation) *sababu* sa·ba·boo
receipt *risiti* ree·see·tee
recently *hivi karibuni*
    hee·vee ka·ree·boo·nee
recommend -*pendekeza* ·payn·day·kay·za
record (music) -*rekodi (muziki)*
    ·ray·koh·dee (moo·zee·kee)
recording (musical) *kanda* kan·da
recyclable *ya kurejeleza*
    ya koo·ray·jay·lay·za
red *nyekundu* nyay·koon·doo
referee *mwamuzi* mwa·moo·zee
reference *marejeo* ma·ray·jay·oh
refrigerator *friji* free·jee
refugee *mkimbizi* m·keem·bee·zee
refund *kurudisha pesa*
    koo·roo·dee·sha pay·sa
refuse -*kataa* ·ka·ta
regional *ya mkoa* ya m·koh·a
registered mail/post *barua ya rejista*
    ba·roo·a ya ray·jee·sta
rehydration salts *dawa ya kuongeza*
    maji mwilini da·wa ya koo·ohn·gay·za
    ma·jee mwee·lee·nee
relationship *uhusiano* oo·hoo·see·a·noh
relax -*jiburudisha* ·jee·boo·roo·dee·sha
relic *mabaki* ma·ba·kee
religion *dini* dee·nee
religious *ya kidini* ya kee·dee·nee
remote *mbali* m·ba·lee
remote control *rimoti* ree·moh·tee
rent -*kodi* ·koh·dee
repair -*tengeneza* ·tayn·gay·nay·za
republic *jamhuri* jam·hoo·ree
reservation (booking) *buking* boo·keeng
rest -*pumzika* ·poom·zee·ka
restaurant *mgahawa* m·ga·ha·wa
résumé (CV) *muhtasari* moo·hta·sa·ree
retired *aliyestaafu* a·lee·yay·sta·a·foo
return (come back) -*rudi* ·roo·dee
return ticket *tiketi ya kwenda na kurudi*
    tee·kay·tee ya kwayn·da na koo·roo·dee
review *mapitio* ma·pee·tee·oh
rhinoceros *kifaru* kee·fa·roo
rhythm *mahadhi* ma·ha·dhee

rib *ubavu* oo·ba·voo
rice (cooked) *wali* wa·lee
rice (uncooked) *mchele* m·chay·lay
rich (wealthy) *tajiri* ta·jee·ree
ride ⓝ *lifti* leef·tee
ride (horse) ⓥ *-panda (farasi)*
·pan·da (fa·ra·see)
right (correct) *sawa* sa·wa
right (direction) *kulia* koo·lee·a
right-wing *mrengo wa kulia*
m·rayn·goh wa koo·lee·a
ring (on finger) *pete* pay·tay
ring (phone) *-piga simu* ·pee·ga see·moo
rip-off *wizi* wee·zee
risk *hatari* ha·ta·ree
river *mto* m·toh
road *barabara* ba·ra·ba·ra
road map *ramani* ra·ma·nee
rob *-iba* ·ee·ba
rock *jiwe* jee·way
rock climbing *upandaji mlamba*
oo·pan·da·jee mee·am·ba
rock group *kundi ya roki*
koon·dee ya roh·kee
rock music *roki* roh·kee
roll (bread) *skonzi* skohn·zee
romantic *kwa wapenzi*
kwa wa·payn·zee
room *chumba* choom·ba
room number *namba ya chumba*
nam·ba ya choom·ba
rope *kamba* kam·ba
round *duara* doo·a·ra
roundabout *kiplefti* keep·layf·tee
route *njia* n·jee·a
rowing *kuvuta makasia*
koo·voo·ta ma·ka·see·a
rubbish *takataka* ta·ka·ta·ka
rug *zulia* zoo·lee·a
rugby *ragbi* rag·bee
ruins *magofu* ma·goh·foo
rule *utawala* oo·ta·wa·la
run *-kimbia* ·keem·bee·a
running *kukimbia* koo·keem·bee·a
Rwanda *Rwanda* r·wan·da

S

sad *masikitiko* ma·see·kee·tee·koh
saddle *tandiko* tan·dee·koh
safe (for money) ⓝ *kasha la fedha*
ka·sha la fay·dha
safe ⓐ *salama* sa·la·ma

safe sex *mapenzi salama*
ma·payn·zee sa·la·ma
saint *mtakatifu* m·ta·ka·tee·foo
salad *saladi* sa·la·dee
salary *mshahara* m·sha·ha·ra
sale *seli* say·lee
sales tax *kodi ya mauzo*
koh·dee ya ma·oo·zoh
salmon *samoni* sa·moh·nee
salt *chumvi* choom·vee
same *sawasawa* sa·wa·sa·wa
sand *mchanga* m·chan·ga
sandal *ndala* n·da·la
sanitary napkin *sodo* soh·doh
sardine *dagaa* da·ga
Saturday *Jumamosi* joo·ma·moh·see
sauce *mchuzi* m·choo·zee
saucepan *sufuria* soo·foo·ree·a
sauna *sauna* sa·oo·na
sausage *soseji* soh·say·jee
say *-sema* ·say·ma
scalp *ngozi ya kichwa*
n·goh·zee ya keech·wa
scarf *skafu* ska·foo
school *shule* shoo·lay
science *sayansi* sa·yan·see
scientist *mwanasayansi*
mwa·na·sa·yan·see
scissors *mkasi* m·ka·see
score *alama* a·la·ma
scoreboard *ubao wa matokeo*
oo·ba·oh wa ma·toh·kay·oh
Scotland *Skotlandi* skoht·lan·dee
scrambled eggs *mayai yallyovurugwa*
ma·ya·ee ya·lee·yoh·voo·roog·wa
sculpture *uchongaji* oo·chohn·ga·jee
sea *bahari* ba·ha·ree
seasickness *kichefuchefu cha bahirini*
kee·chay·foo·chay·foo cha
ba·ha·ree·nee
seaside *ufukwe* oo·fook·way
season *majira* ma·jee·ra
seat (place) *kiti* kee·tee
seatbelt *mkanda wa kiti*
m·kan·da wa kee·tee
second (time unit) *sekundi* say·koon·dee
second ⓐ *ya pili* ya pee·lee
second class *daraja la pili*
da·ra·ja la pee·lee
second-hand *mitumba* mee·toom·ba
second-hand shop *duka la mitumba*
doo·ka la mee·toom·ba
secretary *karani* ka·ra·nee

see -ona ·oh·na
self-employed *ya kujiajiri*
ya koo·jee·a·*jee*·ree
selfish *mwenye choyo*
mway·nyay choh·yoh
self service *ya kujihuduma*
ya koo·jee·hoo·*doo*·ma
sell -*uza* ·oo·za
send -*peleka* ·pay·*lay*·ka
sensible *yenye busara* yay·nyay boo·*sa*·ra
sensual *ya kutamanisha*
ya koo·ta·ma·*nee*·sha
separate *mbalimbali* m·ba·lee·m·*ba*·lee
September *mwezi wa tisa*
mway·zee wa *tee*·sa
serious *makini* ma·*kee*·nee
service *huduma* hoo·*doo*·ma
service charge *malipo ya huduma*
ma·*lee*·poh ya hoo·*doo*·ma
service station *kituo cha petroli*
kee·*too*·oh cha pay·*troh*·lee
serviette *kitambaa cha mkono*
kee·tam·*ba* cha m·*koh*·noh
several *kadhaa* ka·*dha*
sew -*shona* ·*shoh*·na
sex (gender) *jinsia* jeen·*see*·a
sex (intercourse) *mapenzi* ma·*payn*·zee
sexism *ubaguzi wa kijinsia*
oo·ba·*goo*·zee wa kee·jeen·*see*·a
sexy *ya kuchochea ashiki*
ya koo·choh·*chay*·a a·*shee*·kee
shade *kivuli* kee·*voo*·lee
shadow *kivuli* kee·*voo*·lee
shampoo *shampuu* sham·*poo*
shape *umbo* *oom*·boh
share (a dorm etc) -*gawana* ·ga·*wa*·na
share (with) -*shirikiana* ·shee·ree·kee·*a*·na
shave -*nyoa* ·*nyoh*·a
shaving cream *sabuni ya kunyolea*
sa·*boo*·nee ya koo·nyoh·*lay*·a
she *yeye* yay·yay
sheep *kondoo* kohn·*doh*
sheet (bed) *shuka* shoo·ka
shelf *rafu* ra·foo
shingles (illness) *moto ya mungu*
moh·toh ya *moon*·goo
shiny *almasi* al·*ma*·see
ship *meli* may·lee
shirt *shati* sha·tee
shoe *kiatu* kee·*a*·too
shoe shop *duka la viatu*
doo·ka la vee·*a*·too
shoes *viatu* vee·*a*·too

shoot -*piga risasi* ·pee·ga ree·*sa*·see
shop ⓝ *duka* doo·ka
shop ⓥ -*nunua* ·noo·*noo*·a
shopping *ununuzi* oo·noo·*noo*·zee
shopping centre *madukani*
ma·doo·*ka*·nee
short (height) *fupi* foo·pee
shortage *upungufu* oo·poon·*goo*·foo
shorts *kaptura* kap·*too*·ra
shoulder *bega* bay·ga
shout -*piga kelele* ·pee·ga kay·*lay*·lay
show ⓝ *onyesho* oh·*nyay*·shoh
show ⓥ -*onyesha* ·oh·*nyay*·sha
shower *bafuni* ba·*foo*·nee
shrine *ziara* zee·*a*·ra
shut ⓐ *kufungwa* koo·*foon*·gwa
shy *ya aibu* ya a·*ee*·boo
sick *mgonjwa* m·*gohn*·jwa
side *upande* oo·*pan*·day
sign *alama* a·*la*·ma
signature *sahihi* sa·*hee*·hee
silk ⓝ *hariri* ha·*ree*·ree
silver *fedha* fay·dha
silver shop *duka la fedha* doo·ka la fay·dha
SIM card *kadi ya simu (ya mikononi)*
ka·dee ya *see*·moo (ya mee·koh·noh·*nee*)
similar *yenye kufanana*
yay·nyay koo·fa·*na*·na
simple *rahisi* ra·*hee*·see
since (May) *tangu (Mei)* tan·goo (*may*·ee)
sing -*imba* ·*eem*·ba
Singapore *Singapore* seen·ga·*poh*·ray
singer *mwimbaji* mweem·*ba*·jee
single (person) *kapera* ka·*pay*·ra
single room *chumba kwa mtu mmoja*
choom·ba kwa m·too m·*moh*·ja
singlet *fulana ya ndani*
foo·*la*·na ya n·*da*·nee
sister *dada* da·da
sit -*kaa* ·ka
size (general) *saizi* sa·*ee*·zee
skate -*teleza* ·tay·*lay*·za
skateboarding *ubao wa kuteleza*
oo·*ba*·oh wa koo·tay·*lay*·za
ski -*skii* ·skee
skiing *kuskii* koo·skee
skim milk *machunda* ma·*choon*·da
skin *ngozi* n·*goh*·zee
skirt *skati* ska·tee
skull *fuvu* foo·voo
sky *mbingu* m·*been*·goo
sleep -*sinzia* ·seen·zee·a
sleeping bag *mfuko wa kulalia*
m·*foo*·koh wa koo·la·*lee*·a

sleeping berth *kitanda katika behewa* kee·*tan*·da ka·*tee*·ka bay·*hay*·wa
sleeping car *gari la vitanda* *ga*·ree la vee·*tan*·da
sleeping pills *vidonge vya usingizi* vee·*dohn*·gay vya oo·seen·*gee*·zee
sleepy *mwenye usingizi* mway·nyay oo·seen·*gee*·zee
slice ⑪ *slaisi* sla·*ee*·see
slide *filamu ya slaidi* fee·*la*·moo ya sla·*ee*·dee
slow *taratibu* ta·ra·*tee*·boo
slowly *polepole* poh·lay·*poh*·lay
small *-dogo* ·*doh*·goh
smaller *-dogo zaidi* ·*doh*·goh za·*ee*·dee
smallest *-dogo kabisa* ·*doh*·goh ka·*bee*·sa
smart *hodari* hoh·*da*·ree
smell ⑪ *harufu* ha·*roo*·foo
smile *-tabasamu* ·ta·ba·*sa*·moo
smoke *-vuta sigara* ·*voo*·ta see·*ga*·ra
snack *kumbwe* koom·bway
snail *konokono* koh·noh·*koh*·noh
snake *nyoka* nyoh·ka
snow *theluji* thay·*loo*·jee
soap *sabuni* sa·*boo*·nee
soccer *soka* soh·ka
social welfare *ustawi wa jamii* oo·*sta*·wee wa ja·*mee*
socialist *soshalisti* soh·sha·*lee*·stee
socks *soksi* sohk·see
soft drink *soda* soh·da
soft-boiled egg *yai lililochemshwa kidogo* ya·ee lee·lee·loh·*chaym*·shwa kee·*doh*·goh
soldier *askari* a·*ska*·ree
Somalia *Somalia* soh·*ma*·lee·a
some *kadhaa* ka·*dha*
someone *fulani* foo·*la*·nee
something *kitu* kee·too
sometimes *wakati mwingine* wa·*ka*·tee mween·*gee*·nay
son *mwana* mwa·na
song *wimbo* weem·boh
soon *sasa hivi* sa·sa hee·vee
sore *mwenye kuuma* mway·nyay koo·oo·ma
soup *supu* soo·poo
sour cream *malai ya maziwa ya mtindi* ma·*la*·ee ya ma·zee·wa ya m·*teen*·dee
south *kusini* koo·*see*·nee
South Africa *Afrika ya Kusini* a·*free*·ka ya koo·*see*·nee
souvenir *kumbukumbu* koom·boo·*koom*·boo

souvenir shop *duka la kumbukumbu* *doo*·ka la koom·boo·*koom*·boo
soy milk *maziwa ya soya* ma·*zee*·wa ya *soh*·ya
soy sauce *mchuzi wa soya* m·*choo*·zee wa *soh*·ya
(outer) space *angani* an·*ga*·nee
Spain *Uhispania* oo·hee·*spa*·nee·a
speak *-sema* ·*say*·ma
special *maalum* ma·a·loom
specialist *mtaalamu* m·ta·a·*la*·loom
speed (velocity) *mwendo* mwayn·doh
speed limit *kikomo cha mwendo* kee·*koh*·moh cha *mwayn*·doh
speedometer *spidomita* spee·doh·*mee*·ta
spider *buibui* boo·ee·*boo*·ee
spinach *mchicha* m·*chee*·cha
spoilage *uharibifu* oo·ha·ree·*bee*·foo
spoke *spoki* spoh·kee
spoon *kijiko* kee·*jee*·koh
sport *michezo* mee·*chay*·zoh
sports shop *duka la vifaa vya michezo* *doo*·ka la vee·*fa* vya mee·*chay*·zoh
sportsperson *mwanamichezo* mwa·na·mee·*chay*·zoh
sprain *mteguko* m·tay·*goo*·koh
spring (coil) *springi* spreen·gee
spring (season) *majira ya kuchipua* ma·*jee*·ra ya koo·chee·*poo*·a
square (town) *uwanja* oo·*wan*·ja
stadium *uwanja wa michezo* oo·*wan*·ja wa mee·*chay*·zoh
stairway *ngazi* n·*ga*·zee
stale *ya zamani* ya za·ma·nee
stamp *stempu* staym·poo
stand-by ticket *tiketi kutumia kama nafasi ikipatikana* tee·*kay*·tee koo·too·*mee*·a ka·ma na·*fa*·see ee·kee·pa·tee·*ka*·na
star *nyota* nyoh·ta
start ⑪ *mwanzo* mwan·zoh
start ⓥ *-anza* ·an·za
station *stesheni* stay·*shay*·nee
stationer *duka la vifaa vya ofisi* *doo*·ka la vee·*fa* vya o·*fee*·see
statue *sanamu* sa·*na*·moo
stay (at a hotel) *-kaa* ·ka
stay (in one place) *-baki* ·*ba*·kee
steak (beef) *mnofu* m·*noh*·foo
steal *-iba* ·*ee*·ba
steep *ya mwinuko mkali* ya mwee·*noo*·koh m·*ka*·lee
step *hatua* ha·*too*·a

stereo *stirio* stee·*ree*·oh
still water *maji baridi* ma·jee ba·*ree*·dee
stockings *soksi ndefu* sohk·see n·*day*·foo
stolen *ya kuibwa* ya koo·*ee*·bwa
stomach *tumbo* toom·boh
stomachache *maumivu ya tumbo* ma·oo·*mee*·voo ya toom·boh
stone *jiwe* jee·way
stoned (drugged) *-lewa* ·*lay*·wa
stop (bus, etc) ⓝ *kituo* kee·*too*·oh
stop (cease) ⓥ *-simama* ·see·*ma*·ma
stop (prevent) ⓥ *-zuia* ·zoo·*ee*·a
storm *dhoruba* dho·*roo*·ba
story *hadithi* ha·*dee*·thee
stove *jiko* jee·koh
straight *moja kwa moja* moh·ja kwa moh·ja
strange *ya kigeni* ya kee·*gay*·nee
stranger *mgeni* m·*gay*·nee
stream *kijito* kee·*jee*·toh
street *njia* n·jee·a
street children *watoto wa mtaani* wa·*toh*·toh wa m·ta·a·nee
street hawker *mchuuzi* m·choo·oo·zee
street market *soko la mtaani* soh·koh la m·ta·a·nee
strike *mgomo* m·*goh*·moh
string *uzi* oo·zee
stroke (health) *kiharusi* kee·ha·*roo*·see
stroller (pram) *kigari cha mtoto* kee·*ga*·ree cha m·*toh*·toh
strong *madhubuti* ma·dhoo·boo·tee
stubborn *mbishi* m·*bee*·shee
student *mwanafunzi* mwa·na·*foon*·zee
studio *studio* stoo·dee·oh
stupid *pumbavu* poom·*ba*·voo
style *mtindo* m·*teen*·doh
subtitles *maandishi chini* ma·an·*dee*·shee chee·nee
suburb *pembezoni mwa mji* paym·bay·*zoh*·nee mwa m·jee
Sudan *Sudan* soo·*dan*
sugar *sukari* soo·*ka*·ree
suitcase *mzigo* m·zee·goh
sultanas *zabibu nyeupe zilizokaushwa* za·*bee*·boo nyay·oo·*pay* zee·lee·zoh·ka·*oosh*·wa
summer *majira ya joto* ma·jee·ra ya joh·toh
sun *jua* joo·a
sunblock *dawa la kukinga jua* da·wa la koo·*keen*·ga joo·a
sunburn *kuchomwa kwa jua* koo·*chom*·wa kwa joo·a

Sunday *Jumapili* joo·ma·*pee*·lee
sunglasses *miwani ya jua* mee·*wa*·nee ya joo·a
sunny *ya jua* ya joo·a
sunrise *macheo* ma·*chay*·oh
sunset *machweo* ma·*chway*·oh
sunstroke *ugonjwa wa kuchomwa kwa jua* oo·*gohn*·jwa wa koo·*chohm*·wa kwa joo·a
supermarket *duka kubwa* doo·ka koob·wa
superstition *ushirikina* oo·shee·ree·*kee*·na
supporter (politics) *mwungaji mkono* mwoon·*ga*·jee m·*koh*·noh
supporter (sport) *mshabiki* m·sha·*bee*·kee
surface mail (land) *barua kwa lori* ba·*roo*·a kwa *loh*·ree
surface mail (sea) *barua kwa meli* ba·*roo*·a kwa *may*·lee
surfboard *ubao wa kutelezea* oo·*ba*·oh wa koo·tay·lay·*zay*·a
surfing *kuteleza* koo·tay·*lay*·za
surname *jina la baba* jee·na la ba·ba
surprise *mshangao* m·shan·*ga*·oh
sweater *sweta* sway·ta
Sweden *Uswidi* oo·*swee*·dee
sweet ⓐ *tamu* ta·moo
sweets *peremende* pay·ray·*mayn*·day
swelling *uvimbe* oo·*veem*·bay
swim *-ogelea* ·oh·*gay*·lay·a
swimming (sport) *kuogelea* koo·oh·gay·*lay*·a
swimming pool *bwawa la kuogelea* bwa·wa la koo·oh·gay·*lay*·a
swimsuit *vazi la kuogelea* va·zee la koo·oh·gay·*lay*·a
Switzerland *Uswisi* oo·*swee*·see
synagogue *kanisa ya kiyahudi* ka·*nee*·sa ya kee·ya·*hoo*·dee
synthetic *ya usanisia* ya oo·sa·nee·*see*·a
syringe *sindano* seen·*da*·noh

T

table *meza* may·za
tablecloth *kitambaa cha meza* kee·tam·ba cha may·za
table tennis *mpira wa meza* m·pee·ra wa may·za
tail *mkia* m·kee·a
tailor *mshonaji* m·shoh·*na*·jee

take -chukua ·choo·koo·a
take a photo -piga picha ·pee·ga pee·cha
talk -sema ·say·ma
tall mrefu m·ray·foo
tampon sodo soh·doh
tanning lotion dawa la kugeuza rangi
kwenye jua da·wa la koo·gay·oo·za
ran·gee kway·nyay joo·a
Tanzania Tanzania tan·za·nee·a
tap bomba bohm·ba
tap water maji ya bomba
ma·jee ya bohm·ba
tasty tamu ta·moo
tax kodi koh·dee
taxi teksi tayk·see
taxi stand kituo cha teksi
kee·too·oh cha tayk·see
tea chai cha·ee
teacher mwalimu mwa·lee·moo
team timu tee·moo
teaspoon kijiko cha chai
kee·jee·koh cha cha·ee
technique mbinu m·bee·noo
teeth meno may·noh
telecom centre telekom tay·lay·kohm
telegram telegramu tay·lay·gra·moo
telephone ⓝ simu see·moo
telephone ⓥ -piga simu ·pee·ga see·moo
telephone box kibanda cha simu
kee·ban·da cha see·moo
telephone centre kituo cha simu
kee·too·oh cha see·moo
telescope darubini da·roo·bee·nee
television televisheni
tay·lay·vee·shay·nee
tell -ambia ·am·bee·a
temperature (fever) homa hoh·ma
temperature (weather) halijoto
ha·lee·joh·toh
temple hekalu hay·ka·loo
tennis tenesi tay·nay·see
tennis court kiwanja cha tenesi
kee·wan·ja cha tay·nay·see
tent hema hay·ma
tent peg banzi la hema ban·zee la hay·ma
terrible mbaya sana m·ba·ya sa·na
test mtihani m·tee·ha·nee
thank -shukuru ·shoo·koo·roo
that (person) huyo hoo·yoh
that (thing) hiyo hee·yoh
theatre ukumbi wa maonyesho
oo·koom·bee wa ma·oh·nyay·shoh
their yao ya·oh

there huko hoo·koh
they wao wa·oh
thick -zito ·zee·toh
thief mwizi mwee·zee
thin mwembamba mwaym·bam·ba
think -fikiri ·fee·kee·ree
third ya tatu ya ta·too
(to be) thirsty (-sikia) kiu
(·see·kee·a) kee·oo
this (person) huyu hoo·yoo
this (thing) hii hee
thread uzi oo·zee
throat koo koh
thrush (health) ugonjwa wa upele
oo·gohn·jwa wa oo·pay·lay
thunderstorm dhoruba ya radi
dhoh·roo·ba ya ra·dee
Thursday Alhamisi al·ha·mee·see
ticket tiketi/tikiti tee·kay·tee/tee·kee·tee
ticket collector mkusanyaji wa tiketi
m·koo·sa·nya·jee wa tee·kay·tee
ticket machine mashine ya tiketi
ma·shee·nay ya tee·kay·tee
ticket office ofisi ya tiketi
o·fee·see ya tee·kay·tee
tide maji ya kujaa na kupwa
ma·jee ya koo·ja na koopwa
tight ya kubana ya koo·ba·na
time saa sa
time difference tofauti ya wakati
to·fa·oo·tee ya wa·ka·tee
timetable ratiba ra·tee·ba
tin (can) mkebe/kopo m·kay·bay/koh·poh
tin opener kifungua kopo
kee·foon·goo·a koh·poh
tiny ndogo sana n·doh·goh sa·na
tip (gratuity) bakshishi bak·shee·shee
tire tairi ta·ee·ree
tired ya kuchoka ya koo·choh·ka
tissues karatasi za shashi
ka·ra·ta·see za sha·shee
to hadi ha·dee
toast slaisi sla·ee·see
toaster mashine ya kubanika mkate
ma·shee·nay ya koo·ba·nee·ka m·ka·tay
tobacco tumbaku toom·ba·koo
tobacconist duka la tumbaku
doo·ka la toom·ba·koo
today leo lay·oh
toe kidole cha mguu
kee·doh·lay cha m·goo
together pamoja pa·moh·ja
toilet choo choh

toilet paper *karatasi ya choo*
ka·ra·ta·see ya choh
tomato *nyanya* nya·nya
tomato sauce *mchuzi wa nyanya*
m·*choo*·zee wa nya·nya
tomorrow *kesho* kay·shoh
tomorrow afternoon *kesho mchana*
kay·shoh m·*cha*·na
tomorrow evening *kesho jioni*
kay·shoh jee·oh·nee
tomorrow morning *kesho asubuhi*
kay·shoh a·soo·*boo*·hee
tongue *ulimi* oo·*lee*·mee
tonight *usiku huu* oo·*see*·koo hoo
too (expensive etc) *mno* m·noh
tooth *jino* jee·noh
toothache *maumivu ya jino*
ma·oo·*mee*·voo ya jee·noh
toothbrush *mswaki* m·*swa*·kee
toothpaste *dawa la meno*
da·wa la *may*·noh
toothpick *kijiti cha meno*
kee·*jee*·tee cha *may*·noh
torch (flashlight) *tochi* toh·chee
touch *-gusa* ·*goo*·sa
tour *safari ya kutalii* sa·*fa*·ree ya koo·ta·*lee*
tourist *mtalii* m·ta·*lee*
tourist office *ofisi ya watalii*
o·*fee*·see ya wa·ta·*lee*
towards *kuelekea* koo·ay·lay·*kay*·a
towel *taulo* ta·oo·loh
tower *mnara* m·*na*·ra
toxic waste *taka za sumu*
ta·ka za soo·moo
toy shop *duka la vitu vya kuchezea*
doo·ka la *vee*·too vya koo·chay·*zay*·a
track (path) *njia* n·jee·a
track (sport) *michezo ya kukimbia*
mee·*chay*·zoh ya koo·keem·*bee*·a
trade *biashara* bee·a·*sha*·ra
tradesperson *mfanyabiashara*
m·fa·nya·bee·a·*sha*·ra
traffic *magari mengi* ma·*ga*·ree *mayn*·gee
traffic light *taa ya barabarani*
ta ya ba·ra·ba·*ra*·nee
trail *njia* n·jee·a
train *treni* *tray*·nee
train station *stesheni ya treni*
stay·*shay*·nee ya *tray*·nee
transit lounge *chumba cha kupumzikia*
kwa wanaosafiri choom·ba
cha koo·poom·zee·*kee*·a kwa
wa·na·oh·sa·*fee*·ree

translate *-tafsiri* ·taf·*see*·ree
transport *usafirishaji* oo·sa·fee·ree·*sha*·jee
travel *-safiri* ·sa·*fee*·ree
travel agency *uwakala wa safari*
oo·wa·*ka*·la wa sa·*fa*·ree
travellers cheque *hundi ya msafiri*
hoon·dee ya m·sa·*fee*·ree
travel sickness *kichefuchefu cha safari*
kee·chay·foo·*chay*·foo cha sa·*fa*·ree
tree *mti* m·tee
trip (journey) *safari* sa·*fa*·ree
trousers *suruali* soo·roo·a·lee
truck *lori* *loh*·ree
trust *-amini* ·a·*mee*·nee
try (attempt) *-jaribu* ·ja·*ree*·boo
try (taste) *-onja* ·*ohn*·ja
T-shirt *tishati* tee·sha·tee
tube (tyre) *tyubu* *tyoo*·boo
Tuesday *Jumanne* joo·ma·n·nay
tumour *uvimbe* oo·*veem*·bay
tuna *jodari* joh·*da*·ree
tune *wimbo* *weem*·boh
turkey *bata mzinga* ba·ta m·*zeen*·ga
turn *-geuza* ·*gay*·oo·za
TV *televisheni* tay·lay·vee·*shay*·nee
tweezers *twiza* *twee*·za
twice *mara mbili* ma·ra m·*bee*·lee
twin beds *vitanda viwili*
vee·*tan*·da vee·*wee*·lee
twins *mapacha* ma·*pa*·cha
two *mbili* m·*bee*·lee
type *aina* a·*ee*·na
typical *ya mfano hasa* ya m·*fa*·noh *ha*·sa
tyre *tairi* ta·ee·ree

U

Uganda *Uganda* oo·*gan*·da
ultrasound *kupiga picha ya mtoto*
tumboni koo·*pee*·ga *pee*·cha ya
m·*toh*·toh toom·*boh*·nee
umbrella *mwamvuli* mwam·*voo*·lee
uncomfortable *bila raha* bee·la *ra*·ha
understand *-elewa* ·ay·*lay*·wa
underwear *chupi* choo·pee
unemployed *asiye na kazi*
a·*see*·yay na *ka*·zee
unfair *jeuri* jay·oo·ree
uniform ⓝ *nguo rasmi* n·*goo*·oh *ras*·mee
universe *ulimwengu* oo·lee·*mwayn*·goo
university *chuo kikuu* choo·oh kee·*koo*
unleaded *isiyo na risasi*
ee·*see*·yoh na ree·*sa*·see

unsafe *ni hatari* nee ha-*ta*-ree
until *mpaka* m-*pa*-ka
unusual *siyo kawaida* see-yoh ka-wa-ee-da
up *juu* joo
uphill *mwinuko* mwee-*noo*-koh
urgent *muhimu sana* moo-*hee*-moo *sa*-na
urinary infection *ambukizo la mfumo wa mkojo* am-boo-*kee*-zoh la m-*foo*-moh wa m-*koh*-joh
USA *Marekani* ma-ray-*ka*-nee
useful *yenye manufaa* yay-nyay ma-noo-*fa*

V

vacancy *nafasi* na-*fa*-see
vacant *tupu* too-poo
vacation *likizo* lee-*kee*-zoh
vaccination *chanjo* chan-joh
vagina *kuma* koo-ma
validate -*thibitisha* -thee-bee-*tee*-sha
valley *bonde* bohn-day
valuable *ya thamani* ya *tha*-ma-nee
value (price) *thamani* *tha*-ma-nee
veal *nyama ya ndama* nya-ma ya n-*da*-ma
vegetable *mboga* m-*boh*-ga
vegetarian *mlaji wa mboga za majani tu* m-*la*-jee wa m-*boh*-ga za ma-*ja*-nee too
vein *mshipa* m-*shee*-pa
venereal disease *ugonjwa wa zinaa* oo-*gohn*-jwa wa zee-*na*
venue *mahali* ma-*ha*-lee
very *sana* *sa*-na
video recorder *kemra ya video* *kaym*-ra ya vee-*day*-oh
video tape *mkanda wa video* m-*kan*-da wa vee-*day*-oh
view *mandhari* man-*dha*-ree
village *kijiji* kee-*jee*-jee
vine (grape) *mzabibu* m-za-*bee*-boo
vinegar *siki* see-kee
vineyard *shamba la mizabibu* *sham*-ba la mee-za-*bee*-boo
virus *virusi* vee-*roo*-see
visa *viza/visa* vee-za/vee-sa
visit -*tembelea* taym-bay-*lay*-a
vitamins *vitamini* vee-ta-*mee*-nee
voice *sauti* sa-oo-tee
volleyball (sport) *mpira wa wavu* m-*pee*-ra wa wa-voo
volume (sound) *sauti* sa-oo-tee
vote -*piga kura* -*pee*-ga koo-ra
vulture *tumbusi* toom-*boo*-see

W

wage *mshahara* m-sha-*ha*-ra
wait -*subiri* soo-*bee*-ree
wait for -*ngojea* n-goh-*jay*-a
waiter *mhudumu* m-hoo-doo-moo
waiting room *chumba cha wanaosubiri* *choom*-ba cha wa-na-oh-soo-*bee*-ree
wake up -*amka* -*am*-ka
wake someone up -*amsha* -*am*-sha
walk -*tembea* taym-*bay*-a
wall (outer) *ukuta* oo-*koo*-ta
want -*taka* -*ta*-ka
war *vita* vee-ta
wardrobe *kabati ya nguo* ka-*ba*-tee ya n-*goo*-oh
warm *ya joto* ya joh-toh
warn -*onya* -*oh*-nya
wash (oneself) -*oga* -*oh*-ga
wash (something) -*osha* -*oh*-sha
wash cloth (flannel) *kitambaa cha uso* kee-tam-*ba* cha oo-soh
washing machine *mashine ya kufulia* ma-*shee*-nay ya koo-foo-*lee*-a
watch *saa* sa
watch -*tazama* -ta-*za*-ma
water *maji* ma-jee
water bottle (hot) *chupa ya maji (ya moto)* choo-pa ya ma-jee (ya moh-toh)
waterfall *maporomoko ya maji* ma-poh-roh-*moh*-koh ya ma-jee
watermelon *tikiti maji* tee-*kee*-tee ma-jee
waterproof *kutopenyesha maji* koo-to-pay-*nyay*-sha ma-jee
wave *wimbi* weem-bee
way *njia* n-jee-a
we *sisi* see-see
weak *hafifu* ha-*fee*-foo
wealthy *tajiri* ta-*jee*-ree
wear -*vaa* -va
weather *hali ya hewa* ha-lee ya hay-wa
wedding *arusi* a-*roo*-see
wedding cake *keki ya arusi* kay-kee ya a-roo-see
wedding present *zawadi ya arusi* za-*wa*-dee ya a-roo-see
Wednesday *Jumatano* joo-ma-*ta*-noh
week *wiki* wee-kee
weekend *wikendi* wee-*kayn*-dee
weigh -*pima uzito* -*pee*-ma oo-zee-toh
weight *uzito* oo-*zee*-toh

welcome -*karibisha* ·ka·ree·bee·sha
welfare *ustawi* oo·sta·wee
well *vizuri* vee·zoo·ree
west *magharibi* ma·gha·ree·bee
West Afrika *Afrika ya Magharibi*
a·free·ka ya mag·ha·ree·bee
wet ⓐ -*bichi* ·bee·chee
what *nini* nee·nee
wheel *gurudumu* goo·roo·doo·moo
wheelchair *kiti cha magurudumu*
kee·tee cha ma·goo·roo·doo·moo
when *wakati* wa·ka·tee
when *lini* lee·nee
where *wapi* wa·pee
which *gani* ga·nee
white *nyeupe* nyay·oo·pay
who *nani* na·nee
why *kwa nini* kwa nee·nee
wide *pana* pa·na
wife *mke* m·kay
wildebeest *nyumbu* nyoom·boo
win -*shinda* ·sheen·da
wind *upepo* oo·pay·poh
window *dirisha* dee·ree·sha
windscreen *kiwambo upepo*
kee·wam·boh oo·pay·poh
windsurfing *kuteleza na tanga*
koo·tay·lay·za na tan·ga
wine *mvinyo* m·vee·nyoh
wings *mabawa* ma·ba·wa
winner *mshindi* m·sheen·dee
winter *majira ya baridi*
ma·jee·ra ya ba·ree·dee
wire *waya* wa·ya
wish -*tumaini* ·too·ma·ee·nee
with *na* na
without *bila* bee·la
woman *mwanamke* mwan·am·kay
wonderful *ya ajabu* ya a·ja·boo
wood *mbao* m·ba·oh
woodcarver's market
soko la wachonga vinyago
soh·koh la wa·chohn·ga vee·nya·goh
wool *sufu* soo·foo
word *neno* nay·noh
work ⓝ *kazi* ka·zee
work ⓥ -*fanya kazi* ·fa·nya ka·zee
work experience *uzoefu wa kazi*
oo·zoh·ay·foo wa ka·zee
workout *mazoezi* ma·zoh·ay·zee

work permit *ruhusa ya kazi*
roo·hoo·sa ya ka·zee
workshop (place) *karakana* ka·ra·ka·na
workshop (meeting) *warsha* war·sha
world *dunia* doo·nee·a
World Cup *Kombe la Dunia*
kohm·bay la doo·nee·a
worms *minyoo* mee·nyoh
worried *mwenye wasiwasi*
mway·nyay wa·see·wa·see
worship -*abudu* ·a·boo·doo
wrist *kiwiko* kee·wee·koh
write -*andika* ·an·dee·ka
writer *mwandishi* mwan·dee·shee
wrong *kosa* koh·sa

X

x-ray *eksirei* ayk·see·ray·ee

Y

year *mwaka* mwa·ka
yellow *manjano* man·ja·noh
yes *ndiyo* n·dee·yoh
yesterday *jana* ja·na
yogurt *maziwa ganda* ma·zee·wa gan·da
you sg *wewe* way·way
you pl *nyinyi* nyee·nyee
young *ya kijana* ya kee·ja·na
your sg *yako* ya·koh
your pl *yenu* yay·noo
youth hostel *hosteli ya vijana*
hoh·stay·lee ya vee·ja·na

Z

Zaire *Jamhuri ya Kidemokrasia ya Kongo*
jam·hoo·ree ya kee·day·moh·kra·see·a
ya kohn·goh
Zambia *Zambia* zam·bee·a
Zanzibar City *Mji Mkongwe*
m·jee m·kohn·gway
Zanzibar Island *Unguja* oon·goo·ja
zebra *punda milia* poon·da mee·lee·a
zip/zipper *zipu* zee·poo
zodiac *zodiaki* zoh·dee·a·kee
zoo *hifadhi ndogo ya wanyama*
hee·fa·dhee n·doh·goh ya wa·nya·ma

Verbs are shown in the dictionary in their root forms, with a hyphen in front. To express a series of functions in a sentence, the verb can have several prefixes, infixes and suffixes. Some adjectives will also have a hyphen in front as they take different prefixes depending on certain characteristics of the thing being described. For more details on verbs and adjectives, see the **phrasebuilder**. You'll also find words marked as adjective ⓐ, noun ⓝ, verb ⓥ, singular sg, plural pl, adverb adv and preposition prep where necessary. A Swahili dictionary is also available online at www.kamusiproject.org.

A

a/c ay·see *air conditioning*
abiria a·bee·ree·a *a passenger*
-abudu ·a·boo·doo *worship*
-acha ·a·cha *quit*
achari a·cha·ree *pickles*
adapta a·dap·ta *adaptor*
afadhali a·fa·dha·lee *better*
afya af·ya *health*
-agiza ·a·gee·za *order* ⓥ
agizo a·gee·zoh *order* ⓝ
　　— **la daktari** la dak·ta·ree *prescription*
-ahidi ·a·hee·dee *promise*
aibu a·ee·boo *embarrassment*
aina a·ee·na *type*
　　— **ya damu** ya da·moo *blood group*
aiskrimu a·ee·skree·moo *ice cream*
ajali a·ja·lee *accident*
akaunti a·ka·oon·tee *account*
　　— **ya benki** ya bayn·kee *bank account*
akiba za chakula a·kee·ba za cha·koo·la *food supplies*
alama a·la·ma *score • sign*
Alhamisi al·ha·mee·see *Thursday*
aliyestaafu a·lee·yay·sta·a·foo *retired*
almasi al·ma·see *shiny*
amana a·ma·na *deposit (bank)*
amani a·ma·nee *peace*
-ambia ·am·bee·a *tell*
ambukizo am·boo·kee·zoh *infection*
　　— **la mfumo wa mkojo** la m·foo·moh wa m·koh·joh *urinary infection*
amekufa a·may·koo·fa *dead*
-amini ·a·mee·nee *trust*
-amka ·am·ka *wake up*

-amsha ·am·sha *wake someone up*
-amua ·a·moo·a *decide*
anasa a·na·sa *luxury*
-andaa ·an·da *prepare*
-andika ·an·dee·ka *write*
-angalia ·an·ga·lee·a *look*
angani an·ga·nee *airspace • outer space*
-anguka ·an·goo·ka *fall (down)*
anwani an·wa·nee *address*
-anza ·an·za *start*
ardhi ar·dhee *land*
arusi a·roo·see *wedding*
asali a·sa·lee *honey*
asante a·san·tay *thank you*
asilimia a·see·lee·mee·a *per cent*
asiye na hatia a·see·yay na ha·tee·a *innocent*
asiye na kazi a·see·yay na ka·zee *unemployed*
askari a·ska·ree *soldier*
aspirini a·spee·ree·nee *aspirin*
asubuhi a·soo·boo·hee *morning*
au a·oo *or*

B

baa ba *bar (pub)*
baada ya ba·a·da ya *after*
baadaye ba·a·da·yay *later*
baba ba·ba *father*
babamkwe ba·ba·m·kway *father-in-law*
babu ba·boo *grandfather*
-badilisha ·ba·dee·lee·sha *exchange*
　　— **hela** hay·la *change (money)*
bado ba·doh *not yet*
bafu ba·foo *bath*

bafuni ba·*foo*·nee
bathroom (for bathing) • shower
bahari ba·*ha*·ree ocean • sea
bahasha ba·*ha*·sha envelope
bahati ba·*ha*·tee luck
baisikeli ba·ee·see·*kay*·lee bicycle
— **kwenye gia** *kway*·nyay gee·a
mountain bike
— **ya mashindano**
ya ma·sheen·*da*·noh racing bike
bajeti ba·*jay*·tee budget
-baka ·*ba*·ka rape
-baki ·ba·*kee* stay (in one place)
bakshishi bak·*shee*·shee tip (gratuity)
bakuli ba·*koo*·lee bowl
balbu ya taa bal·*boo* ya ta light bulb
balozi ba·*loh*·zee ambassador
balungi ba·*loon*·gee grapefruit
bandari ban·*da*·ree harbour • port (sea)
bangi ban·gee
hash • marijuana • pot (dope)
bango ban·goh poster
banzi la hema ban·zee la *hay*·ma tent peg
bao la kukatia ba·oh la koo·ka·*tee*·a
chopping board
barabara ba·ra·*ba*·ra
avenue • highway • motorway • road
— **kuu** koo main road
barabara ba·ra·ba·ra excellent
barafu ba·*ra*·foo ice
baridi ba·*ree*·dee cold ⓐ
barua ba·*roo*·a letter • mail
— **kwa haraka** kwa ha·*ra*·ka
(by) express mail
— **kwa lori** kwa *loh*·ree
surface mail (land)
— **kwa meli** kwa *may*·lee
surface mail (sea)
— **kwa ndege** kwa n·*day*·gay airmail
— **pepe** *pay*·pay email
— **ya rejista** ya *ray*·jee·sta
(by) registered mail/post
basi ba·see bus (intercity) • coach
bata ba·ta duck
— **mzinga** m·zeen·ga turkey
-beba ·*bay*·ba carry
bega *bay*·ga shoulder
bei bay price
— **ya kuingia** ya koo·een·*gee*·a
cover charge • admission (price)
bekoni bay·*koh*·nee bacon
bendera bayn·*day*·ra flag
benki bayn·kee bank

betri bay·tree battery
Bi bee Mrs • Madam
bia bee·a beer
biashara bee·a·*sha*·ra business • trade
bibi bee·bee grandmother
Bibi bee·bee Ms • Miss
Biblia beeb·*lee*·a Bible
-bichi ·bee·chee fresh • raw • wet
bila bee·la without
— **nyumba** nyoom·ba homeless
— **raha** ra·ha uncomfortable
bili bee·lee cheque (bill)
biliadi bee·lee·a·dee pool (game)
bima bee·ma insurance
binafsi bee·naf·see private
binti bee·n·tee daughter
biri bee·ree cigar
biringani bee·reen·*ga*·nee
aubergine • eggplant
-bisha ·bee·sha argue
biskuti bee·skoo·tee biscuit • cookie
bizari bee·za·ree curry
blanketi blan·*kay*·tee blanket
blue bandi bloo·ban·dee margarine
boga boh·ga pumpkin
bogi la kulia chakula
boh·gee la koo·*lee*·a cha·koo·la dining car
bomba bohm·ba faucet • tap
bonde bohn·day valley
boti boh·tee boat
brandi bran·dee brandy
breki bray·kee brakes
bubu boo·boo mute
bucha boo·cha butcher • butcher's shop
buibui boo·ee·boo·ee spider
buking boo·keeng reservation • booking
buluu boo·loo blue
bunduki boon·doo·kee gun
bunge boon·gay parliament
-buni ·boo·nee guess
burashi boo·ra·shee brush
— **ya nywele** ya nyway·lay hairbrush
bure boo·ray complimentary (free)
burudani boo·roo·da·nee fun
bustani boo·sta·nee garden
— **ya kibotania** ya kee·boh·ta·*nee*·a
botanic garden
busu boo·soo kiss
-busu ·boo·soo kiss
Bwana bwa·na Mr • Sir
bwawa la kuogelea bwa·wa la
koo·oh·gay·*lay*·a swimming pool

C

chache *cha*·chay
few • less • little (not much)

chafu *cha*·foo dirty

-chagua -*cha*·goo·a choose

chai *cha*·ee tea
— **ya asubuhi** ya a·soo·*boo*·hee
breakfast

chakula cha·*koo*·la dish • food
— **cha jioni** cha jee·*oh*·nee dinner
— **cha mchana** cha m·*cha*·na lunch
— **cha mtoto mchanga**
cha m·*toh*·toh m·*chan*·ga baby food

chama *cha*·ma party (politics)

chandarua chan·da·*roo*·a mosquito net

-changanyika -chan·ga·*nyee*·ka mix

chanjo *chan*·joh vaccination

chanuo cha·*noo*·oh comb

chavua cha·*voo*·a pollen

chawa *cha*·wa lice

chaza *cha*·za oyster

-cheka -*chay*·ka laugh

chekechea chay·kay·*chay*·a
kindergarten

chenji *chayn*·jee change

chenza *chayn*·za mandarin

cheti *chay*·tee certificate
— **cha kuzaliwa** cha koo·za·*lee*·wa
birth certificate

-cheza -*chay*·za play (guitar, cards etc)

-cheza densi -*chay*·za *dayn*·see dance

chini *chee*·nee
below • bottom (position) • down • low

chokoleti choh·koh·*lay*·tee chocolate

-choma sindano -*choh*·ma seen·*da*·noh
inject

chombo cha kusaidia kusikia
chohm·boh cha koo·sa·ee·*dee*·a
koo·see·*kee*·a hearing aid

chombo cha majivu
chohm·boh cha ma·*jee*·voo ashtray

chomboni chohm·*boh*·nee aboard

choo choh bathroom (toilet)
— **cha hadhara** cha ha·*dha*·ra
public toilet

choroa choh·*roh*·a oryx

-choshwa -*choh*·shwa bored

chui *choo*·ee leopard

-chukua -*choo*·koo·a take

chumba *choom*·ba room
— **cha dobi** cha *doh*·bee
laundry (room)
— **cha kubadilisha nguo**
cha koo·ba·dee·*lee*·sha n·*goo*·oh
changing room (in shop)
— **cha kulala** cha koo·*la*·la bedroom
— **cha kupumzikia kwa wanaosafiri**
cha koo·poom·zee·*kee*·a kwa
wa·na·oh·*sa·fee*·ree transit lounge
— **cha kuwekea mizigo**
cha koo·way·*kay*·a mee·*zee*·goh
left-luggage room
— **cha makoti** cha ma·*koh*·tee cloakroom
— **cha mali ya kuokota** cha *ma*·lee ya
koo·oh·*koh*·ta lost property office
— **cha wanaosubiri** cha
wa·na·oh·soo·*bee*·ree waiting room
— **kwa watu wawili**
kwa *wa*·too wa·*wee*·lee double room
— **kwa mtu mmoja**
kwa m·*too* m·*moh*·ja single room

chumvi *choom*·vee salt

chungu *choon*·goo
bitter ⓐ • pot (ceramics) ⓝ

chuo *choo*·oh college
— **kikuu** kee·*koo* university

chupa *choo*·pa bottle • jar
— **ya maji (ya moto)**
ya *ma*·jee (ya *moh*·toh) water bottle (hot)

chupi *choo*·pee boxer shorts • underwear

D

dada *da*·da sister

dadu *da*·doo dice

daftari daf·*ta*·ree notebook

dagaa da·*ga* sardine

daima da·*ee*·ma always

dakika da·*kee*·ka minute

daktari dak·*ta*·ree doctor
— **wa akina mama** wa a·*kee*·na *ma*·ma
gynaecologist
— **wa macho** wa *ma*·choh optometrist
— **wa meno** wa *may*·noh dentist

daladala Tan da·la·*da*·la bus (city)

damu *da*·moo blood

daraja da·*ra*·ja bridge
— **la kwanza** la *kwan*·za first class
— **la pili** la *pee*·lee second class
— **la tatu** la *ta*·too economy class
— **la wafanyabiashara**
la wa·fa·nya bee·a·*sha*·ra business class

darubini da-roo-*bee*-nee
binoculars • telescope
dau *da*-oo *bet*
dawa *da*-wa *drug • medicine*
— **la kuendesha** la koo-ayn-*day*-sha
laxative
— **la kugeuza rangi kwenye jua**
la koo-*gay*-oo-za *ran*-gee *kway*-nyay
joo-a *tanning lotion*
— **la kukinga jua** la koo-*keen*-ga *joo*-a
sunblock
— **la kukohoa** la koo-koh-*hoh*-a
cough medicine
— **la meno** la *may*-noh *toothpaste*
— **la midomo** la mee-*doh*-moh
lip balm
— **la sindano** la seen-*da*-noh
injection
— **la kuboresha nywele**
la koo-boh-*ray*-sha *nyway*-lay
conditioner (hair)
— **la kuongeza maji mwilini**
la koo-ohn-*gay*-za *ma*-jee mwee-*lee*-nee
rehydration salts
— **la kusafisha jeraha**
la koo-sa-*fee*-sha jay-*ra*-ha *antiseptic* ⓝ
demokrasia day-moh-kra-*see*-a
democracy
dengu *dayn*-goo *lentil*
densi *dayn*-see *dancing*
dhahabu dha-*ha*-boo *gold*
dhamana dha-*ma*-na *guarantee*
dharura dha-*roo*-ra *emergency*
dhidi ya nyuklia *dhee*-dee ya *nyoo*-klee-a
antinuclear
dhoruba dho-*roo*-ba *storm*
— **ya radi** ya *ra*-dee *thunderstorm*
dini *dee*-nee *religion*
diodorani dee-oh-doh-*ra*-nee
deodorant
dira *dee*-ra *compass*
dirisha dee-*ree*-sha *window*
disketi dees-*kay*-tee *disk (floppy)*
diski *dee*-skee *disk (CD-ROM)*
disko *dee*-skoh *disco*
dobi *doh*-bee *launderette*
-dogo -*doh*-goh *small*
— **kabisa** ka-*bee*-sa *smallest*
— **zaidi** za-*ee*-dee *smaller*
dola *doh*-la *dollar*
dozi kubwa mno ya dawa *doh*-zee
koob-wa m-*noh* ya *da*-wa *overdose*
duara doo-*a*-ra *round*

duka *doo*-ka *shop*
— **kubwa** *koob*-wa *supermarket*
— **la aiskrimu** la a-ee-*skree*-moo
ice-cream parlour
— **la baisikeli** la ba-ee-see-*kay*-lee
bike shop
— **la bidhaa mbalimbali** la bee-*dha*
m-ba-lee-m-*ba*-lee *convenience store*
— **la bidhaa za umeme**
la bee-*dha* za oo-*may*-may *electrical store*
— **la dawa** la *da*-wa *chemist • pharmacy*
— **la fedha** la *fay*-dha *silver shop*
— **la keki** la *kay*-kee *cake shop*
— **la kemra** la *kaym*-ra *camera shop*
— **la kumbukumbu**
la koom-boo-*koom*-boo *souvenir shop*
— **la magazeti** la ma-ga-*zay*-tee
newsstand
— **la maua** la ma-*oo*-a *florist*
— **la mboga** la m-*boh*-ga *greengrocer*
— **la mitumba** la mee-*toom*-ba
second-hand shop
— **la mkate** la m-*ka*-tay *bakery*
— **la muziki** la moo-*zee*-kee *music shop*
— **la nguo** la n-*goo*-oh *clothing store*
— **la pombe kali** la *pohm*-bay *ka*-lee
bottle shop • liquor store
— **la samaki** la sa-*ma*-kee *fish shop*
— **la tumbaku** la toom-*ba*-koo *tobacconist*
— **la viatu** la vee-*a*-too *shoe shop*
— **la vifaa vya kambi**
la vee-*fa* vya *kam*-bee *camping store*
— **la vifaa vya michezo**
la vee-*fa* vya mee-*chay*-zoh *sports store*
— **la vifaa vya ofisi**
la vee-*fa* vya o-*fee*-see *stationer (shop)*
— **la vifaa vya ujenzi**
la vee-*fa* vya oo-*jayn*-zee *hardware store*
— **la vipuli** la vee-*poo*-lee *jewellery store*
— **la vitabu** la vee-*ta*-boo *bookshop*
— **la vitu vya kuchezea**
la *vee*-too vya koo-chay-*zay*-a *toy shop*
— **lenye vitu vingi** *lay*-nyay *vee*-too
veen-gee *department store*
duma *doo*-ma *cheetah*
Dunia *doo*-nee-a *Earth*
dunia doo-*nee*-a *world*

E

-egesha -ay-*gay*-sha *park (a car)*
ekspres ayk-*sprays* *express* ⓐ
ekstasi ayk-sta-see *ecstacy (drug)*

elasto ay·la·stoh *Band-Aid*
-elekeza ay·lay·kay·za *point*
-elewa ay·lay·wa *understand*
elimu ay·lee·moo *education*
embe aym·bay *mango*
   — **mafuta** ma·foo·ta *avocado*
-enda ·ayn·da *go*
   — **dukani** doo·ka·nee *go shopping*
   — **nje** n·jay *go out*
-endesha ·ayn·day·sha *drive*
eskaleta ays·ka·lay·ta *escalator*
euro ay·oo·roh *euro*
eutanasia ay·oo·ta·na·see·a *euthanasia*

F

-fa ·fa *die*
faida fa·ee·da *profit*
faini fa·ee·nee *fine (penalty)*
faksi fak·see *fax machine*
falaki fa·la·kee *horoscope*
familia fa·mee·lee·a *family*
-fanya ·fa·nya *do*
   — **buking** boo·keeng *make a booking*
   — **kazi** ka·zee *work*
farasi fa·ra·see *horse*
faulo fa·oo·loh *foul*
fedha fay·dha *cash • silver*
feni fay·nee *fan (machine)*
fenicha fay·nee·cha *furniture*
figili fee·gee·lee *radish*
figo fee·goh *kidney*
-fika ·fee·ka *arrive*
-fikiri ·fee·kee·ree *think*
-fikisha ·fee·kee·sha *deliver*
filamu fee·la·moo *film (cinema)*
   — **ya hali halisi** ya ha·lee ha·lee·see *documentary (film)*
   — **ya slaidi** ya sla·ee·dee *slide film*
fisi fee·see *hyena*
fleti flay·tee *flat (apartment)*
fluu floo *flu (influenza)*
forodha foh·roh·dha *customs*
foronya foh·roh·nya *pillowcase*
friji free·jee *fridge*
-fuata ·foo·a·ta *follow*
fulana ya ndani foo·la·na ya n·da·nee *singlet*
fulani foo·la·nee *someone*
fundi foon·dee *mechanic*
funga foon·ga *close*
-funga kwa ufunguo ·foon·ga kwa oo·foon·goo·oh *lock*

fungate foon·ga·tay *honeymoon*
-fungua ·foon·goo·a *open*
fupi foo·pee *short (height)*
-furahia ·foo·ra·hee·a *enjoy (oneself) • have fun*
fursa sawa foor·sa sa·wa *equal opportunity*
furushi foo·roo·shee *package*
-futa ·foo·ta *cancel*
futbol ya kimarekani foot·bohl ya kee·ma·ray·ka·nee *American football*
fuvu foo·voo *skull*

G

-ganda ·gan·da *freeze*
gani ga·nee *which*
gari ga·ree *car*
   — **la hospitali** la hoh·spee·ta·lee *ambulance*
   — **la vitanda** la vee·tan·da *sleeping car*
-gawa ·ga·wa *deal (cards)*
-gawana ·ga·wa·na *share (a dorm etc)*
gazeti ga·zay·tee *magazine • newspaper*
gereji gay·ray·jee *garage (to park a car)*
gereza gay·ray·za *jail*
gesti gay·stee *guesthouse • hotel • motel*
-geuza ·gay·oo·za *turn*
ghali ga·lee *expensive*
gharama ga·ra·ma *cost*
   — **kwa mpigiwa simu** kwa m·pee·gee·wa see·moo *collect call*
ghorofa go·ro·fa *floor • storey*
giza gee·za *dark*
glesi glay·see *glass*
godolo goh·doh·loh *mattress*
goli goh·lee *goal*
goti goh·tee *knee*
gramu gra·moo *gram*
gundi goon·dee *glue*
-gundua ·goon·doo·a *find*
gurudumu goo·roo·doo·moo *wheel*
-gusa ·goo·sa *touch*

H

habari ha·ba·ree *news*
hadhi ya kindoa ha·dhee ya kee·n·doh·a *marital status*
hadi ha·dee *to*
hadithi ha·dee·thee *story*
   — **kama riwaya** ka·ma ree·wa·ya *drama*

hafifu ha·*fee*·foo *weak*
haiwezekani ha·ee·way·zay·ka·nee
impossible
haki ya kisheria ya mmiliki wa gari
*ha·*kee ya kee·shay·*ree·*a ya
m·mee·*lee·*kee wa *ga·*ree
car owner's title
haki za binadamu
*ha·*kee za been·a·*da·*moo
civil rights • human rights
-hakikisha (buking) ·ha·kee·*kee·*sha
(*boo·*keeng) *confirm (a booking)*
hakimu ha·*kee·*moo *judge*
hakuna ha·*koo·*na *none*
— **kitu** *kee·*too *nothing*
— **nafasi** na·*fa·*see
booked out • no vacancy
— **sigara** see·*ga·*ra *nonsmoking*
halali ha·*la·*lee *halal • kosher • legal*
hali asili *ha·*le a·*see·*lee *nature*
hali ya hewa *ha·*lee ya *hay·*wa *weather*
halijoto ha·lee·*joh·*toh
temperature (weather)
halisi ha·*lee·*see *pure*
hamna *ham·*na *none*
hapa *ha·*pa *here*
hapana ha·*pa·*na *no • not*
hapo jirani *ha·*poh jee·*ra·*nee *nearby*
hapo karibuni
*ha·*poh ka·ree·*boo·*nee *nearby*
hariri ha·*ree·*ree *silk*
harufu ha·*roo·*foo *smell*
hatari ha·*ta·*ree *dangerous • risk*
hatua ha·*too·*a *step*
hedhi *hay·*dhee *menstruation*
hekalu hay·*ka·*loo *temple*
hela *hay·*la *money*
helmeti hayl·*may·*tee *helmet*
hema *hay·*ma *tent*
herini hay·*ree·*nee *earrings*
heroe hay·*roh·*ay *flamingo*
heroini hay·roh·*ee·*nee *heroin*
-hesabu ·hay·*sa·*boo *count*
hewa *hay·*wa *air (outside) • atmosphere*
hifadhi hee·*fa·*dhee *park*
— **ndogo ya wanyama**
n·*doh·*goh ya wa·*nya·*ma *zoo*
— **ya wanyama** ya wa·*nya·*ma
game park • national park
hii hee *it • this (thing)*
-hisi ·*hee·*see *feel (touch)*
hisia hee·*see·*a *feeling (physical) • feelings*
historia hee·stoh·*ree·*a *history*
-hitaji ·hee·*ta·*jee *need*

hivi karibuni
*hee·*vee ka·ree·*boo·*nee *recently*
hiyo *hee·*yoh *that (thing)*
hodari hoh·*da·*ree *brilliant (smart)*
hoki ya barafuni
*hoh·*kee ya ba·ra·*foo·*nee *ice hockey*
homa *hoh·*ma *fever (temperature)*
— **ya matezi** ya ma·*tay·*zee
glandular fever
— **ya mzio** ya m·*zee·*oh *hay fever*
hongera hohn·*gay·*ra *congratulations*
honi *hoh·*nee *horn*
hospitali hoh·spee·*ta·*lee *hospital*
hosteli ya vijana
hoh·*stay·*lee ya vee·*ja·*na
youth hostel
huduma hoo·*doo·*ma *service*
huko *hoo·*koh *there*
hundi *hoon·*dee *cheque (banking)*
— **ya msafiri** ya m·sa·*fee·*ree
travellers cheque
huru *hoo·*roo *free (not bound)*
husuni hoo·*soo·*nee *castle*
huyo *hoo·*yoh *that (person)*
huyu *hoo·*yoo *this (person)*

I

-iba ·*ee·*ba *rob*
ijayo ee·*ja·*yoh *next*
Ijumaa ee·joo·*ma·*a *Friday*
-imba ·*eem·*ba *sing*
imevunjika ee·may·voon·*jee·*ka
out of order
-ingia ·een·*gee·*a *enter*
ini *ee·*nee *liver*
injini een·*jee·*nee *engine*
intanet kafe een·ta·*nayt* ka·*fay*
Internet café
-ishi ·*ee·*shee *live (somewhere)*
isiyo na risasi
ee·*see·*yoh na ree·*sa·*see *unleaded*
-ita ·*ee·*ta *call*

J

-ja ·ja *come*
jaketi ja·*kay·*tee *jacket*
— **la kuokolea** la koo·oh·koh·*lay·*a
life jacket
jamhuri jam·*hoo·*ree *republic*
jamu ·ja·moo *jam*
— **ya machungwa** ya ma·*choon·*gwa
marmalade

jana *ja*·na *yesterday*
jangwa *jan*·gwa *desert*
jani *ja*·nee *leaf*
-jaribu *ja*·ree·boo *try (attempt)*
-jaza *ja*·za *fill*
-jenga *jayn*·ga *build*
jengo *jayn*·goh *building*
jeraha *jay*·ra·ha *bruise • injury*
   — la moto la *moh*·toh *burn*
jeshi *jay*·shee *military*
jeuri *jay*·oo·ree *unfair*
jibini *jee*·bee·nee *cheese*
jibu *jee*·boo *answer*
-jiburudisha *jee*·boo·roo·*dee*·sha *relax*
jicho *jee*·choh *eye*
-jifunza *jee*·foon·za *learn*
jiko *jee*·koh *kitchen • stove*
jina *jee*·na *name*
   — la baba la *ba*·ba *surname*
   — la familia la fa·mee·*lee*·a
   family name
   — la kwanza la *kwan*·za *Christian name*
   — la utani la oo·*ta*·nee *nickname*
jino *jee*·noh *tooth*
jinsia jeen·*see*·a *sex (gender)*
jinzi jeen·zee *jeans*
jioni jee·oh·nee *evening*
jipi *jee*·pee *jeep*
jiranl *jee*·ra·nee *beside • near*
jiwe *jee*·way *rock • stone*
jodari joh·*da·ree* *tuna*
joko *joh*·koh *oven*
   — la mikrowevu la mee·kroh·*way*·voo
   microwave (oven)
joto *joh*·toh *heat* ⓝ *• heating* ⓝ *• hot* ⓐ
Jua *joo*·a *sun*
-jua *joo*·a *know*
jukwaa *joo*·kwa *platform*
Jumamosi joo·ma·*moh*·see *Saturday*
Jumanne joo·ma·*n*·nay *Tuesday*
Jumapili joo·ma·*pee*·lee *Sunday*
Jumatano joo·ma·*ta*·noh *Wednesday*
Jumatatu joo·ma·*ta*·too *Monday*
jumba *joom*·ba *palace*
   — la opera la *oh*·pay·ra *opera house*
jumuiya ya masista joo·moo·*ee*·ya ya
   ma·*see*·sta *convent*
jusi *joo*·see *juice*
juu joo *high • up*
juu ya joo ya *above* ⓐ *• on* adv
juzi *joo*·zee *day before yesterday*

K

-kaa ·ka *sit • stay (at a hotel)*
-kaanga ·ka·*an*·ga *fry*
kabati ka·*ba*·tee *cupboard*
   — ya nguo ya n·*goo*·oh *wardrobe*
kabichi ka·*bee*·chee *cabbage*
kabla *ka*·bla *before*
kaburi ka·*boo*·ree *grave*
kabuti ka·*boo*·tee *overcoat*
kadhaa ka·*dha* *several • some*
kadi ya benki *ka*·dee ya *bayn*·kee
   credit card
kadi ya simu (ya mikononi) *ka*·dee ya
   see·moo (ya mee·koh·*noh*·nee) *SIM card*
kadi ya simu za vibandani *ka*·dee ya
   see·moo za vee·ban·*da*·nee *phonecard*
-kagua ·ka·*goo*·a *check*
kahawa ka·*ha*·wa *coffee*
kahawia ka·*ha*·wee·a *brown*
kaka *ka*·ka *brother*
kakao ka·*ka*·oh *cocoa*
kalamu ka·*la*·moo *pen (ballpoint)*
kalenda ka·*layn*·da *calendar*
kama *ka*·ma *if*
-kamata ·ka·*ma*·ta *arrest*
kamba *kam*·ba *prawn • rope*
   — ya kukausha nguo
   ya koo·ka·oo·sha n·*goo*·oh *clothesline*
   — za viatu za vee·*a*·too *laces*
kamili ka·*mee*·lee *exactly* adv *• perfect* ⓐ
kamisheni ka·mee·*shay*·nee *commission*
kampuni kam·*poo*·nee *company*
   — ya ndege ya n·*day*·gay *airline*
kamusi ka·*moo*·see *dictionary*
kamwe *kam*·way *never*
kanda *kan*·da *cassette*
   — ya musiki ya moo·*zee*·kee
   musical recording
kando ya *kan*·doh ya *next to*
kanisa ka·*nee*·sa *church*
   — kuu koo *cathedral*
   — ya kiyahudi ya kee·ya·*hoo*·dee
   synagogue
kansa *kan*·sa *cancer*
kapera ka·*pay*·ra *single (person)*
kaptura kap·*too*·ra *shorts*
karakana ka·ra·*ka*·na
   workshop (to make things)
karanga ka·*ran*·ga *groundnut • peanut*
karani ka·*ra*·nee *secretary*

karantini ka·ran·*tee*·nee quarantine
karata ka·*ra*·ta playing cards
karatasi ka·ra·ta·see paper
— **ya choo** ya choh toilet paper
— **za shashi** za sha·shee tissues
-karibisha ·ka·ree·bee·sha invite • welcome
karibu ka·*ree*·boo close (near)
— **na** na almost
— **zaidi** za·ee·dee nearest
karoti ka·*roh*·tee carrot
kasha la fedha ka·sha la fay·dha
safe (for money)
kasino ka·see·noh casino
kaskazini kas·ka·zee·nee north
-kata ·ka·ta cut
-kataa ·ka·ta refuse
katika ka·tee·ka in
— **muda wa (saa moja)**
moo·da wa (sa moh·ja) within (an hour)
katikati ka·tee·*ka*·tee
between adv • centre ⓝ
— **ya mji** ya m·jee city centre
katoni ka·*toh*·nee carton
kaunta ka·*oon*·ta counter (at bar)
-kausha ·ka·oo·sha dry
kavu ka·voo dry
kawaida ka·wa·ee·da ordinary
kazi ka·zee job • work
— **kwenye baa** kway·nyay ba bar work
— **ya mikono** ya mee·*koh*·noh
handicrafts
— **ya nyumbani** ya nyum·*ba*·nee
housework
— **ya ukarani** ya oo·ka·*ra*·nee paperwork
kebo za kuwashia kay·boh za
koo·wa·shee·a jumper leads
kejekeje kay·jay·*kay*·jay loose
keki kay·kee cake
— **ya arusi** ya a·roo·see wedding cake
kemra kaym·ra camera
keshia kay·shee·a cashier
kesho kay·shoh tomorrow
— **asubuhi** a·soo·*boo*·hee
tomorrow morning
— **jioni** jee·oh·nee tomorrow evening
— **kutwa** koot·wa
the day after tomorrow
— **mchana** m·*cha*·na
tomorrow afternoon
kiambato kee·am·*ba*·toh ingredient
kiasi gani kee·a·see ga·nee how much
kiatu kee·*a*·too shoe
kiazi kee·*a*·zee potato

kiazisukari kee·a·zee·soo·*ka*·ree beetroot
kibali kee·*ba*·lee permit
kibanda cha simu
kee·*ban*·da cha see·moo telephone box
kibandiko cha chupi kee·ban·*dee*·koh
cha choo·pee panty liners
kibarua kee·ba·roo·a
casual work • part-time
kibiriti kee·bee·*ree*·tee lighter (match)
kibofu kee·*boh*·foo bladder
kiboko kee·*boh*·koh hippopotamus
kibole kee·*boh*·lay appendix (body)
kichapishi kee·cha·*pee*·shee keyboard
kichefuchefu
kee·chay·foo·*chay*·foo nausea
— **cha asubuhi** cha a·soo·*boo*·hee
morning sickness
— **cha baharini** cha ba·ha·*ree*·nee
seasickness
— **cha safari** cha sa·*fa*·ree travel sickness
kichwa *keech*·wa head
kidole kee·*doh*·lay finger
— **cha mguu** cha m·*goo* toe
kidonge kee·*dohn*·gay pill
— **cha kuzuia mimba**
cha koo·zoo·ee·a *meem*·ba the pill
kifafa kee·*fa*·fa epilepsy
kifaru kee·*fa*·roo rhinoceros
kifiko kee·*fee*·koh destination
kifungo kee·*foon*·goh button
kifungua chupa kee·foon·*goo*·a choo·pa
bottle opener
kifungua kopo kee·foon·*goo*·a koh·poh
tin opener
kifurushi kee·foo·*roo*·shee parcel
kigari cha mtoto
kee·*ga*·ree cha m·*toh*·toh stroller • pram
kiharusi kee·ha·*roo*·see stroke (health)
Kiingereza kee·een·gay·*ray*·za
English (language)
kijani kee·*ja*·nee green
kijiji kee·*jee*·jee village
kijiko kee·*jee*·koh spoon
— **cha chai** cha *cha*·ee teaspoon
kijitabu kee·jee·*ta*·boo brochure
kijiti cha meno kee·*jee*·tee cha *may*·noh
toothpick
kijiti cha pamba safi kee·*jee*·tee cha
pam·ba sa·fee cotton buds
kijito kee·*jee*·toh stream
kijivu kee·*jee*·voo grey
kikaango kee·ka·*an*·goh frying pan
kikapu kee·*ka*·poo basket

kikohozi kee-koh-hoh-zee cough
kikokotoo kee-koh-koh-toh-oh calculator
kikombe kee-kohm-bay cup
kikomo cha mwendo kee-koh-moh cha mwayn-doh speed limit
kikundi kee-koon-dee hand (music)
kila kee-la each • every
kila kitu kee-la kee-too everything
kila siku kee-la see-koo daily
kilainishio kee-la-ee-nee-shee-oh lubricant
kilele kee-lay-lay peak (mountain)
kilema kee-lay-ma paraplegic
kilevi kee-lay-vee alcohol
kilimo kee-lee-moh agriculture
  — **cha bustani** cha boo-sta-nee gardening
kilio kee-lee-oh funeral
kilo kee-loh kilogram
kilomita kee-loh-mee-ta kilometre
-kimbia -keem-bee-a run
kimo kee-moh altitude
-kinga -keen-ga protect
kingamimba keen-ga-meem-ba contraceptives
kinururishi kee-noo-roo-ree-shee radiator
kinyozi kee-nyoh-zee barber
kinyume kee-nyoo-may opposite
kinywaji kee-nywa-jee drink
kiondoa maumivu kee-ohn-doh-a ma-oo-mee-voo painkiller
kiongozi kee-ohn-goh-zee guide (person) • leader
kionyeshi kee-oh-nyay-shee indicator
kioo kee-oh mirror
kioski kee-oh-skee kiosk
kipa kee-pa goalkeeper
kipandauso kee-pan-da-oo-soh migraine
kipande kee-pan-day piece
  — **cha namba ya gari** cha nam-ba ya ga-ree numberplate
kipasha moto kee-pa-sha moh-toh heater
kipepeo kee-pay-pay-oh butterfly
kipima mwanga kee-pee-ma mwan-ga light meter
kipimo cha damu kee-pee-moh cha da-moo blood test
kipindi cha baridi kidogo kee-peen-dee cha ba-ree-dee kee-doh-goh fall (autumn)
kiplefti keep-layf-tee roundabout
kipodozi kee-poh-doh-zee make-up

kipofu kee-poh-foo blind
kirekebisho moyo kee-ray-kay-bee-shoh moh-yoh pacemaker
kemra ya video kaym-ra ya vee-day-oh video recorder
kiroboto kee-roh-boh-toh flea
kisanduku cha huduma ya kwanza kee-san-doo-koo cha hoo-doo-ma ya kwan-za first-aid kit
kishota cha kukatia barafu kee-shoh-ta cha koo-ka-tee-a ba-ra-foo ice axe
kisiwa kee-see-wa island
kisu kee-soo knife
  — **cha mfukoni** cha m-foo-koh-nee penknife • pocket knife
kisukari kee-soo-ka-ree diabetes
kitabu kee-ta-boo book
  — **cha kumbukumbu** cha koom-boo-koom-boo diary
  — **cha misemo** cha mee-say-moh phrasebook
  — **cha mwongozo** cha mwohn-goh-zoh guidebook
  — **cha namba za simu** cha nam-ba za see-moo phone book
kitambaa kee-tam-ba fabric
  — **cha meza** cha may-za tablecloth
  — **cha mkono** cha m-koh-noh face cloth • handkerchief • napkin
  — **cha uso** cha oo-soh wash cloth (flannel)
kitambulisho kee-tam-boo-lee-shoh identification • identification card (ID)
kitanda kee-tan-da bed
  — **cha watu wawili** cha wa-too wa-wee-lee double bed
  — **katika behewa** ka-tee-ka bay-hay-wa sleeping berth
kitani kee-ta-nee linen (material)
kitanzi cha kuzuia kuzaa kee-tan-zee cha koo-zoo-ee-a koo-za IUD
kiti kee-tee chair • seat (place)
  — **cha magurudumu** cha ma-goo-roo-doo-moo wheelchair
  — **cha mtoto** cha m-toh-toh child seat
  — **juu cha mtoto** joo cha m-toh-toh highchair
kitindamlo kee-teen-da-m-loh dessert
kitobosha kee-toh-boh-sha pastry
kitu kee-too something
kitunguu kee-toon-goo onion
  — **saumu** sa-oo-moo garlic

kituo kee·too·oh *stop (bus etc)*
— **cha basi** cha ba·see *bus stop*
— **cha mafuta** cha ma·foo·ta *petrol station • service station*
— **cha petroli** cha pay·troh·lee *service station*
— **cha polisi** cha poh·lee·see *police station*
— **cha simu** cha see·moo *telephone centre*
— **cha teksi** cha tayk·see *taxi stand*
— **cha ukaguzi** cha oo·ka·goo·zee *checkpoint*
(-sikia) kiu (·see·kee·a) kee·oo *(be) thirsty*
kiuavijasumu kee·oo·a·vee·ja·soo·moo *antibiotic*
kiungo kee·oon·goh *connection*
kivuko kee·voo·koh *ferry*
kivuli kee·voo·lee *shade • shadow*
kiwambo cha kizuia mimba kee·wam·boh cha kee·zoo·ee·a meem·ba *diaphragm (contraceptive)*
kiwambo upepo kee·wam·boh oo·pay·poh *windscreen*
kiwanda kee·wan·da *factory • industry*
kiwango cha kubadilishia fedha kee·wan·goh cha koo·ba·dee·lee·shee·a fay·dha *exchange rate*
kiwanja cha kupigia kambi kee·wan·ja cha kuu·pee·gee·a kam·bee *campsite*
kiwanja cha tenesi kee·wan·ja cha tay·nay·see *tennis court*
kiwashio kee·wa·shee·oh *cigarette lighter*
kiwiko kee·wee·koh *wrist*
— **cha mguu** cha m·goo·a *ankle*
kizibo kee·zee·boh *plug (bath)*
kizibuo kee·zee·boo·oh *corkscrew*
kizuizi kee·zoo·ee·zee *blockage*
kizunguzungu kee·zoon·goo·zoon·goo *dizzyness*
— **cha saa kutokana na kwa ndege** cha sa koo·toh·ka·na na koo·sa·fee·ree kwa n·day·gay *jet lag*
klabu ya usiku kla·boo ya oo·see·koo *nightclub*
klachi kla·chee *clutch (car)*
koboko koh·boh·koh *cobra*
-kodi ·koh·dee *hire (rent)*
kodi koh·dee *tax*
— **ya mapato** ya ma·pa·toh *income tax*
— **ya mauzo** ya ma·oo·zoh *sales tax*
— **ya uwanja wa ndege** ya oo·wan·ja wa n·day·gay *airport tax*
kofia koh·fee·a *hat*

kokeini koh·kay·ee·nee *cocaine*
kokteli kohk·tay·lee *cocktail*
kokwa kohk·wa *nut*
koliflawa koh·lee·fla·wa *cauliflower*
Kombe la Dunia kohm·bay la doo·nee·a *World Cup*
kome koh·may *mussel*
kompyuta kohm·pyoo·ta *computer*
— **ya kubeba** ya koo·bay·ba *laptop*
komunyo koh·moo·nyoh *communion*
kona koh·na *corner*
kondom kohn·dohm *condom*
kondoo kohn·doh *sheep*
konokono koh·noh·koh·noh *snail*
koo koh *throat*
-kopa ·koh·pa *borrow*
kopo koh·poh *can • tin*
korosho koh·roh·shoh *cashew*
kosa koh·sa *(someone's) fault* ⓝ • *mistake* ⓝ • *wrong* ⓐ
-kosa ·koh·sa *miss (feel absence of)*
koti koh·tee *coat*
— **la mvua** la m·voo·a *raincoat*
krketi kree·kay·tee *cricket (sport)*
krimu ya kulainisha ngozi kree·moo ya koo·la·ee·nee·sha n·goh·zee *moisturiser*
kuandikwa kitu kimoja kimoja koo·an·deek·wa kee·too kee·moh·ja kee·moh·jah *itemised*
kubadilisha hela koo·ba·dee·lee·sha hay·la *currency exchange*
-kubali ·koo·ba·lee *agree*
kubwa koob·wa *big (large)*
— **kabisa** ka·bee·sa *biggest*
— **sana** sa·na *huge*
— **zaidi** za·ee·dee *bigger*
kucha koo·cha *dawn*
kuchomwa kwa jua koo·chom·wa kwa joo·a *sunburn*
kuchuliwa koo·choo·lee·wa *massage*
kuelekea koo·ay·lay·kay·a *towards*
kufua koo·foo·a *chest (body)*
kufuli koo·foo·lee *lock • padlock*
— **ya baisikeli** ya ba·ee·see·kay·lee *bike lock*
kufungwa koo·foon·gwa *shut*
kuhara koo·ha·ra *diarrhoea*
kuharibu mimba koo·ha·ree·boo meem·ba *miscarriage*
kuharibu misitu koo·ha·ree·boo mee·see·too *deforestation*
kuhusu koo·hoo·soo *about*
kujeruhiwa koo·jay·roo·hee·wa *injured*

kukata nywele koo·ka·ta *nyway·*lay haircut
kukimbia koo·keem·bee·a *running*
— **taratibu** ta·ra·tee·boo *jogging*
kukodi gari koo·koh·dee *ga·*ree *car hire*
kuku *koo·*koo *chicken*
kulia koo·lee·a *right (direction)*
kuma koo·ma *vagina*
-kumbatia ·koom·ba·tee·a *hug*
kumbukumbu
koom·boo·koom·boo *souvenir*
kumbwe koom·bway *snack*
kumi na mbili koo·mee na m·bee·lee *dozen*
kuna mawingu
koo·na ma·ween·goo *cloudy*
kundekunde koon·day·koon·day *legume*
kundi ya roki koon·dee ya roh·kee *rock group*
kuni koo·nee *firewood*
kuogelea koo·oh·gay·lay·a *swimming (sport)*
kuondoka koo·ohn·doh·ka *departure*
kupanda baisikeli
koo·pan·da ba·ee·see·kay·lee *cycling*
kupanda farasi koo·pan·da fa·ra·see *horse riding*
kupanda milima koo·pan·da mee·lee·ma *mountaineering*
kupatikana koo·pa·tee·ka·na *free (available)*
kupiga picha ya mtoto tumboni
koo·pee·ga pee·cha ya m·toh·toh toom·boh·nee *ultrasound*
kupiga simu moja kwa moja koo·pee·ga see·moo moh·ja kwa moh·ja *direct-dial*
kupika koo·pee·ka *cooking*
kuponi koo·pohn·ee *coupon*
kurudisha pesa koo·roo·dee·sha pay·sa *refund*
kushambuliwa na maradhi ya moyo
koo·sham·boo·lee·wa na ma·ra·dhee ya moh·yoh *heart attack*
kushoto koo·shoh·toh *left (direction)*
kusimama kwa mapigo ya moyo
koo·see·ma·ma kwa ma·pee·goh ya moh·yoh *cardiac arrest*
kusini koo·see·nee *south*
kuskii koo·skee *skiing*
-kuta ·koo·ta *meet*
kutaamali koo·ta·a·ma·lee *meditation*
kutalikiwa koo·ta·lee·kee·wa *divorced*
kuteleza koo·tay·lay·za *surfing*
— **na tanga** na tan·ga *windsurfing*

kutembea porini
koo·taym·bay·a poh·ree·nee *hiking*
kutengenezwa kwa mkono
koo·tayn·gay·nayz·wa kwa m·koh·noh *handmade*
kutoa mimba koo·toh·a meem·ba *abortion*
kutoka koo·toh·ka *exit* ⓝ • *from* prep
kutopenyesha maji
koo·to·pay·nyay·sha ma·jee *waterproof*
kutumikia jeshi koo·too·mee·kee·a *jay·*shee *military service*
-kuu ·koo *main*
kuuza madawa ya kulevya
koo·oo·za ma·da·wa ya koo·lay·vya *drug trafficking*
kuvimba kibofu
koo·veem·ba kee·boh·foo *cystitis*
kuvimbiwa koo·veem·bee·wa *indigestion*
kuvuna matunda koo·voo·na ma·toon·da *fruit picking*
kuvuta makasia koo·voo·ta ma·ka·see·a *rowing*
kuwahi koo·wa·hee *be on time* • *early*
kuzamia koo·za·mee·a *diving*
kwa kwa *per (day)*
kwa haraka kwa ha·ra·ka *in a hurry*
kwa heri kwa hay·ree *goodbye*
kwa kuteremka
kwa koo·tay·raym·ka *downhill*
kwa nini kwa nee·nee *why*
kwa sababu kwa sa·ba·boo *because*
kwa sauti kwa sa·oo·tee *loud*
kwa usiku mmoja
kwa oo·see·koo m·moh·ja *overnight*
kwa wapenzi kwa wa·payn·zee *romantic*
kwenye kway·nyay *at* • *to*
— **a/c** ay·see *air-conditioned*

L

-la ·la *eat*
labda lab·da *maybe*
laiseni la·ee·say·nee *license*
lakini la·kee·nee *but*
-lala ·la·la *lie (not stand)*
-lalamika ·la·la·mee·ka *complain*
lalamiko la·la·mee·koh *complaint*
laza la·za *admit*
lazima la·zee·ma *necessary*
lengelenge layn·gay·layn·gay *blister*

lenzi mboni *layn*-zee m-*boh*-nee
contact lenses
leo *lay*-oh today
leseni ya kuendesha gari lay-*say*-nee ya
koo-ayn-*day*-sha *ga*-ree drivers license
-leta -*lay*-ta bring
-lewa -*lay*-wa drunk • stoned (drugged)
lifti *leef*-tee lift • elevator • ride
likizo lee-*kee*-zoh holidays • vacation
limau lee-*ma*-oo lemon
lindo *leen*-doh lookout
lini *lee*-nee when
-lipa -*lee*-pa pay
-lipwa fedha kwa kutoa hundi
-*leep*-wa *fay*-dha kwa koo-*toh*-a
hoon-dee cash (a cheque)
-lisha -*lee*-sha feed
lori *loh*-ree truck
— la wasafiri la wa-sa-*fee*-ree caravan
losheni baada ya kunyoa ndevu
loh-*shay*-nee ba-*a*-da ya koo-*nyoh*-a
n-*day*-voo aftershave
lozi *loh*-zee almond
lugha *loo*-gha language

M

maakuli ma-a-*koo*-lee provisions
maalum ma-a-*loom* special
maandamano ma-an-da-*ma*-noh
demonstration • protest
maandishi chini
ma-an-*dee*-shee *chee*-nee subtitles
maarufu ma-a-*roo*-foo famous
mabaki ma-*ba*-kee relic
mabawa ma-*ba*-wa wings
mabuti ma-*boo*-tee boots (footwear)
— ya kutembea porini
ya koo-taym-*bay*-a poh-*ree*-nee
hiking boots
machela ma-*chay*-la hammock
macheo ma-*chay*-oh sunrise
macho *ma*-choh eyes
machumbwichumbwi
ma-choom-bwee-*choom*-bwee mumps
machunda ma-*choon*-da skim milk
machweo ma-*chway*-oh sunset
madawa (ya kulevya)
ma-*da*-wa (ya koo-*lay*-vya) (illegal) drugs
madhahabu ma-dha-*ha*-boo altar
madhubuti ma-dhoo-*boo*-tee strong

madukani ma-doo-*ka*-nee
shopping centre
maelezo binafsi ya ujuzi ma-ay-*lay*-zoh
bee-*naf*-see ya oo-joo-zee CV • résumé
mafuriko ma-foo-*ree*-koh flood
mafusha ya pamba
ma-*foo*-sha ya *pam*-ba cotton balls
mafuta ma-*foo*-ta gas (petrol) • oil
— ya taa ya ta gas (for cooking)
— ya zaituni ya za-ee-*too*-nee olive oil
magari mengi ma-*ga*-ree *mayn*-gee
traffic
magharibi ma-gha-*ree*-bee west
maglavu ma-*gla*-voo gloves
magofu ma-*goh*-foo ruins
mahadhi ma-*ha*-dhee rhythm
mahakama ma-ha-*ka*-ma court (legal)
mahali ma-*ha*-lee place • venue
— pa kuzaliwa pa koo-za-*lee*-wa
place of birth
maharagwe ma-ha-*rag*-way beans
mahindi ma-*heen*-dee corn
mahojiano ma-hoh-jee-*a*-noh interview
maisha ma-*ee*-sha life
majaribio ya nyuklia ma-ja-ree-*bee*-oh ya
nyook-lee-a nuclear testing
maji *ma*-jee water
— baridi ba-*ree*-dee still water
— ya bomba ya *bohm*-ba tap water
— ya kujaa na kupwa
ya koo-*ja* na *koop*-wa tide
— ya limau ya lee-*ma*-oo lemonade
— ya machungwa ya ma-*choon*-gwa
orange juice
— ya madini ya ma-*dee*-nee
mineral water
— ya moto ya *moh*-toh hot water
majira ma-*jee*-ra season
— ya baridi ya ba-*ree*-dee winter
— ya joto ya *joh*-toh summer
— ya kuchipua ya koo-chee-*poo*-a spring
makaburini ma-ka-boo-*ree*-nee cemetery
makini ma-*kee*-nee serious
maktaba mak-*ta*-ba library
makumbusho ma-koom-*boo*-shoh
museum
malai ya maziwa ya mtindi ma-*la*-ee ya
ma-zee-wa ya m-*teen*-dee sour cream
malaya ma-*la*-ya prostitute
malazi ma-*la*-zee accommodation
malipo ma-*lee*-poh payment
— ya huduma ya hoo-*doo*-ma
service charge

-maliza ·ma-*lee*-za finish
malkia mal-*kee*-a queen
mama *mam*-ba mother
mamamkwe ma-ma-*m*-kway
mother-in law
mamba *mam*-ba crocodile
mandari man-*da*-ree picnic
mandhari man-*dha*-ree view
manjano man-*ja*-noh yellow
maoni ma-*oh*-nee opinion
maonyesho ma-oh-*nyay*-shoh exhibition
mapacha ma-*pa*-cha twins
mapema ma-*pay*-ma early
mapenzi ma-*payn*-zee sex (intercourse)
— **salama** sa-*la*-ma safe sex
mapitio ma-pee-*tee*-oh review
mapokezi ma-poh-*kay*-zee check-in (desk)
maporomoko ya maji
ma-poh-roh-*moh*-koh ya ma-*jee*
waterfall
mapumziko ma-poom-*zee*-koh
intermission
mara mbili *ma*-ra m-*bee*-lee twice
mara moja *ma*-ra moh-ja once
mara nyingi *ma*-ra nyeen-gee often
maradhi ma-*ra*-dhee disease
marashi ma-*ra*-shee perfume
marejeo ma-ray-*jay*-oh reference
Marekani ma-ray-*ka*-nee USA
masaa ya kufunguliwa ma-*sa* ya
koo-foon-*goo*-lee-wa opening hours
mashariki ma-sha-*ree*-kee east
mashindano ya ubingwa
ma-sheen-*da*-noh ya oo-*been*-gwa
championships
mashine ma-*shee*-nay machine
— **ya kubanika mkate** ya
koo-ba-*nee*-ka m-*ka*-tay toaster
— **ya kufulia** ya koo-foo-*lee*-a
washing machine
— **ya kutolea pesa** ya koo-toh-*lay*-a
pay-sa automated teller machine (ATM)
— **ya tiketi** ya tee-*kay*-tee
ticket machine
mashuka ma-*shoo*-ka linen (sheets etc)
masikitiko ma-see-kee-*tee*-koh sad
maskini mas-*kee*-nee poor
mastadi ma-*sta*-dee mustard
matako ma-*ta*-koh bottom (body)
matatu ma-*ta*-too bus (city)
matibabu asilia
ma-tee-*ba*-boo a-see-*lee*-a naturopathy

matone ya macho
ma-*toh*-nay ya *ma*-choh eye drops
matope ma-*toh*-pay mud
matukio ya leo ma-too-*kee*-oh ya *lay*-oh
current affairs
matunda yaliyokaushwa ma-*toon*-da
ya-lee-yoh-ka-*oosh*-wa dried fruit
mauaji ma-oo-*a*-jee murder
maumivu ma-oo-*mee*-voo pain
— **ya jino** ya *jee*-noh toothache
— **ya kichwa** ya *keech*-wa headache
— **ya mwezini** ya mway-*zee*-nee
period pain
maumivu ya tumbo
ma-oo-*mee*-voo ya *toom*-boh
stomachache
mawasiliano ma-wa-see-lee-*a*-noh
communications (profession)
mawe za mizani *ma*-way za mee-*za*-nee
weights
mayai yaliyovurugwa ma-*ya*-ee
ya-lee-yoh-voo-*roog*-wa scrambled eggs
mayonezi ma-yoh-*nay*-zee mayonnaise
mazingira ma-zeen-*gee*-ra environment
maziwa ma-*zee*-wa milk
— **ganda** *gan*-da yoghurt
— **ya soya** ya *soh*-ya soy milk
mazoezi ma-zoh-*ay*-zee workout
mbali m-*ba*-lee far • remote
mbalimbali m-ba-lee-m-*ba*-lee separate
mbao m-*ba*-oh wood
mbaya m-*ba*-ya bad • off (spoiled)
mbaya sana m-*ba*-ya *sa*-na awful • terrible
mbele m-*buy*-lay ahead
— **ya** ya in front of
mbeleni m-bay-*lay*-nee future
mbili m-*bee*-lee both • two
mbilimbili m-bee-lee-m-*bee*-lee double
mbingu m-*been*-goo sky
mbinu m-*bee*-noo technique
mbishi m-*bee*-shee stubborn
mboga m-*boh*-ga vegetable
— **za majani** za ma-*ja*-nee herbs
mboni m-*boh*-nee lens (eye)
mboo m-*boh* penis
mbu m-*boo* mosquito
Mbudisti m-boo-*dee*-stee Buddhist
mbuni m-*boo*-nee ostrich
mbuzi m-*boo*-zee goat
mbwa *m*-bwa dog
— **wa kuongoza** wa koo-ohn-*goh*-za
guide dog
mchana m-*cha*-na afternoon

mchanga m-*chan*-ga sand

mchele m-*chay*-lay rice (uncooked)

mchemuo m-chay-moo-oh exhaust (car)

mchezo m-*chay*-zoh game (sport)

— kwenye kompyuta
kway-nyay kom-*pyoo*-ta computer game

— wa kuigiza wa koo-ee-*gee*-za
play (theatre)

— wa soka wa *soh*-ka football • soccer

mchicha m-*chee*-cha spinach

mchonga vinyago
m-*chohn*-ga vee-*nya*-goh woodcarver

mchuaji m-choo-a-jee masseuse/masseuse

mchumba m-*choom*-ba fiancé/fiancée

mchuuzi m-choo-oo-zee street hawker

— wa samaki wa sa-*ma*-kee
fish monger

mchuzi m-*choo*-zee sauce

— wa nyanya wa *nya*-nya
tomato sauce • ketchup

— wa pilipili hoho
wa pee-lee-*pee*-lee *hoh*-hoh chilli sauce

— wa soya wa *soh*-ya soy sauce

mdanganyi m-dan-*ga*-nyee cheat

mdomo m-*doh*-moh mouth

mdudu m-*doo*-doo bug

-mea -*may*-a grow

mechi *may*-chee match (sports)

meli *may*-lee ship

mende *mayn*-day cockroach

meneja may-*nay*-ja
manager (restaurant, hotel)

meno *may*-noh teeth

menyu *may*-nyoo menu

metali may-*ta*-lee metal ⓝ

meza *may*-za table

— kujihudumia
koo-jee-hoo-doo-*mee*-a buffet

mfalme m-*fal*-may king

mfamasia m-fa-ma-*see*-a
chemist (person) • pharmacist

mfano m-*fa*-noh example

mfanyabiashara m-fa-nya-bee-a-*sha*-ra
business person • tradesperson

mfanyakazi m-fa-nya-*ka*-zee
employee • labourer

— ofisini o-fee-*see*-nee office worker

— wa kiwandani kee-wan-*da*-nee
factory worker

— wa kutumia mikono koo-too-*mee*-a
mee-*koh*-noh manual worker

mfuko m-*foo*-koh bag • pocket

— wa kiunoni wa kee-oo-*noh*-nee
bumbag

— wa kulalia wa koo-la-*lee*-a
sleeping bag

mfumo wa matabaka
m-foo-moh wa ma-ta-*ba*-ka
class system

mfungwa m-*foon*-gwa prisoner

mfupa m-*foo*-pa bone

mgahawa m-ga-*ha*-wa café • restaurant

mganga wa madawa ya kienyeji
m-*gan*-ga wa ma-*da*-wa ya
kee-ay-*nyay*-jee herbalist

mgeni m-*gay*-nee stranger

mgomo m-*goh*-moh strike

mgongano m-gohn-*ga*-noh crash

mgongo m-*gohn*-goh back (body)

mgonjwa m-*gohn*-jwa ill • sick

mguu m-*goo* foot • leg

mhadhiri m-ha-*dhee*-ree lecturer

mhamisishaji m-ha-mee-see-*sha*-jee
activist

mhandisi m-han-*dee*-see engineer

Mhindu m-*heen*-doo Hindu

mhudumu m-hoo-*doo*-moo waiter • waitress

mhuni m-*hoo*-nee hoodlum

mia *mee*-a hundred

miadi mee-*a*-dee date (appointment)

miche ya maharagwe *mee*-chay ya
ma-ha-*rag*-way beansprouts

michezo mee-*chay*-zoh sport

— ya kukimbia ya koo-keem-*bee*-a
track (sport)

— ya riadha ya ree-*a*-dha athletics

Michezo ya Olimpiki mee-*chay*-zoh ya
oh-leem-*pee*-kee Olympic Games

midomo mee-*doh*-moh lips

mieleka mee-ay-*lay*-ka martial arts

mikutano mee-koo-*ta*-noh
conference (big)

mila *mee*-la custom

milele mee-*lay*-lay forever

milimita mee-lee-*mee*-ta millimetre

milioni mee-lee-*oh*-nee million

mimi *mee*-mee I • me

minyoo mee-*nyoh* worms

misa *mee*-sa mass (Catholic)

mita *mee*-ta metre

mitumba mee-*toom*-ba second-hand

miwani mee-*wa*-nee glasses (spectacles)

— ya jua ya *joo*-a sunglasses

— ya kuogelea ya koo-oh-gay-*lay*-a
goggles (swimming)

mizigo mee-*zee*-goh *baggage (luggage)*
— **iliyowekwa** ee-lee-yoh-*wayk*-wa
left luggage
— **ziada** zee-*a*-da *excess baggage*
mjamzlto m-ja-*m*-zee-toh *pregnant*
mjenzi m-*jayn*-zee *builder*
mji m-*jee city*
mjinga m-*jeen*-ga *idiot*
mjukuu m-joo-*koo grandchild*
mjusi m-*joo*-see *lizard*
mkalimani m-ka-lee-*ma*-nee *interpreter*
mkamba m-*kam*-ba *bronchitis*
mkanda wa feni m-*kan*-da wa *fay*-nee
fanbelt
mkanda wa kiti m-*kan*-da wa *kee*-tee
seatbelt
mkanda wa picha m-*kan*-da wa *pee*-cha
film (for camera)
mkanda wa video
m-*kan*-da wa vee-*day*-oh *video tape*
mkarimu m-ka-ree-*moo kind (nice)*
mkasi m-*ka*-see *scissors*
mkasi wa kucha m-*ka*-see wa *koo*-cha
nail clippers
mkataba m-ka-*ta*-ba *contract*
mkate m-*ka*-tay *bread*
— **mkavu** m-*ka*-voo *cracker (biscuit)*
— **wa ngano asilia** wa n-*ga*-noh
a-see-*lee*-a *wholemeal bread*
mke m-*kay wife*
— **anayekaa nyumbani**
a-na-yay-*ka* nyoom-*ba*-nee
homemaker
mkebe m-*kay*-bay *can • tin*
mkeka m-*kay*-ka *mat*
Mkesha wa Krismasi m-*kay*-sha wa
krees-*ma*-see *Christmas Eve*
Mkesha wa Mwaka Mpya m-*kay*-sha wa
mwa-ka m-*pya New Year's Eve*
mkia m-*kee*-a *tail*
mkimbizi m-keem-*bee*-zee *refugee*
mkoba m-*koh*-ba
briefcase • handbag • purse
mkondo m-*kohn*-doh *current (electricity)*
mkono m-*koh*-noh *arm • hand*
mkopo m-*koh*-poh *credit*
Mkristo m-*kree*-stoh *Christian*
mkufu m-*koo*-foo *necklace*
mkulima m-koo-*lee*-ma *farmer*
mkurugenzi m-koo-roo-*gayn*-zee
director • manager
mkusanyaji wa tiketi m-koo-sa-*nya*-jee
wa tee-*kay*-tee *ticket collector*

mkutano m-koo-*ta*-noh *conference (small)*
— **wa hadhara** wa ha-*dha*-ra
rally • public meeting
mlaji wa mboga za majani tu
m-*la*-jee wa m-*boh*-ga za ma-*ja*-nee too
vegetarian ⓝ
mlango m-*lan*-goh *door • gate (airport etc)*
— **wa kuondoka** wa koo-ohn-*doh*-ka
departure gate
mlima m-*lee*-ma *hill • mountain*
mlio wa simu m-*lee*-oh wa see-moo *dial tone*
mlo m-*loh diet • meal*
mmea m-*may*-a *plant*
mnada m-*na*-da *fleamarket*
mnara m-*na*-ra *monument • tower*
mno m-*noh too (expensive etc)*
mnofu m-*noh*-foo *steak*
mnyama m-*nya*-ma *animal*
mnyororo m-*nyoh*-roh-roh *chain*
— **wa baisikeli** wa ba-ee-see-*kay*-lee
bike chain
moja *moh*-ja *one*
— **kwa moja** kwa *moh*-ja
direct • straight
motaboti moh-ta-*boh*-tee *motorboat*
moto *moh*-toh *fire*
— **ya mungu** ya *moon*-goo
shingles (illness)
moyo *moh*-yoh *heart*
mpaka m-*pa*-ka *border* ⓝ *• until* prep
mpanda baisikeli m-*pan*-da
ba-ee-see-*kay*-lee *cyclist*
mpenzi m-*payn*-zee
boyfriend • girlfriend • lover
mpigapicha m-pee-ga-*pee*-cha
photographer
mpira m-*pee*-ra
ball • chewing gum • gum
— **wa gofu** wa *goh*-foo *golf ball*
— **wa kikapu** wa kee-*ka*-poo
basketball
— **wa meza** wa *may*-za *table tennis*
— **wa mikono** wa mee-*koh*-noh
handball
— **wa wavu** wa *wa*-voo
volleyball
— **wa wavu ufukoni** wa *wa*-voo
oo-foo-*koh*-nee *beach volleyball*
mpishi m-*pee*-shee *chef • cook*
mpya m-*pya new*
mradi m-*ra*-dee *program*
mrefu m-*ray*-foo *tall*

243

mrembo m-*raym*-boh handsome
mrengo wa kulia
m-*rayn*-goh wa koo-*lee*-a right-wing
mrengo wa kushoto
m-*rayn*-goh wa koo-*shoh*-toh left-wing
mruko m-*roo*-koh flight (of a bird)
msaada m-sa-*a*-da help
msagaji m-sa-*ga*-jee lesbian
msalaba m-sa-*la*-ba cross (religious)
msanifu wa majengo
m-sa-*nee*-foo wa ma-*jayn*-goh
architect
msanii m-sa-*nee* artist
— **wa rangi** wa *ran*-gee painter
msenge m-*sayn*-gay gay (homosexual)
mshabiki m-sha-*bee*-kee fan (sport, etc)
— **wa utawala huria**
wa oo-ta-*wa*-la hoo-*ree*-a anarchist
mshahara m-sha-*ha*-ra salary • wage
mshangao m-shan-*ga*-oh surprise
mshindi m-*sheen*-dee winner
mshipa m-*shee*-pa vein
mshonaji m-shoh-*na*-jee tailor
mshtuko wa ubongo m-*shtoo*-koh wa
oo-*bohn*-goh concussion
mshumaa m-shoo-*ma* candle
mshushio m-shoo-*shee*-oh orgasm
msichana m-see-*cha*-na girl
msikiti m-see-*kee*-tee mosque
msitu m-*see*-too forest
mstari m-*sta*-ree queue
msusi m-*soo*-see hairdresser
mswaki m-*swa*-kee toothbrush
mtaalamu m-ta-a-*la*-moo specialist
mtabiri m-ta-*bee*-ree fortune teller
mtakatifu m-ta-ka-*tee*-foo saint
mtalii m-ta-*lee* tourist
mtandao wa kompyuta
m-tan-*da*-oh wa kohm-*pyoo*-ta
Internet
mtawa m-*ta*-wa monk
mteguko m-tay-*goo*-koh sprain
mteja m-*tay*-ja client
mtembezi m-taym-*bay*-zee pedestrian
mti m-*tee* tree
mtihani m-tee-*ha*-nee test
mtindi m-*teen*-dee cream
mtindo m-*teen*-doh fashion • style
mto m-*toh* pillow • river
mtoto m-*toh*-toh child
— **mchanga** m-*chan*-ga baby
mtu m-*too* person
— **mzima** m-*zee*-ma adult ⓜ

mtumiaji wa madawa ya kulevya
m-too-mee-*a*-jee wa ma-*da*-wa ya
koo-*lay*-vya drug user
mtungi wa gesi m-*toon*-gee wa *gay*-see
gas cartridge
mtunza bustani m-*toon*-za boo-*sta*-nee
gardener
muhafidhina moo-ha-fee-*dhee*-na
conservative
muhimu moo-*hee*-moo important
— **sana** *sa*-na urgent
muhtasari mooh-*ta*-sa-ree résumé (CV)
mume *moo*-may husband
mumunye ya kula moo-*moo*-nyay ya
koo-la courgette • zucchini
Mungu *moon*-goo God
musuli moo-*soo*-lee muscle
muziki moo-*zee*-kee music
mvinyo m-*vee*-nyoh wine
— **mwenye povu** *mway*-nyay poh-*voo*
sparkling wine
mvivu m-*vee*-voo lazy
mvua m-*voo*-a rain
mvulana m-voo-*la*-na boy
mwajiri mwa-*jee*-ree employer
mwaka *mwa*-ka year
— **huu** hoo this year
mwalimu mwa-*lee*-moo
instructor • teacher
mwamba *mwam*-ba cliff • ledge
mwamuzi mwa-*moo*-zee referee
mwamvuli mwam-*voo*-lee umbrella
mwana *mwa*-na son
mwanachama mwa-na-*cha*-ma member
mwanafunzi mwa-na-*foon*-zee student
mwanakondoo mwa-na-kohn-*doh* lamb
mwanamichezo mwa-na-mee-*chay*-zoh
sportsperson
mwanamke mwan-*am*-kay woman
mwanamume mwa-na-*moo*-may man
mwanamuziki mwa-na-moo-*zee*-kee
musician
mwanasayansi mwa-na-sa-*yan*-see
scientist
mwanasesere mwa-na-say-*say*-ray doll
mwanasheria mwa-na-shay-ree-a lawyer
mwanasiasa mwa-na-see-*a*-sa politician
mwandishi mwan-*dee*-shee writer
— **wa habari** wa ha-*ba*-ree journalist
mwanga *mwan*-ga light ⓜ
mwanzo *mwan*-zoh start
mwasho *mwa*-shoh itch
mwema *mway*-ma nice

mwembamba mwaym-*bam*-ba *thin*
mwendo mwayn-doh *speed (velocity)*
— **wa mkanda** wa m-*kan*-da
film speed
mwenye *mway*-nyay *owner*
— **bahati** ba-*ha*-tee *lucky*
— **choyo** *choh*-yoh *selfish*
— **furaha** foo-*ra*-ha *happy*
— **haiba** ha-*ee*-ba *charming*
— **hasira** ha-*see*-ra *angry*
— **hatia** ha-*tee*-a *guilty*
— **hisia** hee-*see*-a *emotional*
— **kichaa** kee-*cha crazy*
— **kuuma** koo-oo-ma *sore*
— **nyumba** *nyoom*-ba
landlady/landlord
— **shughuli nyingi**
shoo-goo-lee nyeen-gee *busy (person)*
— **shukrani** shook-*ra*-nee *grateful*
— **usingizi** oo-seen-*gee*-zee *sleepy*
— **wasiwasi** wa-see-*wa*-see *worried*
— **wivu** wee-voo *jealous*
mwenyekiti mway-nyay-kee-tee *mayor*
mwenzi *mwayn*-zee *companion*
— **wangu** *wan*-goo *colleague*
mwezi *mway*-zee *month • moon*
— **wa kumi** wa koo-mee *October*
— **wa kumi na mbili**
wa koo-mee na m-bee-lee *December*
— **wa kumi na moja**
wa koo-mee na moh-ja *November*
— **wa kwanza** wa *kwan*-za *January*
— **wa nane** wa *na*-nay *August*
— **wa nne** wa *n*-nay *April*
— **wa pili** wa pee-lee *February*
— **wa saba** wa *sa*-ba *July*
— **wa sita** wa *see*-ta *June*
— **wa tano** wa *ta*-noh *May*
— **wa tatu** wa *ta*-too *March*
— **wa tisa** wa *tee*-sa *September*
mwigizaji mwee-gee-*za*-jee *actor*
mwili *mwee*-lee *body*
mwimbaji mweem-*ba*-jee *singer*
— **barabarani** ba-ra-ba-*ra*-nee *busker*
mwingilio mween-gee-*lee*-oh *entry (access)*
mwinuko mwee-*noo*-koh *uphill*
mwisho *mwee*-shoh *end (finish)*
Mwislamu mwee-*sla*-moo *Muslim*
mwizi *mwee*-zee *thief*
mwombaji mwohm-*ba*-jee *beggar*
mwongo mwohn-goh *liar*
mwongozo (wa sauti) mwohn-*goh*-zoh
(wa sa-oo-tee) *(audio) guide*

mwongozo wa burudani
mwohn-*goh*-zoh wa boo-roo-*da*-nee
entertainment guide
mwuguzi mwoo-goo-zee *nurse*
mwungaji mkono mwoon-*ga*-jee
m-*koh*-noh *supporter (politics)*
mwuzaji wa chakula
mwoo-*za*-jee wa cha-*koo*-la
food vendor
mwuzaji wa madawa ya kulevya
mwoo-*za*-jee wa ma-*da*-wa ya
koo-*lay*-vya *drug dealer*
mwuzaji wa magazeti mwoo-*za*-jee wa
ma-ga-*zay*-tee *newspaper vendor*
Myahudi m-ya-*hoo*-dee *Jewish*
myeyuko wa lenzi mboni
m-*yay*-*yoo*-koh wa *layn*-zee m-*boh*-nee
contact lens solution
mzabibu m-za-*bee*-boo *vine (grape)*
mzawa m-*za*-wa *descendent*
mzee m-*zay old person • pensioner*
mzigo m-zee-goh *suitcase*
mzio m-*zee*-oh *allergy*

N

na na *and • with*
nadra na-dra *rare (uncommon)*
nafaka na-*fa*-ka *cereal*
nafasi na-*fa*-see *chance • vacancy*
namba *nam*-ba *number*
— **ya chumba** ya *choom*-ba
room number
— **ya gari** ya *ga*-ree
license plate number
— **ya pasipoti** ya pa-see-*poh*-tee
passport number
namna *nam*-na *how*
nanasi na-*na*-see *pineapple*
nani na-nee *who*
nauli na-oo-lee *fare*
nazi na-zee *coconut*
nchi n-chee *country*
— **za nje** za *n*-jay *abroad (overseas)*
ndala n-*da*-la *sandal*
ndani n-*da*-nee *indoor • inside*
— **yake** ya-kay *included*
ndefu n-*day*-foo *long*
ndege n-*day*-gay
airplane • bird • flight (scheduled)
ndimu n-*dee*-moo *lime*
ndiyo n-*dee*-yoh *yes*

ndizi n-*dee*-zee *banana*
ndoa n-*doh*-a *marriage*
ndogo sana n-*doh*-goh *sa*-na *tiny*
ndondi n-*dohn*-dee *boxing*
ndoo n-*doh* *bucket*
ndoto n-*doh*-toh *dream*
ndovu n-*doh*-voo *elephant*
nene *nay*-nay *fat*
neno *nay*-noh *word*
nepi *nay*-pee *diaper • nappy*
neti *nay*-tee *net*
ng'ambo ng-*am*-boh *across*
ng'ombe ng-*ohm*-bay *cow*
ngamia n-ga-*mee*-a *camel*
ngazi n-*ga*-zee *stairway*
-ngoja -n-*goh*-ja *wait*
-ngojea -n-goh-*jay*-a *wait for*
ngoma n-*goh*-ma *drum*
　— ya kuigiza hadithi
　ya koo-ee-*gee*-za ha-*dee*-thee *ballet*
ngozi n-*goh*-zee *leather • skin*
　— ya kichwa ya *keech*-wa *scalp*
ngumu n-*goo*-moo *hard (not soft)*
nguo n-*goo*-oh *clothing*
　— kufua koo-*foo*-a *laundry (clothes)*
　— rasmi *ras*-mee *uniform*
　— za kuogelea za koo-oh-gay-*lay*-a
　bathing suit
nguruwe n-*goo*-roo-way *pig*
nguvu n-*goo*-voo *power*
ni hatari nee ha-*ta*-ree *unsafe*
nimechumbiwa nee-may-*choom-bee*-wa
　(I'm) engaged
nimeoa nee-may-*oh*-a *(I'm) married (man)*
nimeolewa nee-may-oh-*lay*-wa
　(I'm) married (woman)
nini *nee*-nee *what*
nishati ya nyuklia
　nee-sha-tee ya *nyook*-lee-a *nuclear energy*
njaa n-*ja* *hunger*
nje n-*jay* *outside*
njegere n-jay-*gay*-ray *pea*
njia n-*jee*-a *aisle (on plane) • path • route •*
　street • track • way
　— mkato m-*ka*-toh *shortcut*
　— ya baisikeli ya ba-ee-see-*kay*-lee
　bike path
　— ya kupanda mlimani ya koo-*pan*-da
　m-lee-*ma*-nee *mountain path*
　— ya kutembea porini
　ya koo-taym-*bay*-a poh-*ree*-nee
　hiking route
　— ya miguu ya mee-*goo* *footpath*

noti *noh*-tee *banknote*
nukta *nook*-ta *point*
-nunua -noo-*noo*-a *buy • shop*
nusu *noo*-soo *half*
nyama *nya*-ma *meat*
nyani *nya*-nee *baboon*
nyanya *nya*-nya *tomato*
nyasi *nya*-see *grass*
nyati *nya*-tee *buffalo*
nyekundu nyay-*koon*-doo *red*
nyepesi nyay-*pay*-see
　light (not heavy) • quick
nyeupe nyay-*oo*-pay
　light (of colour) • white
nyeusi nyay-*oo*-see *black • dark (of colour)*
　— na nyeupe na nyay-*oo*-pay *B&W (film)*
nyika *nyee*-ka *countryside*
nyingi *nyeen*-gee *a lot • many*
nyingine nyeen-*gee*-nay *another • other*
nyinyi *nyee*-nyee *you* pl
-nyoa -*nyoh*-a *shave*
nyoka *nyoh*-ka *snake*
-nyonyesha -nyoh-*nyay*-sha *breast-feed*
nyonyo bandia nyoh-nyoh ban-*dee*-a
　dummy • pacifier
nyota nyoh-ta *star*
nyuki *nyoo*-kee *bee*
nyuma *nyoo*-ma
　back (position) • behind • rear (seat etc)
nyumba *nyoom*-ba *house*
　— ya sanaa ya sa-*na* *art gallery*
　— ya utawa wa wanaume
　ya oo-*ta*-wa wa wa-na-*oo*-may *monastery*
　— ya wageni ya wa-*gay*-nee
　boarding house
nyumbani nyoom-*ba*-nee *home*
nyumbu *nyoom*-boo *wildebeest*
nyundo *nyoon*-doh *hammer*
nyuzi *nyoo*-zee *degrees (temperature)*
-nywa -*nywa* *drink*
nywele *nyway*-lay *hair*
nzito n-*zee*-toh *heavy*
nzuri n-*zoo*-ree *fine • good*
　— kabisa ka-*bee*-sa *best*
　— sana *sa*-na *great (fantastic)*

O

-oa -*oh*-a *marry (man)*
ofisi oh-*fee*-see *office*
　— ya tiketi ya tee-*kay*-tee *ticket office*
　— ya watalii ya wa-ta-*lee* *tourist office*

-oga ·oh·ga wash (oneself)
-ogelea ·oh·gay·lay·a swim
okestra oh·kay·stra orchestra
oksijeni ohk·see·jay·nee oxygen
-olewa ·oh·lay·wa marry (woman)
-omba ·ohm·ba ask (for something)
　— **lifti** leef·tee hitchhike
ombi ohm·bee petition
omlet ohm·layt omelette
-ona ·oh·na see
-ondoka ohn·doh·ka depart
-onja ·ohn·ja try (taste)
-onya oh·nya warn
-onyesha oh·nyay·sha show
onyesho oh·nyay·shoh
　gig (musical) • performance • show
　— **la muziki** la moo·zee·kee concert
opareta oh·pa·ray·ta operator
opena ya kopo oh·pay·na ya koh·poh
　can opener
opera oh·pay·ra opera
operesheni oh·pay·ray·shay·nee
　operation (medical)
-osha ·oh·sha wash (something)
ovari oh·va·ree ovary

P

-pa ·pa give
padri pa·dree priest
pafu pa·foo lung
paka pa·ka cat
pakiti pa·kee·tee packet (general)
palahala pa·la·ha·la antelope
pamba pam·ba cotton
pamoja pa·moh·ja together
pampu pam·poo pump
pana pa·na wide
pancha pan·cha puncture
-panda ·pan·da
　board (a plane, ship etc) • climb
　— **baisikeli** ba·ee·see·kay·lee cycle
　— **farasi** fa·ra·se ride a horse
pango pan·goh cave
panya pa·nya mouse • rat
Pasaka pa·sa·ka Easter
pasheni pa·shay·nee passionfruit
pasi pa·see iron (for clothes)
pasi ya kupanda ndege pa·see ya
　koo·pan·da n·day·gay boarding pass
pasipoti pa·see·poh·tee passport
-pata ·pa·ta earn • get

pauda kwa mtoto
　pa·oo·da kwa m·toh·toh baby powder
paundi pa·oon·dee pound (money, weight)
pea pay·a pear
pedeli pay·day·lee pedal
pekee pay·kay alone
-peleka ·pay·lay·ka send
pembezoni mwa mji
　paym·bay·zoh·nee mwa m·jee suburb
-penda ·payn·da like • love
-pendekeza ·payn·day·kay·za recommend
-pendelea ·payn·day·lay·a prefer
pensili payn·see·lee pencil
peremende pay·ray·mayn·day sweets
pesa pay·sa change
　— **kichele** kee·chay·lay loose change
pete pay·tay ring (on finger)
pia pee·a also
picha pee·cha painting (a work) • photo
pichi pee·chee peach
-piga kambi ·pee·ga kam·bee camp
-piga kelele ·pee·ga kay·lay·lay shout
-piga kura ·pee·ga koo·ra vote
-piga picha ·pee·ga pee·cha take a photo
-piga risasi ·pee·ga ree·sa·see shoot
-piga simu ·pee·ga see·moo ring (phone)
-piga teke ·pee·ga tay·kay kick
pigano pee·ga·noh fight
-pika ·pee·ka cook
pikipiki pee·kee·pee·kee motorcycle
pilipili pee·lee·pee·lee pepper
　— **hoho** pee·lee·pee·lee hoh·hoh
　capsicum • chilli
　— **mbichi** pee·lee·pee·lee m·bee·chee
　pepper (bell)
-pima uzito ·pee·ma oo·zee·toh weigh
-pinda ·peen·da turn
-pinga ·peen·ga protest
pinki peen·kee pink
pipa la taka pee·pa la ta·ka garbage can
pipi pee·pee candy (lollies)
-pita ·pee·ta pass
plagi pla·gee plug (electricity)
plamu pla·moo plum
　— **kavu** ka·voo prune
plasta pla·sta bandage
plastiki pla·stee·kee plastic
poda poh·da powder
polepole poh·lay·poh·lay slowly
polisi poh·lee·see police • police officer
pombe pohm·bay drink (alcoholic)
　— **ya kienyeji** ya kee·ay·nyay·jee
　home brew

posho *poh*·shoh *dole*
posta *poh*·sta
    mail (postal system) • *post office*
postikadi poh·stee·*ka*·dee *postcard*
-potea ·poh·*tay*·a *lose*
printa *preen*·ta *printer (computer)*
projekta proh·*jayk*·ta *projector*
pua *poo*·a *nose*
    — **yenye makamasi**
    yay·nyay ma·ka·*ma*·see *runny nose*
pumbavu poom·*ba*·voo *stupid*
pumu *poo*·moo *asthma*
-pumua ·poo·*moo*·a *breathe*
-pumzika ·poom·*zee*·ka *rest*
punda milia *poon*·da mee·*lee*·a *zebra*
punguzo poon·*goo*·zoh *discount*
pwani *pwa*·nee *coast*

R

rafiki ra·*fee*·kee *friend*
-rafikiana ·ra·fee·kee·*a*·na *go out with*
rafu *ra*·foo *shelf*
ragbi *rag*·bee *rugby*
rahisi ra·*hee*·see *cheap* • *easy* • *simple*
raia ra·*ee*·a *nationality*
rais ra·*ees president*
raketi ra·*kay*·tee *racquet*
ramani ra·*ma*·nee *map* • *road map*
rangi *ran*·gee *colour*
    — **ya machungwa** ya ma·*choon*·gwa
    orange (colour)
    — **ya mdomo** ya m·*doh*·moh *lipstick*
rasimu ra·*see*·moo *design*
ratiba ra·*tee*·ba *timetable*
    — **ya safari** ya sa·*fa*·ree *itinerary*
redio ray·*dee*·oh *radio*
-refu ·*ray*·foo *deep*
-rejeleza ·ray·jay·*lay*·za *recycle*
rejista ray·*gee*·sta *cash register*
-rekodi ·ray·*koh*·dee *record*
rimoti ree·*moh*·tee *remote control*
risiti ree·*see*·tee *receipt*
robo *roh*·boh *quarter*
roki *roh*·kee *rock (music)*
Romani roh·*ma*·nee
    Catholic (denomination)
-rudi ·*roo*·dee *return (come back)*
ruhusa roo·*hoo*·sa *permission*
    — **ya kazi** ya *ka*·zee *work permit*
-ruhusiwa ·roo·hoo·*see*·wa
    can (have permission)
-ruka ·*roo*·ka *fly* • *jump*

S

saa sa *clock* • *hour* • *time* • *watch*
    — **sita mchana** *see*·ta m·*cha*·na
    midday (noon)
    — **sita usiku** *see*·ta oo·*see*·koo
    midnight
    — **yenye kengele**
    yay·nyay kayn·*gay*·lay *alarm clock*
sababu sa·*ba*·boo *reason*
sabuni sa·*boo*·nee *soap*
    — **ya kunyolea** ya koo·nyoh·*lay*·a
    shaving cream
safari sa·*fa*·ree *trip (journey)*
    — **kwa biashara** kwa bee·a·*sha*·ra
    business trip
    — **ya kutalii** ya koo·ta·*lee tour*
    — **yenye kiongozi**
    yay·nyay kee·ohn·*goh*·zee
    guided tour
safi *sa*·fee *clean*
-safiri ·sa·*fee*·ree *travel*
-safisha ·sa·*fee*·sha *clean*
safu ya milima *sa*·foo ya mee·*lee*·ma
    mountain range
sahani sa·*ha*·nee *plate*
-sahau ·sa·*ha*·oo *forget*
sahihi sa·*hee*·hee *signature*
-saidia ·sa·ee·*dee*·a *help*
saizi sa·*ee*·zee *size (general)*
sakafu sa·*ka*·foo *floor*
sakitu sa·*kee*·too *frost*
sala *sa*·la *prayer*
salama sa·*la*·ma *safe*
-sali ·*sa*·lee *pray*
saloni sa·*loh*·nee *beauty salon*
samaki sa·*ma*·kee *fish*
-samehe ·sa·*may*·hay *forgive*
sana *sa*·na *very*
sanaa sa·*na art*
    — **ya uchoraji wa rangi**
    ya oo·choh·*ra*·jee wa *ran*·gee
    painting (the art)
sanamu sa·*na*·moo *statue*
sanduku san·*doo*·koo *box*
    — **la kuhifadhia mizigo**
    la koo·hee·fa·*dhee*·a mee·*zee*·goh
    luggage locker
    — **la posta** la *poh*·sta *mailbox*
sarafu sa·*ra*·foo *change (coins)*
sarakasi sa·ra·*ka*·see *circus* • *gymnastics*
sarara sa·*ra*·ra *fillet*

sasa *sa*·sa *now • present (time)*
— **hivi** *hee*·vee *soon*
sataranji sa·ta·*ran*·jee *chess*
sauna *sa*·oo·na *sauna*
sauti sa·*oo*·tee *voice • volume (sound)*
sawa *sa*·wa *right (correct)*
sawasawa sa·wa·*sa*·wa *same*
sayansi sa·*yan*·see *science*
— **za jamii** za ja·*mee* *humanities*
sayari sa·*ya*·ree *planet*
sebule say·*boo*·lay *foyer*
sehemu say·*hay*·moo *part (component)*
— **ya kuchukulia mizigo**
ya koo·choo·koo·*lee*·a mee·*zee*·goh
baggage claim
— **ya kuegeshea magari**
ya koo·ay·gay·*shay*·a ma·*ga*·ree *car park*
sekundi say·*koon*·dee *second (time unit)*
seli *say*·lee *sale*
-sema ·*say*·ma *say • speak • talk*
senti *sayn*·tee *cent*
sentimita sayn·tee·*mee*·ta *centimetre*
sera *say*·ra *policy*
seremala say·ray·*ma*·la *carpenter*
serikali say·ree·*ka*·lee *government*
shaba *sha*·ba *copper*
shairi pl sha·*ee*·ree *poetry*
shamba *sham*·ba *farm*
— **la mizabibu** la mee·za·*bee*·boo
vineyard
shampeni sham·*pay*·nee *champagne*
shampuu sham·*poo* *shampoo*
shangazi shan·*ga*·zee *aunt*
shanta *shan*·ta *backpack*
shashi *sha*·shee *gauze*
shati *sha*·tee *shirt*
shayiri sha·*yee*·ree *oats*
sherehe shay·*ray*·hay
celebration • party (night out)
sheria shay·*ree*·a
legislation • law (study, profession)
shifta *sheef*·ta *derailleur*
-shinda ·*sheen*·da *win*
shindano sheen·*da*·noh *race (sport)*
shinikizo shee·nee·*kee*·zoh *pressure*
— **la damu** la *da*·moo *blood pressure*
shirika la habari shee·*ree*·ka la ha·*ba*·ree
newsagency
-shirikiana ·shee·ree·kee·*a*·na *share (with)*
-shona ·*shoh*·na *sew*
shuka *shoo*·ka *bed linen • sheet*
— **na tandiko** na tan·*dee*·koh *bedding*
-shuka ·*shoo*·ka *get off (a train, etc)*

-shukuru ·shoo·koo·*roo* *thank*
shule *shoo*·lay *school*
— **ya msingi** ya m·*seen*·gee *high school*
shupavu shoo·*pa*·voo *brave*
siagi see·*a*·gee *butter*
siasa see·*a*·sa *politics*
sidiria see·dee·*ree*·a *bra*
sifa *see*·fa *quality*
— **za kielimu** za kee·ay·*lee*·moo
qualifications
sigara see·*ga*·ra *cigarette*
siki *see*·kee *vinegar*
-sikia ·*see*·kee·a *hear*
-sikiliza ·see·kee·*lee*·za *listen*
-sikilizia ·see·kee·lee·*zee*·a *listen to*
sikio see·*kee*·oh *ear*
siku *see*·koo *day*
Siku ya Krismasi *see*·koo ya krees·*ma*·see
Christmas Day
Siku ya Mwaka Mpya
see·koo ya *mwa*·ka m·pya
New Year's Day
sikukuu see·koo·*koo* *holiday*
— **ya kuzaliwa** ya koo·za·*lee*·wa
birthday
-simama ·see·*ma*·ma *stop (cease)*
simba *seem*·ba *lion*
simbo ya posta *seem*·boh ya *poh*·sta
post code
simu *see*·moo *telephone*
— **ya mkononi** ya m·koh·*noh*·nee
cell phone • mobile phone
— **ya mtaani** ya m·*ta*·nee
public telephone
sindano (ya dawa)
seen·*da*·noh (ya *da*·wa) *needle (syringe)*
sindano (ya kushonea) seen·*da*·noh (ya
koo·shoh·*nay*·a) *needle (sewing)*
sinema see·*nay*·ma *cinema*
-sinzia ·seen·*zee*·a *sleep*
sisi *see*·see *we*
sista *see*·sta *nun*
siyo kawaida *see*·yoh ka·wa·*ee*·da
unusual
skafu *ska*·foo *scarf*
skati *ska*·tee *skirt*
-skii ·*skee* *ski*
skonzi *skohn*·zee *bread rolls*
slaidi sla·*ee*·dee *slide (film)*
soda *soh*·da *soft drink*
sodo *soh*·doh *sanitary napkin • tampon*
soga *soh*·ga *joke*
soka *soh*·ka *football (soccer)*

soko *soh*·koh *market*
— **la mtaani** la m·ta·*a*·nee
street market
— **la wachonga vinyago**
la wa·*chohn*·ga vee·*nya*·goh
woodcarver's market

soksi *sohk*·see *socks • condom (slang)*
— **ndefu** n·*day*·foo *stockings*

-soma ·*soh*·ma *read*

somo *soh*·moh *reading*

soshalisti soh·sha·*lee*·stee *socialist*

spidomita spee·doh·*mee*·ta
speedometer

spishi zilizo hatarini
spee·shee zee·*lee*·zoh ha·ta·*ree*·nee
endangered species

spishi zilizo hifadhiwa
spee·shee zee·*lee*·zoh hee·fa·*dhee*·wa
protected species

spoki *spoh*·kee *spoke*

springi *spreen*·gee *spring (coil)*

stempu *staym*·poo *postage • stamp*

stendi ya basi *stayn*·dee ya *ba*·see
bus station

stesheni stay·*shay*·nee *station*
— **ya treni** ya *tray*·nee *railway station*

stirio stee·*ree*·oh *stereo*

studio stoo·*dee*·oh *studio*

-subiri ·soo·*bee*·ree *wait*

sufu *soo*·foo *wool*

sufuria soo·foo·*ree*·a *saucepan*

sukari soo·*ka*·ree *sugar*

-sukuma ·soo·*koo*·ma *push*

sungura soon·*goo*·ra *rabbit*

sungusungu soon·goo·*soon*·goo *ant*

supu *soo*·poo *soup*

surua soo·*roo*·a *measles*

suruali soo·roo·*a*·lee *pants (trousers)*

sururu soo·*roo*·roo *pickaxe*

swala *swa*·la *gazelle*

swalapala swa·la·*pa*·la *impala*

swali *swa*·lee *question*

sweta *sway*·ta *jumper (sweater)*

T

taa ta *light (lamp)*
— **ya barabarani** ya ba·ra·ba·*ra*·nee
traffic light
— **za mbele** za m·*bay*·lay *headlights*

taarifa ta·a·*ree*·fa *information*

tabaka ta·*ba*·ka *class (category)*
— **la hewa ya ozoni**
la *hay*·wa ya oh·*zoh*·nee *ozone layer*

-tabasamu ·ta·ba·*sa*·moo *smile*

tabibu wa maungo
ta·*bee*·boo wa ma·*oon*·goh *chiropractor*

-tafsiri ·taf·*see*·ree *translate*

-tafuta ·ta·*foo*·ta *look for*

tairi ta·ee·ree *tyre*

tajiri ta·*jee*·ree *rich (wealthy)*

-taka ·*ta*·ka *want*

taka za sumu *ta*·ka za *soo*·moo
toxic waste

takataka ta·ka·*ta*·ka *garbage*
— **za nyuklia** za *nyook*·lee·a
nuclear waste

tamasha ta·*ma*·sha *festival*

tambalale tam·ba·*la*·lay *flat* ⓐ

tambi *tam*·bee *noodles • pasta*

tamu *ta*·moo *sweet • tasty*

tandiko tan·*dee*·koh *saddle*

tangazo tan·*ga*·zoh *advertisement*

tango *tan*·goh *cucumber*

tangu (Mei) *tan*·goo (*may*·ee) *since (May)*

taratibu ta·ra·*tee*·boo *slow*

tarehe ta·*ray*·hay *date (day)*
— **ya kuzaliwa** ya koo·za·*lee*·wa
date of birth

taulo ta·oo·loh *towel*

taya ta·ya *jaw*

tayari ta·*ya*·ree *already* adv• *ready* ⓐ

-tazama ·ta·za·ma *watch*

teknolojia ya maarifa
tayk·noh·loh·*jee*·a ya ma·a·*ree*·fa *IT*

teksi *tayk*·see *taxi*

telegramu tay·lay·*gra*·moo *telegram*

telekom *tay*·lay·kohm *telecom centre*

televisheni tay·lay·vee·*shay*·nee
television

-teleza ·tay·*lay*·za *skate*

-tembea ·*taym*·bay·a *walk*
— **porini** poh·*ree*·nee *hike*

-tembelea ·taym·bay·*lay*·a *visit*

tembo *taym*·boh *elephant*

tena *tay*·na *again*

tende *tayn*·day *date (fruit)*

tenesi tay·*nay*·see *tennis*

-tengeneza ·tayn·gay·*nay*·za
make • repair

tetekuwanga tay·tay·koo·*wan*·ga
chicken pox

tetemeko la ardhi
tay·tay·*may*·koh la ar·dhee *earthquake*
thamani *tha*·ma·nee *value (price)*
theluji thay·*loo*·jee *snow*
-thibitisha ·thee·bee·*tee*·sha *validate*
tiba ya harufu tee·ba ya ha·*roo*·foo
aromatherapy
tiba ya kuchoma na sindano
tee·ba ya koo·*choh*·ma na seen·*da*·noh
acupuncture
tiketi tee·*kay*·tee *ticket*
— kutumia kama nafasi ikipatikana
koo·too·*mee*·a *ka*·ma na·*fa*·see
ee·kee·pa·tee·*ka*·na *stand-by ticket*
— ya kwenda tu ya *kwayn*·da too
one-way (ticket)
— ya kwenda na kurudi ya *kwayn*·da
na koo·*roo*·dee *return (ticket)*
— ya mzigo ya m·*zee*·goh *luggage tag*
tikiti tee·*kee*·tee *ticket*
timu *tee*·moo *team*
tini *tee*·nee *fig*
tishati *tee*·sha·tee *T-shirt*
titi *tee*·tee *breast (body)*
-toa rushwa ·toh·a *roosh*·wa *bribe*
tochi *toh*·chee *torch (flashlight)*
tofaa to·*fa apple*
tofauti to·fa·*oo*·tee *different*
— ya wakatl ya wa·*ka*·tee *time difference*
treni *tray*·nee *train*
tu too *only*
-tulivu ·too·*lee*·voo *quiet*
-tumaini ·too·ma·*ee*·nee *wish*
tumbaku toom·*ba*·koo *tobacco*
tumbili toom·*bee*·lee *monkey*
tumbo *toom*·boh *stomach*
tumbusi toom·*boo*·see *vulture*
tunda *toon*·da *fruit*
-tunza ·*toon*·za
care (for someone) · *look after*
tupu *too*·poo *empty* · *vacant*
twiga *twee*·ga *giraffe*
twiza *twee*·za *tweezers*
tyubu *tyoo*·boo *inner tube* · *tyre*

U

ua *oo*·a *flower*
-ua ·*oo*·a *murder*
ubaguzi oo·ba·*goo*·zee *discrimination*
— wa kijinsia wa kee·jeen·*see*·a *sexism*
— wa rangi wa *ran*·gee *racism*

ubakaji oo·ba·*ka*·jee *rape*
ubalozi oo·ba·*loh*·zee *embassy*
— mdogo m·*doh*·goh *consulate*
ubao wa kuteleza oo·*ba*·oh wa
koo·tay·*lay*·za *skateboarding*
ubao wa kutelezea
oo·*ba*·oh wa koo·tay·lay·*zay*·a *surfboard*
ubao wa matokeo
oo·*ba*·oh wa ma·toh·*kay*·oh *scoreboard*
ubao wa sataranji
oo·*ba*·oh wa sa·ta·*ran*·jee *chessboard*
ubaraza oo·ba·*ra*·za *balcony*
ubatizo oo·ba·*tee*·zoh *baptism*
ubavu oo·*ba*·voo *rib*
uchafuzi oo·cha·*foo*·zee *pollution*
uchaguzi oo·cha·*goo*·zee *election*
ucheleweshaji oo·chay·lay·way·*sha*·jee
delay
uchongaji oo·chohn·*ga*·jee *sculpture*
uchumba oo·*choom*·ba *engagement*
udaktari oo·dak·*ta*·ree
medicine (study, profession)
udobi oo·*doh*·bee *laundry (place)*
udongo oo·*dohn*·goh *clay*
uelekeo oo·ay·lay·*kay*·oh *direction*
ufinyanzi oo·fee·*nyan*·zee *ceramics*
ufukwe oo·*fook*·way *beach* · *seaside*
ufunguo oo·foon·*goo*·oh *key*
ugonjwa wa kuchomwa kwa jua
oo·*gohn*·jwa wa koo·*chohm*·wa kwa
joo·a *sunstroke*
ugonjwa wa moyo oo·*gohn*·jwa wa
moh·yoh *heart condition*
ugonjwa wa upele oo·*gohn*·jwa wa
oo·*pay*·lay *thrush (health)*
ugonjwa wa zinaa
oo·*gohn*·jwa wa zee·*na venereal disease*
uhamiaji oo·ha·mee·*a*·jee *immigration*
uhandisi oo·han·*dee*·see *engineering*
uharibifu oo·ha·ree·*bee*·foo *spoilage*
uhusiano oo·hoo·see·*a*·noh *relationship*
— wa jamii wa ja·*mee public relations*
ujangili oo·jan·*gee*·lee *poached (game)*
ujao oo·*ja*·oh *next*
ujenzi oo·*jayn*·zee *architecture*
ujumbe oo·*joom*·bay *message*
ukarimu oo·ka·*ree*·moo *hospitality*
ukimwi oo·*keem*·wee *AIDS*
ukumbi oo·*koom*·bee *gym (place)*
— wa maonyesho
wa ma·oh·*nyay*·shoh *theatre*
ukungu oo·*koon*·goo *fog*
ukurasa oo·koo·*ra*·sa *page*

ukurutu oo·koo·roo·too *eczema*

ukuta oo·koo·ta *wall (outer)*

Ulaya oo·la·ya *Europe*

ulezi wa mtoto oo·lay·zee wa m·toh·toh *childminding*

ulimi oo·lee·mee *tongue*

ulimwengu oo·lee·mwayn·goo *universe*

-uliza ·oo·lee·za *ask (a question)*

uma oo·ma *bite (dog, insect)* • *fork*

-uma ·oo·ma *hurt*

umaskini oo·ma·skee·nee *poverty*

umbo oom·boh *shape*

umeme oo·may·may *electricity*

umri oom·ree *age*

ungamo oon·ga·moh *confession*

ununuzi oo·noo·noo·zee *shopping*

uongezaji wa visa oo·ohn·gay·za·jee wa vee·sa *extension (visa)*

upandaji miamba oo·pan·da·jee mee·am·ba *rock climbing*

upande oo·pan·day *side*

upele oo·pay·lay *rash*

— wa nepi wa nay·pee *nappy rash*

upendo oo·payn·doh *love*

upepo oo·pay·poh *air (in a tyre)* • *wind*

upigaji picha oo·pee·ga·jee pee·cha *photography*

upimaji mimba oo·pee·ma·jee meem·ba *pregnancy test kit*

upungufu oo·poon·goo·foo *shortage*

— wa damu wa da·moo *anaemia*

uraia oo·ra·ee·a *citizenship*

urari oo·ra·ree *balance (account)*

usafi oo·sa·fee *cleaning*

usafirishaji oo·sa·fee·ree·sha·jee *transport*

usajili wa gari oo·sa·jee·lee wa ga·ree *car registration*

usawa oo·sa·wa *equality*

ushauri oo·sha·oo·ree *advice*

ushirikina oo·shee·ree·kee·na *superstition*

usiku oo·see·koo *night*

— huu hoo *tonight*

— nje n·jay *night out*

usimamizi oo·see·ma·mee·zee *administration*

uso oo·soh *face*

ustawi oo·sta·wee *welfare*

— wa jamii wa ja·mee *social welfare*

usukani pl oo·soo·ka·nee *handlebars*

usumbufu oo·soom·boo·foo *harassment*

utawala oo·ta·wa·la *rule*

utegemezi wa madawa ya kulevya oo·tay·gay·may·zee wa ma·da·wa ya koo·lay·vya *drug addiction*

utumiaji oo·too·mee·a·jee *exploitation*

uvimbe oo·veem·bay *inflammation* • *lump* • *swelling* • *tumour*

— wa mboni wa m·boh·nee *conjunctivitis*

— wa ovari wa oh·va·ree *ovarian cyst*

uvimbi wa ini oo·veem·bee wa ee·nee *hepatitis*

uvuvi oo·voo·vee *fishing*

uwakala wa safari oo·wa·ka·la wa sa·fa·ree *travel agency*

uwanda wa juu oo·wan·da wa joo *plateau*

uwanja oo·wan·ja *square (town)*

— wa gofu wa goh·foo *golf course*

— wa kupigia kambi wa kuu·pee·gee·a kam·bee *camping ground*

— wa mbio wa m·bee·oh *racetrack*

— wa michezo wa mee·chay·zoh *stadium*

— wa ndege wa n·day·gay *airport*

uwezo wa watu oo·way·zoh wa wa·too *human resources*

uwindaji oo·ween·da·jee *hunting*

uyabisi wa tumbo oo·ya·bee·see wa toom·boh *constipation*

uyoga oo·yoh·ga *mushroom*

-uza ·oo·za *sell*

uzi oo·zee *string* • *thread*

— wa meno wa may·noh *dental floss*

uzito oo·zee·toh *weight*

— usiolipiwa oo·see·oh·lee·pee·wa *baggage allowance*

uzoefu oo·zoh·ay·foo *experience*

— wa kazi wa ka·zee *work experience*

uzushi oo·zoo·shee *fiction*

V

-vaa ·va *wear*

vazi va·zee *dress*

— la kuogelea la koo·oh·gay·lay·a *swimsuit*

viatu vee·a·too *shoes*

vibiriti vee·bee·ree·tee *matches (for lighting)*

vidonge vya usingizi vee·dohn·gay vya oo·seen·gee·zee *sleeping pills*

vifaa vee·fa *equipment*

— vya kuzamia vya koo·za·mee·a *diving equipment*

vigumu vee·goo·moo *difficult*

vipengele vee·payn·gay·lay *details*

vipuli vee·poo·lee *jewellery*

virusi *vee-roo-see* virus
visa *vee-sa* visa
visu *vee-soo* cutlery
vita *vee-ta* war
vitamini *vee-ta-mee-nee* vitamins
vitanda viwili *vee-tan-da vee-wee-lee* twin beds
vitu vya sanaa *vee-too vya sa-na* crafts
viza *vee-za* visa
vizibo vya masikio *vee-zee-boh vya ma-see-kee-oh* earplugs
vizuri *vee-zoo-ree* well
-vunja *-voon-ja* break
-vunjika *-voon-jee-ka* break down
-vuta *-voo-ta* pull
  — sigara *see-ga-ra* smoke
VVU *vee-vee-yoo* HIV
vyakula *vya-koo-la* groceries
vyombo vya habari *vyohm-boh vya ha-ba-ree* media
vyombo vya udongo *vyohm-boh vya oo-dohn-goh* pottery

W

-wa *-wa* be
  — marafiki *ma-ra-fee-kee* date (a person)
  — mgonjwa *m-gohn-jwa* have a cold
  — na *na* have
  — na deni *na day-nee* owe
wakala wa maeneo *wa-ka-la wa ma-ay-nay-oh* real estate agent
wakala wa shamba *wa-ka-la wa sham-ba* estate agency
wakati *wa-ka-tee* when
  — mwingine *mween-gee-nay* sometimes
wala *wa-la* neither
wali *wa-lee* rice (cooked)
-wa na maumivu ya tumbo *-wa na ma-oo-mee-voo ya toom-boh* to have a stomachache
wanaofika *wa-na-oh-fee-ka* arrivals
wao *wa-oh* they • their
wapi *wa-pee* where
warsha *war-sha* workshop (meeting)
wasiojiweza *wa-see-oh-jee-way-za* disabled
watoto *wa-toh-toh* children
  — wa mtaani *wa m-ta-a-nee* street children

watu *wa-too* people
wawili wawili *wa-wee-lee wa-wee-lee* pair (couple)
waya *wa-ya* wire
wazazi *wa-za-zee* parents
wazi *wa-zee* open (premises)
wazimu *wa-zee-moo* hallucination
waziri mkuu *wa-zee-ree m-koo* prime minister
-weka *-way-ka* put
wembe *waym-bay* razor • razor blade
wengi *wayn-gee* many
wewe *way-way* you *sg*
-weza *-way-za* can (be able)
wigo *wee-goh* fence
wikendi *wee-kayn-dee* weekend
wiki *wee-kee* week
  — iliyopita *ee-lee-yoh-pee-ta* last week
  — mbili *m-bee-lee* fortnight
wimbi *weem-bee* wave
wimbo *weem-boh* song • tune
wingu *ween-goo* cloud
wizi *wee-zee* rip-off
wote *woh-tay* everyone

Y

ya aibu *ya a-ee-boo* shy
ya ajabu *ya a-ja-boo* wonderful
ya awali *ya a-wa-lee* original
ya baridi *ya ba-ree-dee* cool
ya chujwa *ya chooj-wa* filtered
ya elimu kale *ya ay-lee-moo ka-lay* archaeological
ya hakika *ya ha-kee-ka* positive
ya jadi *ya ja-dee* classical
ya joto *ya joh-toh* warm
ya jua *ya joo-a* sunny
ya kabla *ya kab-la* last (previous)
ya kale *ya ka-lay* ancient
ya kasi *ya ka-see* fast
ya kidini *ya kee-dee-nee* religious
ya kienyeji *ya kee-ayn-nyay-jee* local
ya kigeni *ya kee-gay-nee* foreign • strange
ya kihistoria *ya kee-hee-stoh-ree-a* historical
ya kijana *ya kee-ja-na* young
ya kike *ya kee-kay* female
ya kimataifa *ya kee-ma-ta-ee-fa* international
ya kisasa *ya kee-sa-sa* modern
ya kuachwa *ya koo-ach-wa* excluded
ya kubana *ya koo-ba-na* tight

ya kuchekesha ya koo·chay·*kay*·sha comedy • funny

ya kuchelewa ya koo·chay·*lay*·wa late

ya kuchochea ashiki ya koo·choh·*chay*·a a·*shee*·kee sexy

ya kuchoka ya koo·*choh*·ka tired

ya kuchomwa ya koo·*chohm*·wa burnt

ya kuchosha ya koo·*choh*·sha boring

ya kufungwa ya koo·*foon*·gwa closed • locked

ya kugandwa ya koo·*gan*·dwa frozen

ya kuharibika ya koo·ha·ree·*bee*·ka broken down

ya kuibwa ya koo·*ee*·bwa stolen

ya kujaa ya koo·*ja* full

ya kujazana ya koo·ja·*za*·na crowded

ya kujiajiri ya koo·jee·a·*jee*·ree self-employed

ya kujihuduma ya koo·jee·hoo·*doo*·ma self-service

ya kukana ya koo·*ka*·na negative

ya kukaushwa ya koo·ka·*oosh*·wa dried

ya kula rushwa ya *koo*·la *roosh*·wa corrupt

ya kupendeza ya koo·payn·*day*·za beautiful • pretty

ya kupendwa ya koo·*payn*·dwa popular

ya kupotezwa ya koo·poh·*tayz*·wa lost

ya kurejeleza ya koo·ray·jay·*lay*·za recyclable

ya kutamanisha ya koo·ta·ma·*nee*·sha sensual

ya kutosha ya koo·*toh*·sha enough

ya kuumiza ya koo·oo·*mee*·za painful

ya kuvunjika ya koo·voon·*jee*·ka broken — **kirahisi** kee·ra·*hee*·see fragile

ya kuvutia ya koo·voo·*tee*·a interesting

ya kuwezekana ya koo·way·zay·*ka*·na possible

ya kwanza ya *kwan*·za first

ya mfano hasa ya m·*fa*·noh *ha*·sa typical

ya mkoa ya m·*koh*·a regional

ya moto ya *moh*·toh heated

ya muda kamili ya *moo*·da ka·*mee*·lee full-time

ya mwinuko mkali ya mwee·*noo*·koh m·*ka*·lee steep

ya mwisho ya *mwee*·shoh last (final)

ya pili ya *pee*·lee second ⑧

ya starehe ya sta·*ray*·hay comfortable

ya tatu ya *ta*·too third

ya thamani ya *tha*·ma·nee valuable

ya usanisia ya oo·sa·nee·*see*·a synthetic

ya zamani ya za·*ma*·nee antique • old • stale

yai ya·*ee* egg

yake ya·*kay* her • his

yako ya·*koh* your sg

yangu yan·*goo* my

yao ya·*oh* their

yaya ya·*ya* babysitter

yenu yay·*noo* your pl

yenye busara yay·nyay boo·*sa*·ra sensible

yenye kelele yay·nyay kay·*lay*·lay noisy

yenye kosa yay·nyay *koh*·sa faulty

yenye kufanana yay·nyay koo·fa·*na*·na similar

yenye manufaa yay·nyay ma·noo·*fa* useful

yenye sumu yay·nyay *soo*·moo poisonous

yenye uhalisi yay·nyay oo·ha·*lee*·see realistic

yetu yay·*too* our

yeye yay·*yay* he • she

yoyote yoh·*yoh*·tay any

Z

zabibu za·*bee*·boo grapes — **kavu** *ka*·voo raisin

zaidi za·*ee*·dee more

zaituni za·ee·*too*·nee olive

-zalisha ·za·*lee*·sha produce

zamani za·*ma*·nee past

zambarau zam·ba·*ra*·oo purple

zao za·*oh* crop

zawadi za·*wa*·dee present (gift) — **ya arusi** ya a·*roo*·see wedding present

zeze zay·*zay* guitar

ziara zee·*a*·ra shrine

zingizi zeen·*gee*·zee premenstrual tension

zipu zee·*poo* zip/zipper

-zito ·zee·*toh* thick

ziwa *zee*·wa lake

ziwi zee·*wee* deaf

zodiaki zoh·dee·*a*·kee zodiac

zote zoh·*tay* all

-zuia ·zoo·*ee*·a stop (prevent)

zulia zoo·*lee*·a rug

A

abbreviations	10
accidents	60, 179
accommodation	67, 197
addresses	65, 67, 76, 96
addressing people	109
adjectives (grammar)	17
admission (sightseeing)	96
adverbs (grammar)	17
age	114
airport	52
alcoholic drinks	163, 164
allergies	172, 185, 187, 190
alphabet	14
alternative treatments	191
ambulance	179
amounts	38, 168
animals	98, 151, 197
appointment (business)	99
architecture	140
arranging to meet	129
art	139
articles (grammar)	18
asking someone out	131
assault	181
automated teller machine	46, 93

B

babies	103, 106, 187
baggage	51, 53, 73
banking	93
bargaining	79
bars	127, 153, 161, 165
basic phrases (general)	107, 153, 159
be (verb)	19
beach	55, 150
beliefs	137
bicycle	61
bill (restaurant)	45, 156, 158

blind	102
boat	55, 146
body language	107, 113
body parts (diagram)	192
booking (accommodation)	68
booking (lesson)	145
booking (restaurant)	154
booking (taxi)	56, 73
booking (tickets)	49
books	83
border crossing	63
breast-feeding	106
bus	48, 53
business	99

C

calendar	41
camping	67, 74, 148, 149
car (diagram)	59
car (general)	58
cardinal numbers	37
cell phone	91
changing money	45, 70, 93
check (banking)	45, 93
check (restaurant)	45, 156, 158
checking in	50, 68
checking out	73
children	103
children (discounts)	49, 97, 103
children (health)	105, 184, 186
children's menu	103, 154
cinema	122
clothes	80, 113
coach (transport)	53
coffee	127, 153, 162, 163
communications	87
compass points	66
complaints (accommodation)	72
complaints (banking)	94
complaints (photographs)	86
complaints (restaurant)	158, 160

KEY PATTERNS

When's (the next bus)?	(Basi ijayo) itaondoka lini?	(*ba*·see ee·*ja*·yoh) ee·ta·ohn·*doh*·ka *lee*·nee
Where's (the station)?	(Stesheni) iko wapi?	(stay·*shay*·nee) ee·koh *wa*·pee
Where do I buy (a ticket)?	Ninunue (tiketi) wapi?	nee·noo·*noo*·ay (tee·*kay*·tee) *wa*·pee
How much is (a room)?	(Chumba) ni bei gani?	(*choom*·ba) nee bay *ga*·nee
I'm looking for (a hotel).	Natafuta (hoteli).	na·ta·*foo*·ta (hoh·*tay*·lee)
Do you have (a map)?	Una (ramani)?	*oo*·na (ra·*ma*·nee)
Please bring (the bill).	Lete (bili).	*lay*·tay (*bee*·lee)
I'd like (the menu)	Nataka (menyu).	na·*ta*·ka (*may*·nyoo)
I'd like (to hire a car).	Nataka (kukodi gari).	na·*ta*·ka (koo·*koh*·dee *ga*·ree)
I have (a reservation).	Nina (buking).	*nee*·na (*boo*·keeng)
Could you please (help me)?	(Saidia), tafadhali.	(sa·ee·*dee*·a) ta·fa·*dha*·lee
Do I have to (get a visa)?	Ni lazima (nipate viza)?	nee *la*·zee·ma (nee·*pa*·tay *vee*·za)